双语名著无障碍阅读丛书

经典集锦

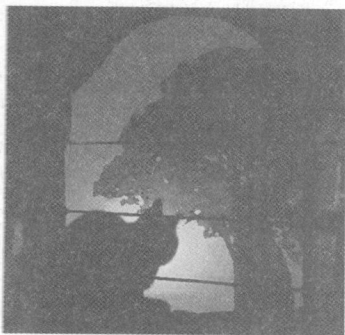

爱伦·坡短篇小说选

Selected Short Stories of
Edgar Allan Poe

［美国］埃德加·爱伦·坡 著

夏百娜 译

中国出版集团

中译出版社

图书在版编目（CIP）数据

爱伦·坡短篇小说选：英汉对照/（美）埃德加·爱伦·坡（Edgar Allan Poe）著；夏百娜译. —北京：中译出版社，2018.6（2023.2 重印）

（双语名著无障碍阅读丛书）

ISBN 978-7-5001-5578-2

Ⅰ.①爱… Ⅱ.①埃… ②夏… Ⅲ.①英语—汉语—对照读物 ②中篇小说—小说集—美国—近代 ③短篇小说—小说集—美国—近代 Ⅳ.①H319.4：Ⅰ

中国版本图书馆 CIP 数据核字（2018）第 084527 号

出版发行/中译出版社

地　　址/北京市西城区新街口外大街 28 号普天德胜主楼四层

电　　话/(010) 68359827；68359303（发行部）；68359725（编辑部）

邮　　编/100044

传　　真/(010) 68357870

电子邮箱/book@ ctph.com.cn

网　　址/http：//www.ctph.com.cn

责任编辑/范祥镇　王诗同　杨佳特

封面设计/潘　峰

排　　版/北京竹页文化传媒有限公司

印　　刷/永清县晔盛亚胶印有限公司

经　　销/新华书店

规　　格/710 毫米×1000 毫米　1/16

印　　张/16.75

字　　数/264 千字

版　　次/2018 年 6 月第一版

印　　次/2023 年 2 月第四次

ISBN 978-7-5001-5578-2　　　　　　定价：57.00 元

多年以来，中译出版社有限公司（原中国对外翻译出版有限公司）凭借国内一流的翻译和出版实力及资源，精心策划、出版了大批双语读物，在海内外读者中和业界内产生了良好、深远的影响，形成了自己鲜明的出版特色。

二十世纪八九十年代出版的英汉（汉英）对照"一百丛书"，声名远扬，成为一套最权威、最有特色且又实用的双语读物，影响了一代又一代英语学习者和中华传统文化研究者、爱好者；还有"英若诚名剧译丛""中华传统文化精粹丛书""美丽英文书系"，这些优秀的双语读物，有的畅销，有的常销不衰反复再版，有的被选为大学英语阅读教材，受到广大读者的喜爱，获得了良好的社会效益和经济效益。

"双语名著无障碍阅读丛书"是中译专门为中学生和英语学习者精心打造的又一品牌，是一个新的双语读物系列，具有以下特点：

选题创新——该系列图书是国内第一套为中小学生量身打造的双语名著读物，所选篇目均为教育部颁布的语文新课标必读书目，或为中学生以及同等文化水平的社会读者喜闻乐见的世界名著，重新编译为英汉（汉英）对照的双语读本。这些书既给青少年读者提供了成长过程中不可或缺的精神食粮，又让他们领略到原著的精髓和魅力，对他们更好地学习英文大有裨益；同时，丛书中入选的《论语》《茶馆》《家》等汉英对照读物，亦是热爱中国传统文化的中外读者所共知的经典名篇，能使读者充分享受阅读经典的无限乐趣。

无障碍阅读——中学生阅读世界文学名著的原著会遇到很多生词和文化难点。针对这一情况，我们给每一本读物原文中的较难词汇和不易理解之处都加上了注释，在内文的版式设计上也采取英汉（或汉英）对照方式，扫清了学生阅读时的障碍。

优良品质——中译双语读物多年来在读者中享有良好口碑，这得益于作者和出版者对于图书质量的不懈追求。"双语名著无障碍阅读丛书"继承了中译双语读物的优良传统——精选的篇目、优秀的译文、方便实用的注解，秉承着对每一个读者负责的精神，竭力打造精品图书。

愿这套丛书成为广大读者的良师益友，愿读者在英语学习和传统文化学习两方面都取得新的突破。

目录 CONTENTS

Edgar Allan Poe

The Black Cat

For the most wild, yet most homely **narrative**① which I am about to pen, I neither expect nor **solicit**② belief. Mad indeed would I be to expect it, in a case where my very senses reject their own evidence. Yet, mad am I not — and very surely do I not dream. But to-morrow I die, and to-day I would unburthen my soul. My immediate purpose is to place before the world, plainly, **succinctly**③, and without comment, a series of mere household events. In their consequences, these events have terrified—have **tortured**④ — have destroyed me. Yet I will not attempt to **expound**⑤ them. To me, they have presented little but Horror — to many they will seem less terrible than *barroques*⑥. Hereafter, perhaps, some intellect may be found which will reduce my **phantasm**⑦ to the common-place — some intellect more calm, more logical, and far less excitable than my own, which will **perceive**⑧, in the circumstances I detail with **awe**⑨, nothing more than an ordinary succession of very natural causes and effects.

From my **infancy**⑩ I was noted for the **docility**⑪ and humanity of my **disposition**⑫. My tenderness of heart was even so **conspicuous**⑬ as to make me the jest of my companions. I was especially fond of animals, and was **indulged**⑭ by my parents with a great variety of pets. With these I spent most of my time, and never was so happy as when feeding and caressing them. This **peculiarity**⑮ of character grew with my growth, and in my **manhood**⑯,

夺魂黑猫

我要给你讲的是一个荒诞至极又平淡无奇的故事。要指望或祈求你相信，那我定是疯了；连我自己都一度觉得这不可能是我的亲身经历。我确确实实没疯，也的的确确不是在做梦。明天是我的死期，今天我要一股脑儿地把这些事讲出来，以救赎我的灵魂。我只是不加修饰地把这些家长里短的事简短道来，并不作过多的评论。这些事令我惊魂不定，饱受折磨，最终走向毁灭。我并不想作过多的解释，因为对我来说，这些事留给我的只有恐怖。很多人会认为这些事与其可怕，不如说离奇古怪，或许将来一些聪明人——更冷静更理性更能看透世事的聪明人——会发现我满脑子恐惧的不过是普通事件，而我心怀畏惧所讲述的那些事都不过是一连串因果相关的自然事件罢了。

我从小性情就出了名的温和善良。同伴们经常嘲笑我那软得出奇的心肠。我特别喜欢小动物，我的父母也对我百般宠爱，给我弄来各种各样的宠物。我大部分时间都和小动物们在一起，给他们喂食、照顾他们让我幸福无比。这种癖好在我

I derived from it one of my principal sources of pleasure. To those who have cherished an **affection**① for a faithful and **sagacious**② dog, I need hardly be at the trouble of explaining the nature or the intensity of the gratification thus derivable. There is something in the unselfish and self-sacrificing love of a **brute**③, which goes directly to the heart of him who has had frequent occasion to test the **paltry**④ friendship and **gossamer**⑤ fidelity of mere *Man*.

I married early, and was happy to find in my wife a disposition not **uncongenial**⑥ with my own. Observing my **partiality**⑦ for domestic pets, she lost no opportunity of **procuring**⑧ those of the most agreeable kind. We had birds, gold-fish, a fine dog, rabbits, a small monkey, and *a cat*.

This latter was a remarkably large and beautiful animal, entirely black, and sagacious to an astonishing degree. In speaking of his intelligence, my wife, who at heart was not a little **tinctured**⑨ with **superstition**⑩, made frequent **allusion**⑪ to the ancient popular notion, which regarded all black cats as witches in **disguise**⑫. Not that she was ever serious upon this point — and I mention the matter at all for no better reason than that it happens, just now, to be remembered.

Pluto — this was the cat's name — was my favorite pet and playmate. I alone fed him, and he **attended**⑬ me wherever I went about the house. It was even with difficulty that I could prevent him from following me through the streets.

Our friendship lasted, in this manner, for several years, during which my general temperament and character — through the instrumentality of the Fiend Intemperance — had (I **blush**⑭ to **confess**⑮ it) experienced a radical alteration for the worse. I grew, day by day, more moody, more irritable, more regardless of the feelings of others. I suffered myself to use **intemperate**⑯ language to my wife. At length, I even offered her personal violence. My pets, of course, were made to feel the change in my disposition. I not only neglected, but ill-used them. For Pluto, however, I still retained sufficient regard to restrain me from **maltreating**⑰ him, as I made no **scruple**⑱ of maltreating the rabbits, the monkey, or even the dog, when by accident, or through affection, they came in my way.

① affection [əˈfekʃən] n. 喜爱

② sagacious [səˈgeiʃəs] a. 聪明的，睿智的

③ brute [bruːt] n. 畜生，野兽

④ paltry [ˈpɔːltri] a. 无价值的，微不足道的

⑤ gossamer [ˈgɔsəmə] a. 脆弱的，薄弱的

⑥ uncongenial [ˌʌnkənˈdʒiːnjəl] a. 志趣不相投的

⑦ partiality [ˌpɑːʃiˈæliti] n. 偏爱

⑧ procure [prəuˈkjuə] v.（设法）获得

⑨ tincture [ˈtiŋktʃə] v. 使带有……的意味

⑩ superstition [ˌsjuːpəˈstiʃən] n. 迷信

⑪ allusion [əˈljuːʒən] n. 暗指，提及

⑫ disguise [disˈgaiz] n. 掩饰，伪装

⑬ attend [əˈtend] v. 陪伴，陪同

⑭ blush [blʌʃ] v. 惭愧，羞愧

⑮ confess [kənˈfes] v. 承认，坦白

⑯ intemperate [inˈtempərət] a.（言辞）激烈的，过激的

⑰ maltreat [mælˈtriːt] v. 虐待

⑱ scruple [ˈskruːpl] n. 顾虑，顾忌

成年后也丝毫未减，竟成了我生活中最大的乐趣。如果你钟爱忠实又有灵气的狗，那么我就无须多费口舌向你解释其中满溢着怎样的喜悦了。兽类无私又自我牺牲的爱总能挑动那些亲历过淡薄人情的人们那脆弱的心灵。

我结婚早，妻子和我性情相投，这让我感到十分幸福。知道我喜欢养宠物，她就不失时机地给我弄些中意的宠物来养。我们养过许多鸟、金鱼、一条好狗、兔子、一只小猴儿，还有一只猫。

那只猫体形硕大，通体乌黑，美丽无比，十分机灵。我妻子骨子里就迷信，一说到这只猫的灵性，她总会绕到猫都是巫婆变的这一旧说。当然啦，这点她从来也没当真，我之所以提到这点，没别的，就是刚巧想到而已。

那猫叫布鲁托[1]，它是我的爱宠，也是我的玩伴。它由我一个人喂，在家里它如影随形地跟着我。就连我上街去，也很难甩开它。

就这样，我和它相交甚欢。然而几年间，我如恶魔般在酒精里纵欲，性情大变。纵然我羞于承认，但是我的性格确实越变越糟。我一天比一天喜怒无常，动辄发怒，我行我素。对妻子，我也是恶语相向，甚至到后来还对她拳脚相加。那些宠物当然也感受到了我的变化，被我忽视也算不了什么，被我虐待成了家常便饭。那些兔子、猴子，甚至狗，无意碰到我或有意跑来与我亲近，我都毫不怜惜地蹂躏他们一番；但对于布鲁托，我并没有下手，我还是有所

---

1 这个名字在希腊语中的意思是冥王。

But my disease grew upon me — for what disease is like Alcohol! — and at length even Pluto, who was now becoming old, and consequently somewhat **peevish**① — even Pluto began to experience the effects of my ill temper.

One night, returning home, much **intoxicated**②, from one of my haunts about town, I fancied that the cat avoided my presence. I seized him; when, in his fright at my violence, he **inflicted**③ a slight wound upon my hand with his teeth. The **fury**④ of a demon instantly possessed me. I knew myself no longer. My original soul seemed, at once, to take its flight from my body and a more than **fiendish**⑤ **malevolence**⑥, gin-nurtured, thrilled every fibre of my frame. I took from my waistcoat-pocket a pen-knife, opened it, grasped the poor beast by the throat, and deliberately cut one of its eyes from the socket! I blush, I burn, I shudder, while I pen the **damnable**⑦ **atrocity**⑧.

When reason returned with the morning — when I had slept off the **fumes**⑨ of the night's **debauch**⑩ — I experienced a sentiment half of horror, half of **remorse**⑪, for the crime of which I had been guilty; but it was, at best, a **feeble**⑫ and **equivocal**⑬ feeling, and the soul remained untouched. I again plunged into excess, and soon drowned in wine all memory of the deed.

In the meantime the cat slowly recovered. The socket of the lost eye presented, it is true, a frightful appearance, but he no longer appeared to suffer any pain. He went about the house as usual, but, as might be expected, fled in extreme terror at my approach. I had so much of my old heart left, as to be at first grieved by this evident dislike on the part of a creature which had once so loved me. But this feeling soon gave place to irritation. And then came, as if to my final and **irrevocable**⑭ overthrow, the spirit of **PERVERSENESS**⑮. Of this spirit philosophy takes no account. Yet I am not more sure that my soul lives, than I am that perverseness is one of the primitive impulses of the human heart — one of the indivisible primary faculties, or sentiments, which give direction to the character of Man. Who has not, a hundred times, found himself committing a **vile**⑯ or a silly action, for no other reason than because he knows he should not? Have we not a **perpetual**⑰ inclination, in the teeth of our best

① peevish ['pi:viʃ] a. 易怒的，暴躁的

② intoxicated [in'tɔksikeitid] a. 喝醉的

③ inflict [in'flikt] v. 施予（打击等）

④ fury ['fjuəri] n. 狂怒，暴怒

⑤ fiendish ['fi:ndiʃ] a. 恶魔似的，残忍的

⑥ malevolence [mə'levələns] n. 恶意，怨恨

⑦ damnable ['dæmnəbl] a. 可恶的，该死的

⑧ atrocity [ə'trɔsəti] n. 暴行

⑨ fume [fju:m] n. 愤怒

⑩ debauch [di'bɔ:tʃ] n. 放荡

⑪ remorse [ri'mɔ:s] n. 懊悔，悔恨

⑫ feeble ['fi:bl] a. 软弱的，虚弱的

⑬ equivocal [i'kwivəkəl] a. 模棱两可的，含糊的

⑭ irrevocable [i'revəkəbl] a. 不可改变的

⑮ perverseness [pə'və:snis] n. 堕落

⑯ vile [vail] a. 邪恶的

⑰ perpetual [pə'petʃuəl] a. 永久的，永恒的

顾忌的。酗酒真是病中之病啊，它让我病情日益严重。终于布鲁托——因年老体衰而有些脾气乖戾的布鲁托——也开始遭受我的坏脾气带来的厄运了。

有一晚，我从常去的城里酒馆醉酒而归。我以为那猫是在故意躲着我，我就一把揪住它；惊愕之中，它用牙把我的手背划破了一点儿。我顿时愤怒得像恶魔附体一般，也不知道自己是怎么了，原来善良的灵魂也不知飞逃到哪儿去了，恶魔的邪恶和酒精的熏染令我浑身都是狠劲儿。我从背心口袋里拿出削笔刀，打开，攥住那可怜畜生的脖子，存心不良地挖出来一颗眼珠！写到这暴行，我不禁面红耳赤，浑身颤抖。

过了一晚，我酒也醒了，神智也恢复了，想到自己犯下的罪行，我感到一半恐惧一半悔恨。但这充其量不过是一种微弱而模棱两可的感觉，并没有触及我的心灵。我又开始放纵自己，很快把这段事儿都泡在酒里一饮而尽。

我沉迷于酒精的同时，那猫的伤口慢慢愈合了。那没有眼珠的空空眼窝看着真吓人，但看起来它应该感觉不到疼了。它像往常一样在房间里走动，只是一见到我靠近就仓皇逃命，这是意料之中的事了。良心未泯的我起初看到曾如此爱我的猫现在对我如此嫌恶也是悲从中来。但这悲伤很快就化作了愤怒，进而化作邪念，这邪念最终注定了我的沉沦。哲学上并不承认这种邪念，但比起相信灵魂存在，我更相信这种邪念是人类心灵的一种原始冲动，还是决定人性格的一种不可分割的原始能力或原始感

judgment, to violate that which is *Law*, merely because we understand it to be such? This spirit of perverseness, I say, came to my final overthrow. It was this **unfathomable**[1] longing of the soul *to vex*[2] *itself* — to offer violence to its own nature — to do wrong for the wrong's sake only — that urged me to continue and finally to **consummate**[3] the injury I had inflicted upon the unoffending brute. One morning, in cool blood, I slipped a **noose**[4] about its neck and hung it to the limb of a tree; — hung it with the tears streaming from my eyes, and with the bitterest remorse at my heart; — hung it *because* I knew that it had loved me, and because I felt it had given me no reason of offence; — hung it because I knew that in so doing I was committing a sin — a deadly sin that would so **jeopardize**[5] my immortal soul as to place it — if such a thing were possible — even beyond the reach of the infinite mercy of the Most Merciful and Most Terrible God.

On the night of the day on which this cruel deed was done, I was aroused from sleep by the cry of fire. The curtains of my bed were in flames. The whole house was blazing. It was with great difficulty that my wife, a servant, and myself, made our escape from the **conflagration**[6]. The destruction was complete. My entire **worldly**[7] wealth was swallowed up, and I resigned myself thenceforward to despair.

I am above the weakness of seeking to establish a sequence of cause and effect, between the disaster and the atrocity. But I am detailing a chain of facts — and wish not to leave even a possible link imperfect. On the day succeeding the fire, I visited the ruins. The walls, with one exception, had fallen in. This exception was found in a **compartment wall**[8], not very thick, which stood about the middle of the house, and against which had rested the head of my bed. The **plastering**[9] had here, in great measure, resisted the action of the fire — a fact which I attributed to its having been recently spread. About this wall a dense crowd were collected, and many persons seemed to be examining a particular portion of it with very minute and eager attention. The words "strange!" "**singular**[10]!" and other similar expressions, excited my curiosity. I

① unfathomable
[ʌn'fæðəməbəl] *a.* 高深
莫测的

② vex [veks] *v.* 使烦恼，
使恼怒

③ consummate
['kɔnsə,meit] *v.* 使完整
或圆满

④ noose [nu:s] *n.* 套索，绞
索

⑤ jeopardize ['dʒepədaiz] *v.*
危及，危害

⑥ conflagration
[,kɔnflə'greiʃən] *n.* 大火，
大火灾

⑦ worldly [wə:ldli] *a.* 世间
的，人世的

⑧ compartment wall 分隔
墙

⑨ plastering ['plɑ:stəriŋ] *n.*
灰泥墙面

⑩ singular ['siŋgjulə] *a.* 异
常的，奇异的

情。谁敢说自己没有干过一箩筐蠢事，不为别的，
正是因为自己不应该做才要去做？难道我们不是一
直不顾理智的判断知法犯法，正是因为知道那是法
律才要去破坏吗？要我说，就是这种邪念让我沉
沦。内心神秘的渴望让灵魂违逆自我，摧残本性，
让我为了作恶而作恶，它推动着我继续对那无辜的
畜生下狠手，最终把它折磨致死。一天早上，我冷
酷地用索套勒住它的脖子把它吊在了树枝上。当它
吊起时我满眼泪水，内心懊悔万分。而我要吊死它，
正是因为它曾爱过我，因为它让我找不到作恶的理
由，因为我知道这是在犯罪，是让我的灵魂不得超
生的死罪。如果可能，这罪连最慈悲最可畏的上帝
也无法宽恕。

　　就在做下这恶行的当天晚上，正在睡梦中的我
被救火声吵醒。床上的幔帐已经着火，整幢房子被
大火吞噬。我和妻子连同一个仆人侥幸从火海逃脱。
房子全毁了，我世上的财产都被大火烧光，从那以
后，我陷入绝望。

　　我还没脆弱到在灾难和恶行之间寻找因果联系。
但我还是详细地把这一连串的事实讲出来，希望不
落下任何环节。火灾后那天我去查看废墟，所有的
墙都塌了，只有一面墙还立在那儿。那墙不太厚，
也不是承重墙，就在房屋中间，是我的床头靠着的
那面墙。墙上我新刷的灰泥很大程度上阻碍了火势。
墙跟前密密麻麻挤满了人，他们都目不转睛又急切
地看着墙上的一处，都惊呼着"怪事啊""没见过啊"。
我好奇心顿起，也靠过去看。老天哪！白色墙面上

approached and saw, as if graven in ***bas relief***[1] upon the white surface, the figure of a gigantic *cat*. The impression was given with an accuracy truly **marvellous**[2]. There was a rope about the animal's neck.

When I first beheld this **apparition**[3] — for I could scarcely regard it as less — my wonder and my terror were extreme. But at length reflection came to my aid. The cat, I remembered, had been hung in a garden adjacent to the house. Upon the alarm of fire, this garden had been immediately filled by the crowd — by some one of whom the animal must have been cut from the tree and thrown, through an open window, into my **chamber**[4]. This had probably been done with the view of arousing me from sleep. The falling of other walls had compressed the victim of my cruelty into the substance of the freshly-spread plaster; the lime of which, with the flames, and the ***ammonia***[5] from the **carcass**[6], had then accomplished the **portraiture**[7] as I saw it.

Although I thus readily accounted to my reason, if not altogether to my conscience, for the **startling**[8] fact just detailed, it did not the less fail to make a deep impression upon my fancy. For months I could not rid myself of the phantasm of the cat; and, during this period, there came back into my spirit a half-sentiment that seemed, but was not, remorse. I went so far as to regret the loss of the animal, and to look about me, among the vile haunts which I now habitually frequented, for another pet of the same species, and of somewhat similar appearance, with which to supply its place.

One night as I sat, half stupified, in a den of more than **infamy**[9], my attention was suddenly drawn to some black object, reposing upon the head of one of the **immense**[10] **hogsheads**[11] of **Gin**[12], or of **Rum**[13], which constituted the chief furniture of the apartment. I had been looking steadily at the top of this hogshead for some minutes, and what now caused me surprise was the fact that I had not sooner perceived the object thereupon. I approached it, and touched it with my hand. It was a black cat — a very large one — fully as large as Pluto, and closely resembling him in every respect but one. Pluto had not a white hair upon any portion of his body; but this cat had a large, although indefinite

① bas relief 浅浮雕
② marvellous ['mɑ:vələs] *a.*
不可思议的，惊人的
③ apparition [ˌæpə'riʃən] *n.*
幻影，幽灵

④ chamber ['tʃeimbə] *n.* 房
间，（尤指）卧室

⑤ ammonia [ə'məunjə] *n.*
氨气
⑥ carcass ['kɑːkəs] *n.* 动物
尸体
⑦ portraiture ['pɔːtritʃə] *n.*
肖像画
⑧ startling ['stɑːtliŋ] *a.* 惊
人的，令人震惊的

⑨ infamy ['infəmi] *n.* 声名
狼藉
⑩ immense [i'mens] *a.* 巨
大的
⑪ hogshead ['hɔgzhed] *n.*
大桶
⑫ gin [dʒin] *n.* 杜松子酒
⑬ rum [rʌm] *n.* 朗姆酒

赫然呈现出一个浅浮雕——一只硕大的猫！那雕刻栩栩如生，那畜生的脖子上还缠着一条绳子！

我乍一看到这幽灵，怎能不觉得自己是见鬼了，我惊恐至极。但转念想，松了一口气。我记得那猫被我吊在房子旁边的花园里了。火警一响，花园里马上聚满了人群，肯定有人把猫卸下来，看着窗户开着就扔进了我的房间，可能是为了把我从火中叫醒。其他墙倒下来就把我那残忍罪行的牺牲品挤压在了那面新涂了灰泥的墙上。石灰和尸体中的氨气连同火焰一同作用，就形成了墙上赫然的浮雕了吧。

对于刚刚详述的骇人事实，若说我在良心上不能得安，但于道理上却也说得过去，然而这件事却成功地在我的脑海中刻下深深的印记。接下来的好几个月，我都无法摆脱那猫的幻影的纠缠。在此期间我的心中竟然生发出一种貌似悔恨又不是悔恨的情绪。这情绪让我后悔失去那猫，于是我开始在我现在经常出入的龌龊场所蹅摸一只外貌多少相似的猫，来填补那猫的位置。

有一晚，我坐在一个臭名昭著的酒寮里，半醉半醒间我兀地注意到一个黑东西，就在这屋子的一件主要家什，那个装着金酒或是朗姆酒的巨大酒桶上头趴着。我目不转睛地盯着那酒桶上边也有几分钟了，怪就怪在我早没察觉到那东西的存在。我走近它，用手摸了一下。原来那是一只黑猫——个头还不小——大得赶上布鲁托了，和它也极相似，唯一不同的是这猫胸前有一大块白斑，虽然不清晰却几乎盖住整个胸前，而布鲁托周身都是黑色的。我一摸它，它就立刻站起来，大声地咕噜咕噜叫着蹭向我的手，对

splotch① of white, covering nearly the whole region of the breast. Upon my touching him, he immediately arose, **purred**② loudly, rubbed against my hand, and appeared delighted with my notice. This, then, was the very creature of which I was in search. I at once offered to purchase it of the landlord; but this person made no claim to it — knew nothing of it — had never seen it before.

I continued my caresses, and, when I prepared to go home, the animal **evinced**③ a disposition to accompany me. I permitted it to do so; occasionally stooping and patting it as I proceeded. When it reached the house it **domesticated**④ itself at once, and became immediately a great favorite with my wife.

For my own part, I soon found a dislike to it arising within me. This was just the reverse of what I had anticipated; but — I know not how or why it was — its evident fondness for myself rather disgusted and annoyed. By slow degrees, these feelings of disgust and annoyance rose into the bitterness of hatred. I avoided the creature; a certain sense of shame, and the remembrance of my former deed of cruelty, preventing me from physically abusing it. I did not, for some weeks, strike, or otherwise violently ill use it; but gradually — very gradually — I came to look upon it with **unutterable**⑤ **loathing**⑥, and to flee silently from its **odious**⑦ presence, as from the breath of a **pestilence**⑧.

What added, no doubt, to my hatred of the beast, was the discovery, on the morning after I brought it home, that, like Pluto, it also had been deprived of one of its eyes. This circumstance, however, only **endeared**⑨ it to my wife, who, as I have already said, possessed, in a high degree, that humanity of feeling which had once been my distinguishing trait, and the source of many of my simplest and purest pleasures.

With my **aversion**⑩ to this cat, however, its partiality for myself seemed to increase. It followed my footsteps with a **pertinacity**⑪ which it would be difficult to make the reader comprehend. Whenever I sat, it would **crouch**⑫ beneath my chair, or spring upon my knees, covering me with its loathsome caresses. If I arose to walk it would get between my feet and thus nearly throw me down, or, fastening its long and sharp claws in my dress, **clamber**⑬, in this

① splotch [splɔtʃ] *n.* 斑点
② pur [pɔ:] *v.* 咕噜咕噜叫

③ evince [i'vins] *v.* 表明，
表示
④ domesticate
[dəu'mestikeit] *v.* 使习惯
于家庭生活

⑤ unutterable [ˌʌn'ʌtərəbl]
a. 难以言表的
⑥ loathing ['ləuðiŋ] *n.* 厌
恶，憎恶
⑦ odious ['əudiəs] *a.* 可憎
的，讨厌的
⑧ pestilence ['pestiləns] *n.*
瘟疫
⑨ endear [in'diə] *v.* 使受喜
爱，使受爱慕

⑩ aversion [ə'və:ʃən] *n.* 厌
恶，嫌恶
⑪ pertinacity [ˌpɔ:ti'næsiti]
n. 顽固，固执
⑫ crouch [krautʃ] *v.* 蜷伏
⑬ clamber ['klæmbə] *v.* 攀
登，爬上

我的关注表示欢喜。好吧，这就是我苦苦寻找的猫了。我当场就向店主表示我愿出钱买下它；但那店主却表示这猫并不是他的，不知道它的来历，也从没见过它。

我一直爱抚着那猫，当我起身要回家的时候，这畜生却露出要跟着我走的样子。我就让它跟着，一边走着一边偶尔弯下腰拍拍它。一到家，它就把这儿当成了自己家，立刻赢得了我妻子的欢心。

而我，心里却很快燃起对它的憎恶。这完全出乎我的预料；不知怎的，也不知为何，它对我表现出很明显的眷爱却令我厌烦又恼火。逐渐地，这些情绪升级为深恶痛绝。我故意躲着那畜生；或出于某种羞愧心理，抑或忆起早先的暴行，我并没有虐待它。有几周时间，我都没有打它，也没有粗暴地踩躏它；但渐渐地，渐渐地，我一看到它就说不出来地厌恶。见到它那可憎的模样我就像遇到瘟疫一般悄悄溜开。

我把它带回家的第二天早上，发现它像布鲁托一样也有一只眼睛被挖掉了，不用说，这使我打心底里对它的憎恶又加深一层。然而见这情形，我妻子却更疼爱它了。我说过，我妻子她极富同情心，那种同情心也曾是我突出的美德，也曾是我简单纯洁的快乐的源泉。

然而我越是反感这猫，它却越和我亲热。它和我寸步不离，那股惹人烦的黏人劲儿读者你根本无法理解。我一坐下，它就蹲在我椅子下面，或者跳到我的膝盖上，在我身上到处蹭，实在令人厌恶。要是我站起来走开，要么它就缠在我脚下，险些把我绊倒，要么用它那长长的尖爪子勾住我的衣服攀爬到我胸前。每每此时，我真想一拳揍死它，但却

manner, to my breast. At such times, although I longed to destroy it with a blow, I was yet withheld from so doing, partly by a memory of my former crime, but chiefly — let me confess it at once — by absolute dread of the beast.

This dread was not exactly a dread of physical evil — and yet I should be at a loss how otherwise to define it. I am almost ashamed to own — yes, even in this **felon**①'s cell, I am almost ashamed to own — that the terror and horror with which the animal inspired me, had been heightened by one of the merest **chimaeras**② it would be possible to conceive. My wife had called my attention, more than once, to the character of the mark of white hair, of which I have spoken, and which constituted the sole visible difference between the strange beast and the one I had destroyed. The reader will remember that this mark, although large, had been originally very indefinite; but, by slow degrees — degrees nearly **imperceptible**③, and which for a long time my Reason struggled to reject as fanciful — it had, at length, assumed a rigorous distinctness of outline. It was now the representation of an object that I shudder to name — and for this, above all, I loathed, and dreaded, and would have rid myself of the monster *had I dared* — it was now, I say, the image of a **hideous**④ — of a **ghastly**⑤ thing — of the **GALLOWS**⑥! — oh, mournful and terrible engine of Horror and of Crime — of Agony and of Death!

And now was I indeed **wretched**⑦ beyond the wretchedness of mere Humanity. And *a brute beast* — whose fellow I had **contemptuously**⑧ destroyed — *a brute beast* to work out for *me* — for me a man, fashioned in the image of the High God — so much of insufferable wo! Alas! neither by day nor by night knew I, the blessing of Rest any more! During the former the creature left me no moment alone; and, in the latter, I started, hourly, from dreams of unutterable fear, to find the hot breath of *the thing* upon my face, and its vast weight — an **incarnate**⑨ Night-Mare that I had no power to shake off — **incumbent**⑩ eternally upon my *heart*!

Beneath the pressure of torments such as these, the feeble **remnant**⑪ of the good within me **succumbed**⑫. Evil thoughts became my sole intimates — the

不能这么做，也许是由于我对之前的罪行仍记忆犹新，但，还是直说了吧，主要还是因为我真是怕极了这畜生。

确切地说，这种怕和对实实在在的恶魔的怕又不是一回事儿——而我又不知该如何定义它。我羞于承认——是的，即使在这死牢，我还是羞于承认——这畜生在我心中激发起的恐惧和厌恶与日俱增，在我脑海中幻化成妖魔鬼怪。我妻子不止一次提醒我注意，我以前也提到过，这奇怪的猫和我虐杀的那只猫之间唯一的不同就在于那片白斑。读者你可能也记得，这白斑虽然很大，原来也不明显，但是慢慢地，慢慢地，几乎在不知不觉中，它终于显现出清晰的轮廓，长久以来我的理智一直挣扎着拒绝承认，并当它是幻象。一提起那白斑代表的东西，我就不寒而栗——对于这点，我尤其厌恶和惧怕，如果我有胆量，我早就把它弄死了——告诉你吧，那白斑现在变成了一个可怕的东西的图案——绞刑架！——天哪！多么可悲、多么可怕的刑具！让人受苦、让人送命的刑具！

这时的我真的是可怜得不能再可怜。我若无其事地杀死了一只没有理性的畜生，它的同类却令我这个至高的上帝按照自己的样子创造出来的人遭受如此令人难以忍受的灾祸！天哪！无论白天黑夜，我再也得不到安宁啦！白天，那畜生一刻也不离开我；晚上，我时不时地从说不出多可怕的梦魇中惊醒，每每醒来都会发现那梦魇化身的东西对着我的脸喷着热气，而它那沉重的身躯就那样一直压在我的心头，我甩都甩不掉。

在这百般痛苦的煎熬下，我心底仅存的一丝善良被耗尽了。最黑暗、最邪恶的念头一直在我心头萦绕。

① felon ['felən] *n.* 重罪犯，恶棍

② chimaera [kai,mərə] *n.*（希腊神话）吐火怪的喀迈拉，假想的怪物

③ imperceptible [,impə'septəbl] *a.* 感觉不到的，极细微的

④ hideous ['hidiəs] *a.* 可怕的，丑恶的

⑤ ghastly ['gɑ:stli] *a.* 可怕的，令人毛骨悚然的

⑥ gallows ['gæləuz] *n.* 绞刑架

⑦ wretched ['retʃid] *a.* 可怜的，卑鄙的

⑧ contemptuously [kən'temptjuəsli] *ad.* 轻蔑地

⑨ incarnate [in'kɑ:nit] *a.* 化身的，极典型的

⑩ incumbent [in'kʌmbənt] *a.* 成为责任的，必须履行的

⑪ remnant ['remnənt] *n.* 剩余

⑫ succumb [sə'kʌm] *v.* 屈服，屈从

darkest and most evil of thoughts. The moodiness of my usual temper increased to hatred of all things and of all mankind; while, from the sudden, frequent, and ungovernable outbursts of a fury to which I now blindly abandoned myself, my uncomplaining wife, alas! was the most usual and the most patient of sufferers.

One day she accompanied me, upon some household **errand**①, into the **cellar**② of the old building which our poverty compelled us to inhabit. The cat followed me down the steep stairs, and, nearly throwing me headlong, **exasperated**③ me to madness. Uplifting an axe, and forgetting, in my **wrath**④, the childish dread which had hitherto stayed my hand, I aimed a blow at the animal which, of course, would have proved instantly fatal had it descended as I wished. But this blow was arrested by the hand of my wife. **Goaded**⑤, by the **interference**⑥, into a rage more than **demoniacal**⑦, I withdrew my arm from her grasp and buried the axe in her brain. She fell dead upon the spot, without a **groan**⑧.

This hideous murder accomplished, I set myself forthwith, and with entire deliberation, to the task of concealing the body. I knew that I could not remove it from the house, either by day or by night, without the risk of being observed by the neighbors. Many projects entered my mind. At one period I thought of cutting the corpse into minute fragments, and destroying them by fire. At another, I resolved to dig a grave for it in the floor of the cellar. Again, I deliberated about casting it in the well in the yard — about packing it in a box, as if merchandize, with the usual arrangements, and so getting a **porter**⑨ to take it from the house. Finally I hit upon what I considered a far better **expedient**⑩ than either of these. I determined to wall it up in the cellar — as the monks of the middle ages are recorded to have walled up their victims.

For a purpose such as this the cellar was well adapted. Its walls were loosely constructed, and had lately been plastered throughout with a rough plaster, which the dampness of the atmosphere had prevented from hardening. Moreover, in one of the walls was a projection, caused by a false **chimney**⑪, or fireplace, that had been filled up, and made to resemble the rest of the cellar. I

以往的喜怒无常变本加厉地升级到痛恨一切人一切事。我盲目地放任自己，经常突然无法控制地暴怒。我那逆来顺受的妻子，哎呀，就成了最惯常最隐忍的受虐者啦。

因为穷，我和妻子只能住在一栋旧房子里。一天，她陪我去房子的地窖里干点儿家务活。那猫尾随我走下陡峭的楼梯，差点儿把我绊了个倒栽葱，我顿时火往上蹿。盛怒之下我忘却了那之前还阻止我动手的幼稚的恐惧，我提起斧子，照着那畜生就抡过去。如果按照我的意愿落下去，这一下无疑是致命的。不料这一挥却被我妻子用手拦在半空。正在气头上的我被这一挡更是激怒得如同恶魔，从她手中挣出胳膊，一斧子就砍进她的脑壳。她哼都没哼一声，当场就断气了。

犯下这杀人的罪孽，我开始深思熟虑如何隐藏尸体。我知道无论白天黑夜，只要我把尸体搬出屋子，就有被邻居发现的危险。我头脑中构想出几个方案。一度我还想到将尸体肢解成小块，用火焚烧。我还想到在地窖里挖一个坑将她埋了。我还考虑过把她丢进院子的井里，抑或把她装进箱子，像安排货物一样找个脚夫把箱子抬走。最后我灵光一现，撇开诸多权宜之计，想到一个万全之策。我决定把她砌进地窖的墙里——据记载，中世纪的僧侣也曾将他们的殉葬品砌进墙里。

这个地窖正合适派上这个用场。它的墙壁砌得很松，近期刚用粗灰泥粉刷过，由于地窖空气潮湿，灰泥还没完全硬化。更妙的是，有一面墙壁因为有个假烟囱或是壁炉而突出一块，已经被填实了，做

① errand ['erənd] *n.* 差事
② cellar ['selə] *n.* 地窖，地下室
③ exasperate [ig'zæspəreit] *v.* 激怒，触怒
④ wrath [ræθ] *n.* 愤怒

⑤ goad [gəud] *v.* (不断地) 招惹，激怒
⑥ interference [,intə'fiərəns] *n.* 干扰，冲突
⑦ demoniacal [,di:məu'naiəkəl] *a.* 恶魔似的，狂暴的
⑧ groan [grəun] *n.* 呻吟

⑨ porter ['pɔ:tə] *n.* 搬运工人
⑩ expedient [ik'spi:diənt] *n.* 权宜之计，应急手段

⑪ chimney ['tʃimni] *n.* 烟囱

made no doubt that I could readily displace the bricks at this point, insert the corpse, and wall the whole up as before, so that no eye could detect any thing **suspicious**①. And in this calculation I was not deceived. By means of a **crow-bar**② I easily **dislodged**③ the bricks, and, having carefully deposited the body against the inner wall, I propped it in that position, while, with little trouble, I re-laid the whole structure as it originally stood. Having procured **mortar**④, sand, and hair, with every possible precaution, I prepared a plaster which could not be distinguished from the old, and with this I very carefully went over the new brickwork. When I had finished, I felt satisfied that all was right. The wall did not present the slightest appearance of having been disturbed. The rubbish on the floor was picked up with the minutest care. I looked around triumphantly, and said to myself — "Here at least, then, my labor has not been in vain."

My next step was to look for the beast which had been the cause of so much wretchedness; for I had, at length, firmly resolved to put it to death. Had I been able to meet with it, at the moment, there could have been no doubt of its fate; but it appeared that the **crafty**⑤ animal had been alarmed at the violence of my previous anger, and forebore to present itself in my present mood. It is impossible to describe, or to imagine, the deep, the **blissful**⑥ sense of relief which the absence of the detested creature occasioned in my bosom. It did not make its appearance during the night — and thus for one night at least, since its introduction into the house, I soundly and tranquilly slept; aye, slept even with the burden of murder upon my soul!

The second and the third day passed, and still my **tormentor**⑦ came not. Once again I breathed as a freeman. The monster, in terror, had fled the premises forever! I should behold it no more! My happiness was supreme! The guilt of my dark deed disturbed me but little. Some few inquiries had been made, but these had been readily answered. Even a search had been instituted — but of course nothing was to be discovered. I looked upon my future **felicity**⑧ as secured.

Upon the fourth day of the **assassination**⑨, a party of the police came, very unexpectedly, into the house, and proceeded again to make rigorous

① suspicious [sə'spiʃəs] *a.*
可疑的，容易引起怀疑
的

② crow-bar 铁撬棍

③ dislodge [dis'lɔdʒ] *v.*（从
特定位置上）强行取出
（或去除、移开、移动）

④ mortar ['mɔ:tə] *n.* 砂浆

⑤ crafty ['krɑ:fti] *a.* 狡猾
的

⑥ blissful ['blisful] *a.* 充满
喜悦的

⑦ tormentor [tɔ:'mentə] *n.*
使人痛苦的人或物

⑧ felicity [fi'lisiti] *n.* 幸福，
快乐

⑨ assassination
[ə,sæsi'neiʃən] *n.* 暗杀

得跟地窖其他部分浑然一体。我确信可以轻而易举
地将这里的砖挖开，塞入尸体，再把墙重新垒好如
初，谁也看不出破绽来。如此算计果然不错。我用
撬棍将砖轻松撬开，小心翼翼地把尸体靠在内墙撑
好，这样一来我就毫不费力地把墙照原样砌回去了。
备好灰浆、沙子和杂毛，做好一切防范措施，我拌
好了和原来的粗灰泥一样的泥浆，把它小心翼翼地
抹在新砌的墙上。等我干完活，看到一切顺当才心
满意足。那墙表面一点儿也看不出被动过的痕迹。
地上的垃圾也被细心地捡起来了。我扬扬得意地环
顾四周，自言自语道："至少这回没白忙活。"

　　紧接着就是要找到那个让我如此悲惨的畜生，
我终于横下心要置它于死地。当时若让我见到它，
它死定了；可似乎那狡猾的畜生被我之前的暴怒惊
到了，故意躲着我的这种情绪不敢露脸。压在我心
头的那可憎的畜生终于没有了，那种充斥着喜悦的
无比释然之感真是难以形容难以想象。当晚，那畜
生也没露面——这样，自从它侵入这房子，至少我
能有一晚能够酣然入睡；哎，纵然灵魂还背负着谋杀
的罪恶，我还是安稳地睡着了。

　　第二天过去了，第三天过去了，那折磨我的猫还
是没出现。我又可以呼吸着自由的空气啦。那畜生说
不定吓得溜着墙根儿逃之夭夭，再也不回来了。眼
前从此清静啦！真是幸福至极！就连犯下罪恶勾当
也没令我内心有多少不安。有人来调查过几次，但
都被我轻易搪塞过去了。甚至还来屋子里搜查过一
次——当然也是毫无收获。看来我未来是有保障高
枕无忧啦。

　　我杀妻第四天，一帮警察不期而至，再次对房子
进行严密的搜查。藏尸地点是他们想不到的，绝对

investigation of the premises. Secure, however, in the inscrutability of my place of concealment, I felt no embarrassment whatever. The officers **bade**① me accompany them in their search. They left no **nook**② or corner unexplored. At length, for the third or fourth time, they descended into the cellar. I quivered not in a muscle. My heart beat calmly as that of one who **slumbers**③ in innocence. I walked the cellar from end to end. I folded my arms upon my bosom, and **roamed**④ easily to and fro. The police were thoroughly satisfied and prepared to depart. The **glee**⑤ at my heart was too strong to be restrained. I burned to say if but one word, by way of triumph, and to render doubly sure their assurance of my guiltlessness.

"Gentlemen," I said at last, as the party ascended the steps, "I delight to have **allayed**⑥ your suspicions. I wish you all health, and a little more courtesy. By the bye, gentlemen, this — this is a very well constructed house." [In the **rabid**⑦ desire to say something easily, I scarcely knew what I uttered at all.] — "I may say an *excellently* well constructed house. These walls — are you going, gentlemen? — these walls are solidly put together;" and here, through the mere phrenzy of **bravado**⑧, I rapped heavily, with a **cane**⑨ which I held in my hand, upon that very portion of the brick-work behind which stood the corpse of the wife of my bosom.

But may God shield and deliver me from the fangs of the Arch-Fiend! No sooner had the **reverberation**⑩ of my blows sunk into silence, than I was answered by a voice from within the tomb! — by a cry, at first **muffled**⑪ and broken, like the sobbing of a child, and then quickly swelling into one long, loud, and continuous scream, utterly **anomalous**⑫ and inhuman — a howl — a **wailing**⑬ **shriek**⑭, half of horror and half of triumph, such as might have arisen only out of hell, conjointly from the throats of the dammed in their agony and of the demons that **exult**⑮ in the **damnation**⑯.

Of my own thoughts it is folly to speak. **Swooning**⑰, I **staggered**⑱ to the opposite wall. For one instant the party upon the stairs remained motionless,

① bade [beid] *v.* (bid 的一种过去式) 命令
② nook [nuk] *n.* 隐蔽处
③ slumber ['slʌmbə] *v.* 打盹
④ roam [rəum] *v.* 闲逛，漫步
⑤ glee ['gliː] *n.* 高兴，欢乐

⑥ allay [ə'lei] *v.* 减轻
⑦ rabid ['ræbid] *a.* 狂暴的，激烈的
⑧ bravado [brə'vɑːdəu] *n.* 虚张声势，冒险
⑨ cane [kein] *n.* 手杖，藤杖
⑩ reverberation [ri,və:bə'reiʃən] *n.* 回响
⑪ muffled ['mʌfld] *a.* (声音因隔着门、墙等) 沉闷，模糊不清的
⑫ anomalous [ə'nɔmələs] *a.* 反常的，异常的
⑬ wail [weil] *v.* 哀号，恸哭
⑭ shriek [ʃriːk] *n.* 尖叫声
⑮ exult [ig'zʌlt] *v.* 狂喜，欢欣鼓舞
⑯ damnation [dæm'neiʃən] *n.* 诅咒，遭天罚
⑰ swoon [swuːn] *v.* 晕厥，昏倒
⑱ stagger ['stæɡə] *v.* 蹒跚

安全，所以我表现得波澜不惊。那些警察让我陪同他们搜查。他们把犄角旮旯都查看了，搜了三四遍，最后搜到了地窖里。我丝毫不紧张，心跳平稳得好像没做亏心事不怕鬼叫门一般。我从地窖一头走到另一头，双手抱在胸前，若无其事地来回踱步。这下警察们彻底满意了，准备离开。我抑制不住心头那股强烈的窃喜劲儿。胜利在望，我恨不得开口哪怕说一个字，好让他们更加确定我是无罪的。

"各位，"正当那帮人走上楼梯时，我终于还是忍不住开口了，"你们不怀疑我了，我很高兴。愿你们健康，给你们请安。再见吧，先生们，这，这房子结实着呢。"（太努力想让自己说些轻松的话了，我都不知道自己说了什么。）"可以说这房子建得完美极了。这些墙——先生们，要走了吗？——这些墙砌得很牢固。"说到这儿，我真是昏了头，虚张声势地拿手里的一根棒子用力地敲击那堵将我的爱妻砌在后面的砖墙。

上帝保佑，请从恶魔的利齿下将我拯救吧！那棍子敲击的回音刚消失，我就听见坟墓里发出了声音！——是哭声，一开始瓮声瓮气，断断续续，像婴儿哭泣，紧接着一下子变成连声长啸，十分诡异，惨绝人寰——一声哀嚎——一声尖利的哀鸣，一半惊恐，一半得意，这声音好似来自地狱，夹杂着冤魂痛苦的嘶鸣和魔鬼见了他们遭到天谴时发出的欢呼。

要说当时我的想法真是愚蠢至极。我晕晕乎乎地踉跄着走到那堵墙旁边。出于极度惊恐和畏惧，站在楼梯上的警察们一时间没缓过神来，都愣住了，

through extremity of terror and of awe. In the next, a dozen **stout**[1] arms were toiling at the wall. It fell bodily. The corpse, already greatly decayed and **clotted**[2] with **gore**[3], stood **erect**[4] before the eyes of the spectators. Upon its head, with red extended mouth and **solitary**[5] eye of fire, sat the hideous beast whose craft had seduced me into murder, and whose informing voice had consigned me to the **hangman**[6]. I had walled the monster up within the tomb!

① stout [staut] *a.* 肥胖粗壮
的

② clot [klɔt] *v.*（血液等）
凝结成块

③ gore [gɔ:] *n.*（伤口流出
的）血，污血

④ erect [i'rekt] *a.* 直立的，
竖立的

⑤ solitary ['sɔlitəri] *a.* 孤独
的

⑥ hangman ['hæŋmən] *n.*
绞刑执行人

而下一秒，十来条健壮的臂膀开始奋力拆墙。那墙整面倒下来。只见那尸体已经腐烂不堪，凝满血块，赫然立在众人面前。而那只可恶的诱使我实施谋杀的狡猾的猫正张着它那血盆大口，瞪着火红的独眼，站在尸体的头顶上；也正是这畜生报警似的叫声把我送上了绞刑架。原来我竟把这畜生砌进了这堵墓墙！

The Gold-Bug

What ho! what ho! this fellow is dancing mad!
He hath been bitten by the Tarantula.
                    — All in the Wrong.

Many years ago, I contracted an **intimacy**① with a Mr. William Legrand. He was of an ancient Huguenot family, and had once been wealthy; but a series of misfortunes had reduced him to want. To avoid the **mortification**② consequent upon his disasters, he left New Orleans, the city of his forefathers, and took up his residence at Sullivan's Island, near Charleston, South Carolina. This Island is a very singular one. It consists of little else than the sea sand, and is about three miles long. Its breadth at no point exceeds a quarter of a mile. It is separated from the main land by a scarcely **perceptible**③ **creek**④, **oozing**⑤ its way through a wilderness of **reeds**⑥ and **slime**⑦, a favorite resort of the **marsh hen**⑧. The vegetation, as might be supposed, is **scant**⑨, or at least **dwarfish**⑩. No trees of any magnitude are to be seen. Near the western extremity, where Fort Moultrie stands, and where are some miserable frame buildings, **tenanted**⑪, during summer, by the **fugitives**⑫ from Charleston dust and fever, may be found, indeed, the **bristly**⑬ **palmetto**⑭; but the whole island, with the exception of this western point, and a line of hard, white beach on the seacoast, is covered with a

金甲虫

喂！快瞧！这家伙在疯跳！
他被毒狼蛛咬啦。

——《无人脱责》

① intimacy ['intiməsi] *n.* 亲
密，亲近

② mortification
[,mɔ:tifi'keiʃən] *n.* 屈辱

③ perceptible [pə'septibl] *a.*
看得见的

④ creek [kri:k] *n.* 小溪

⑤ ooze [u:z] *v.* 渗出

⑥ reed [ri:d] *n.* 芦苇

⑦ slime [slaim] *n.* 烂泥

⑧ marsh hen 沼泽鸡

⑨ scant [skænt] *a.* 不足的，
欠缺的

⑩ dwarfish ['dwɔ:fiʃ] *a.* 矮
小的

⑪ tenant ['tenənt] *v.* 租借

⑫ fugitive ['fju:dʒitiv] *n.* 逃
亡者，逃犯

⑬ bristly ['brisli] *a.* 有刚毛
的

⑭ palmetto [pæl'metəu] *n.*
美洲蒲葵（棕榈科植物）

多年前，我与一位威廉·勒格朗先生交往甚密。他来自一个古老的胡格诺教徒家族，曾经家道富贵，但接连灾祸却使他一贫如洗。因惧怕人穷遭欺，他便离开了祖辈居住的新奥尔良，在南卡罗莱纳州靠近查尔斯顿的沙利文岛屿落脚住下。此岛独一无二，几乎全部由海沙堆成，三英里长，宽度也不过四百米。这小岛和大陆之间，一条几乎看不清的小溪挣扎着流淌过一片杂生的软泥芦苇荡，水鸡喜欢在这里栖息。这里的植被即使有，也十分稀少，抑或低矮，更是见不到参天大树了。靠近小岛最西头能看到短硬的蒲葵，那里建有一座穆特里城堡，还有几幢破败的建筑，一到夏天，就有人为了躲避查尔斯顿的灰尘和炎热而租住在这里。除了这个角落，整个岛的海岸都是坚硬的白沙，其他地方都密密麻麻地长满了芬芳的桃金娘，这种植物颇受英格兰的园艺家

dense undergrowth of the sweet myrtle, so much prized by the **horticulturists**[①] of England. The shrub here often attains the height of fifteen or twenty feet, and forms an almost impenetrable **coppice**[②], burthening the air with its fragrance.

In the inmost recesses of this coppice, not far from the eastern or more remote end of the island, Legrand had built himself a small hut, which he occupied when I first, by mere accident, made his acquaintance. This soon **ripened**[③] into friendship — for there was much in the recluse to excite interest and esteem. I found him well educated, with unusual powers of mind, but infected with **misanthropy**[④], and subject to perverse moods of alternate enthusiasm and **melancholy**[⑤]. He had with him many books, but rarely employed them. His chief amusements were gunning and fishing, or **sauntering**[⑥] along the beach and through the myrtles, in quest of shells or **entomological**[⑦] **specimens**[⑧]; — his collection of the latter might have been envied by a Swammerdamm. In these excursions he was usually accompanied by an old negro, called Jupiter, who had been **manumitted**[⑨] before the reverses of the family, but who could be induced, neither by threats nor by promises, to abandon what he considered his right of attendance upon the footsteps of his young "Massa Will." It is not improbable that the relatives of Legrand, conceiving him to be somewhat unsettled in intellect, had contrived to **instil**[⑩] this **obstinacy**[⑪] into Jupiter, with a view to the supervision and guardianship of the wanderer.

The winters in the latitude of Sullivan's Island are seldom very severe, and in the fall of the year it is a rare event indeed when a fire is considered necessary. About the middle of October, 18—, there occurred, however, a day of remarkable chilliness. Just before sunset I scrambled my way through the **evergreens**[⑫] to the hut of my friend, whom I had not visited for several weeks — my residence being, at that time, in Charleston, a distance of nine miles from the Island, while the facilities of passage and re-passage were very far behind those of the present day. Upon reaching the hut I rapped, as was my custom, and getting no reply, sought for the key where I knew it was secreted, unlocked the door and went in. A fine fire was blazing upon the **hearth**[⑬]. It was a novelty, and by no means an

① horticulturist
[ˌhɔ:ti'kʌltʃərist] *n.* 园艺
家

② coppice ['kɔ,pis] *n.* 矮
林，小灌木丛

③ ripen ['raipən] *v.*（思想、
感情等）变得成熟

④ misanthropy
[mi'zænθrəpi] *n.* 厌世

⑤ melancholy ['melənkəli]
n. 忧郁

⑥ saunter ['sɔ:ntə] *v.* 漫步，
闲逛

⑦ entomological
[ˌentəmə'lɔdʒikəl] *a.* 昆
虫学的

⑧ specimen ['spesimin] *n.*
样品，样本

⑨ manumit [ˌmænju'mit] *v.*
解放，释放

⑩ instil [in'stil] *v.* 逐渐灌
输

⑪ obstinacy ['ɔbstinəsi] *n.*
固执，顽固

⑫ evergreen ['evəgri:n] *n.*
常绿植物，常绿树

⑬ hearth [hɑ:θ] *n.* 壁炉

们的青睐。这些桃金娘都高达十五到二十英尺[1]，连成浓密的树丛，几乎无从下脚，散发出馥郁香气，弥漫小岛。

离小岛东头不远，也就是较偏远那头的密林深处，勒格朗建了一座小屋，我最初偶然结识他就在这里。我们很快成了朋友——这个隐士激起了我的兴趣又令我敬佩。他富有教养，脑力过人，但是染上了厌世情绪，做事有悖常理，时而热情洋溢，时而郁郁寡欢。他有许多藏书，但很少看。他的主要消遣就是去打猎钓鱼，有时沿海滩散步，抑或钻进桃金娘树丛去寻找贝壳或者昆虫标本；他的昆虫标本收藏令施旺麦丹[2]之流都羡慕不已。每次出门，都有一个叫作朱庇特的老黑奴跟着他。在勒格朗家道中落之前这黑奴就被解放了，但是无论威逼利诱都无法将他赶走，他认为寸步不离地侍奉小"威尔少爷"就是他的使命。想必是勒格朗家的亲戚认为朱庇特有些弱智，所以才想办法养成他这种艮脾气，既能监督这个流浪汉，又能保护他。

在沙利文岛所在的纬度，冬天很少严寒，秋季也不必生火。然而在18××年的十月中旬，有一日居然冷得彻骨。日落前，我深一脚浅一脚地穿过长青木丛来到我朋友的小屋。有几周没来看他了——当时我住在查尔斯顿，距离这个小岛九英里远，往返的交通工具也不如现在便利。我在屋外如往常一样敲门，却没人应答，我知道钥匙藏在哪，于是我找到钥匙，开门进了屋。只见壁炉里烈火熊熊，这倒稀奇，我却求之不得。于是我脱了外套，坐在炉

1　4.5米到6米。

2　荷兰生物学家，在昆虫学研究方面成就突出。

ungrateful one. I threw off an overcoat, took an arm-chair by the crackling logs, and awaited patiently the arrival of my hosts.

Soon after dark they arrived, and gave me a most **cordial**① welcome. Jupiter, grinning from ear to ear, bustled about to prepare some marsh-hens for supper. Legrand was in one of his fits — how else shall I term them? — of enthusiasm. He had found an unknown **bivalve**②, forming a new genus, and, more than this, he had hunted down and secured, with Jupiter's assistance, a **scarabaeus**③ which he believed to be totally new, but in respect to which he wished to have my opinion on the morrow.

"And why not to-night?" I asked, rubbing my hands over the blaze, and wishing the whole tribe of scarabæi at the devil.

"Ah, if I had only known you were here!" said Legrand, "but it's so long since I saw you; and how could I foresee that you would pay me a visit this very night of all others? As I was coming home I met **Lieutenant**④ G — , from the fort, and, very foolishly, I lent him the bug; so it will be impossible for you to see it until the morning. Stay here to-night, and I will send Jup down for it at sunrise. It is the loveliest thing in creation!"

"What? — sunrise?"

"Nonsense! no! — the bug. It is of a brilliant gold color — about the size of a large hickory-nut — with two jet black spots near one extremity of the back, and another, somewhat longer, at the other. The **antennae**⑤ are — "

"Dey aint no tin in him, Massa Will, I keep a tellin on you," here interrupted Jupiter; "de bug is a goole bug, solid, ebery bit of him, inside and all, sep him wing — neber feel half so hebby a bug in my life."

"Well, suppose it is, Jup," replied Legrand, somewhat more earnestly, it seemed to me, than the case demanded, "is that any reason for your letting the birds burn? The color" — here he turned to me — "is really almost enough to **warrant**⑥ Jupiter's idea. You never saw a more brilliant **metallic**⑦ **lustre**⑧ than

边的扶手椅上，一边听着木块燃烧的噼啪声，一边耐心等待屋主归来。

他们天黑不久就回来了，十分热情地招待了我。朱庇特笑得合不拢嘴，嘴角都快咧到耳朵了，满屋忙乱着准备把水鸡做成晚餐。勒格朗的"热情洋溢"病正发作——除了"病"我还真想不出别的词来形容。他找到了一种不知名的双壳贝，是个新品种；此外，在朱庇特的协助下他还成功追踪并捕获了一只金龟子，照他看来也是个新品种，但想在明天听听我的看法。

"为什么不在今晚？"我问，一边搓着手烤着炉火，一边心里想着让金龟子那类东西都见鬼去吧。

"嗨，早知道你来就好啦！"勒格朗说，"许久没见你，我怎么也没料到你偏偏在今晚来找我啊。我回来的路上遇到穆特里城堡的 G 中尉，一时犯傻，把虫子借给了他；所以今晚你是见不到它啦，明天早上吧。你在这儿过夜，等到太阳一升起，我就让老朱把它取回来。那是世上最妙的东西！"

"什么？日出吗？"

"胡说！当然不是！——虫子。它浑身金光闪闪——像大山胡桃那么大——后背一端有两颗如玉般黑亮的圆点，另一端也有一颗，稍长一点儿。那触须……"

"它身上可没锡，威尔少爷，我还是那句话，"这时朱庇特打断道，"那虫子是金甲虫，纯金，里里拜拜斗是金子，就翅膀拔是——我这辈子豆没掂过这么粽的虫子。"

"行，就算是，老朱，"勒格朗搭腔道，在我看来，他大可不必说得那么认真，"就凭这点你就让水鸡烧糊啦？那颜色"——说到这儿，他转身看着我——"实在是足以证实朱庇特的想法。那甲壳上发出的铿

① cordial ['kɔ:djəl] *a.* 热情的，诚恳的

② bivalve ['baivælv] *n.* 双壳贝

③ scarabaeus [ˌskærə'bi:əs] *n.* 圣甲虫

④ lieutenant [lu:'tenənt] *n.* 中尉

⑤ antennae [æn'teni:] *n.* [复数]（昆虫的）触须

⑥ warrant ['wɔrənt] *v.* 使有正当理由，成为……的根据

⑦ metallic [mi'tælik] *a.* 金属的

⑧ lustre ['lʌstə] *n.* 光泽，光彩

the scales **emit**① — but of this you cannot judge till tomorrow. In the mean time I can give you some idea of the shape." Saying this, he seated himself at a small table, on which were a pen and ink, but no paper. He looked for some in a drawer, but found none.

"Never mind," said he at length, "this will answer;" and he drew from his waistcoat pocket a scrap of what I took to be very dirty foolscap, and made upon it a rough drawing with the pen. While he did this, I retained my seat by the fire, for I was still chilly. When the design was complete, he handed it to me without rising. As I received it, a loud **growl**② was heard, succeeded by a scratching at the door. Jupiter opened it, and a large Newfoundland, belonging to Legrand, rushed in, leaped upon my shoulders, and loaded me with caresses; for I had shown him much attention during previous visits. When his **gambols**③ were over, I looked at the paper, and, to speak the truth, found myself not a little puzzled at what my friend had **depicted**④.

"Well!" I said, after **contemplating**⑤ it for some minutes, "this is a strange scarabæus, I must confess: new to me: never saw anything like it before — unless it was a skull, or a death's-head — which it more nearly resembles than anything else that has come under my observation."

"A death's-head!" echoed Legrand — "Oh — yes — well, it has something of that appearance upon paper, no doubt. The two upper black spots look like eyes, eh? and the longer one at the bottom like a mouth — and then the shape of the whole is oval."

"Perhaps so," said I; "but, Legrand, I fear you are no artist. I must wait until I see the beetle itself, if I am to form any idea of its personal appearance."

"Well, I don't know," said he, a little **nettled**⑥, "I draw tolerably — should do it at least — have had good masters, and **flatter**⑦ myself that I am not quite a **blockhead**⑧."

"But, my dear fellow, you are joking then," said I, "this is a very **passable**⑨ skull — indeed, I may say that it is a very excellent skull, according to the

① emit [i'mit] v. 发出，散发

② growl [graul] v. 嗥叫，狂吠

③ gambol ['gæmbəl] n. 雀跃，嬉戏

④ depict [di'pikt] v. 描绘，描写

⑤ contemplate ['kɔntəm,pleit] v. 注视，凝视

⑥ nettle ['netl] v. 惹恼

⑦ flatter ['flætə] v. 奉承

⑧ blockhead ['blɔkhed] n. 笨人，蠢人

⑨ passable ['pɑ:səbl] a. 合格的，尚可的

亮的金属光泽你肯定从没见过——等明天你一见便知。现在，我可以给你看看它的大概样子。"说着，他就坐到一张小小的桌子旁，桌上有笔墨却没有纸，抽屉里也没找到能写字的纸。

"算了，"最后他说，"这个也行。"然后他从坎肩口袋里抽出一大张像是脏兮兮的纸的东西，在那上边用笔画起来。趁着这功夫，我又坐回火炉边，因为我还没暖和过来。他画完，也没起身，直接把图递给了我。刚拿到画，就听见一声咆哮，紧接着就是一阵嚓嚓的抓门声。朱庇特打开门，他家那只体型硕大的纽芬兰犬就冲进来就扒在我肩膀上跟我百般亲热；因为以前我来他家做客也很关照它。等它嬉闹够了，我再看那张纸，说实话，我还真是对我这位朋友的画疑惑不解。

"呃！"仔细端详了几分钟后，我说，"我不得不说，这只金龟子真稀奇，真新鲜，我可没见过——莫不是个头颅骨，或者死人的头颅——照我看，这东西真是像极了骷髅头。"

"骷髅头！"勒格朗应声说道，"哦——对——啊，无疑，画在纸上是很像。那两个黑点看起来就像骷髅头的眼睛，对吧？下面较长的那个黑点就像嘴——整体又是椭圆形。"

"或许是吧"我说；"可是勒格朗，你可能不太擅长画画。我得等看到那个真的金龟子，才能确定它长的到底是什么样子。"

"啊，随便你吧，"他说道，显然有点生气了，"我的画还说得过去吧——至少画个虫子还是可以的吧——我也曾师从几位大家，我敢自诩还不是太笨。"

"可是我的老兄，你可真能开玩笑，"我说，"这确实看着像骷髅头，照这类生物学标本大致的样子

vulgar notions about such specimens of physiology — and your scarabæus must be the **queerest**① scarabæus in the world if it resembles it. Why, we may get up a very thrilling bit of superstition upon this **hint**②. I presume you will call the bug scarabæus **caput**③ hominis, or something of that kind — there are many similar titles in the Natural Histories. But where are the antennæ you spoke of?"

"The antennæ!" said Legrand, who seemed to be getting **unaccountably**④ warm upon the subject; "I am sure you must see the antennæ. I made them as distinct as they are in the original insect, and I presume that is **sufficient**⑤."

"Well, well," I said, "perhaps you have — still I don't see them;" and I handed him the paper without additional remark, not wishing to **ruffle**⑥ his temper; but I was much surprised at the turn affairs had taken; his ill humor puzzled me — and, as for the drawing of the beetle, there were positively no antennæ visible, and the whole did bear a very close **resemblance**⑦ to the ordinary cuts of a death's-head.

He received the paper very peevishly, and was about to **crumple**⑧ it, **apparently**⑨ to throw it in the fire, when a casual glance at the design seemed suddenly to **rivet**⑩ his attention. In an instant his face grew violently red — in another as excessively pale. For some minutes he continued to **scrutinize**⑪ the drawing minutely where he sat. At length he arose, took a candle from the table, and proceeded to seat himself upon a sea-chest in the farthest corner of the room. Here again he made an anxious examination of the paper; turning it in all directions. He said nothing, however, and his conduct greatly astonished me; yet I thought it **prudent**⑫ not to **exacerbate**⑬ the growing moodiness of his temper by any comment. Presently he took from his coat pocket a wallet, placed the paper carefully in it, and deposited both in a writing-desk, which he locked. He now grew more **composed**⑭ in his **demeanor**⑮; but his original air of enthusiasm had quite disappeared. Yet he seemed not so much **sulky**⑯ as abstracted. As the evening wore away he became more and more absorbed in **reverie**⑰, from which no sallies of mine could arouse him. It had been my intention to pass the night at the hut, as I had frequently done before, but, seeing

① queer [kwiə] *a.* 奇怪的，异乎寻常的

② hint [hint] *n.* 提示，暗示

③ caput ['keipət] *n.*〈拉〉头

④ unaccountably ['ʌnə'kauntəbli] *ad.* 莫名其妙地，无法解释地

⑤ sufficient [sə'fiʃənt] *a.* 充足的，足够的

⑥ ruffle ['rʌfl] *v.* 触怒

⑦ resemblance [ri'zembləns] *n.* 相似

⑧ crumple ['krʌmpl] *v.* 弄皱，起皱

⑨ apparently [ə'pærəntli] *ad.* 显然地

⑩ rivet ['rivit] *v.*（把目光、注意力等）集中于

⑪ scrutinize ['skru:tinaiz] *v.* 仔细检查

⑫ prudent [pru:dənt] *a.* 谨慎的

⑬ exacerbate [ig'zæsəbeit] *v.* 加重，使恶化

⑭ composed [kəm'pəuzd] *a.* 镇定的，沉着的

⑮ demeanor [di'mi:nə] *n.* 举止，行为

⑯ sulky ['sʌlki] *a.* 愠怒的，生气的

⑰ reverie ['revəri] *n.* 幻想

来讲，我不得不说，这是一幅很完美的头颅骨——你那金龟子果真卡成这个样子，那它一定是世上最怪的甲虫。哎呀，就凭这点提示，总能生出点骇人听闻的迷信来。我猜想，你可以把这只甲虫称作人头金龟子之类的 ——反正《博物志》中有很多类似的称呼。再者说，你说的触须在哪呢？"

"触须！"勒格朗说，这个话题不知怎的让他来了脾气；"你肯定看到触须了。我画的就跟它长得一样分明，我觉得我画得够清楚的了。"

"得得得，"我说，"或许你画得分明，我可就是没看见触须。"我也不想再说什么惹他发火，就把画递给了他；但我着实惊讶事情竟闹得这么尴尬，他的这股无名火让我大惑不解——至于金龟子的图画，那上面确实没什么触须可见，整个形状和普通的骷髅头相差无几。

他恼火地接过那张纸，正想揉成一团，显然是打算把它扔进火里，无意中看了那图一眼仿佛就无法错神了。突然他的脸一会儿红一会儿白。他就那样坐在那里仔细端详着那幅画。许久，他方起身端走桌上的蜡烛，然后坐在角落里的一只大储物箱上，重又带着焦虑的神情翻来覆去地检查起那幅画来，却不发一言。这反常的举动令我吃惊，但我认为还是缄口不言为妙，以免激化他那反复无常的情绪病。过了一会儿，他从外衣口袋里取出钱包，小心翼翼地把画装进去，然后放进写字台的抽屉里，又上了锁。现在他慢慢冷静下来了，而他起初那股热情洋溢的情绪也没了。看他那副模样，与其说闷闷不乐，倒不如说是心不在焉。夜色越来越深，他也越来越深地陷入冥想，我再怎么用俏皮话逗他，他都不理。本打算像以前一样在小屋过夜，但看到屋主这么心

my host in this mood, I deemed it proper to take leave. He did not press me to remain, but, as I departed, he shook my hand with even more than his usual **cordiality**①.

It was about a month after this (and during the interval I had seen nothing of Legrand) when I received a visit, at Charleston, from his man, Jupiter. I had never seen the good old negro look so **dispirited**②, and I feared that some serious disaster had **befallen**③ my friend.

"Well, Jup," said I, "what is the matter now? — how is your master?"

"Why, to speak de troof, massa, him not so berry well as mought be."

"Not well! I am truly sorry to hear it. What does he complain of?"

"Dar! dat's it! — him neber plain of notin — but him berry sick for all dat."

"Very sick, Jupiter! — why didn't you say so at once? Is he confined to bed?"

"No, dat he aint! — he aint find nowhar — dat's just whar de shoe pinch — my mind is got to be berry hebby bout poor Massa Will."

"Jupiter, I should like to understand what it is you are talking about. You say your master is sick. Hasn't he told you what **ails**④ him?"

"Why, massa, taint worf while for to git mad about de matter — Massa Will say noffin at all aint de matter wid him — but den what make him go about looking dis here way, wid he head down and he soldiers up, and as white as a gose? And den he keep a syphon all de time — "

"Keeps a what, Jupiter?"

"Keeps a syphon wid de figgurs on de slate — de queerest figgurs I ebber did see. Ise gittin to be skeered, I tell you. Hab for to keep mighty tight eye pon him noovers. Todder day he gib me slip fore de sun up and was gone de whole ob de blessed day. I had a big stick ready cut for to gib him deuced good beating when he did come — but Ise sich a fool dat I hadn't de heart arter all — he look so berry poorly."

"Eh? — what? — ah yes! — upon the whole I think you had better not be

① cordiality [ˌkɔːdi'æliti] *n.*
热诚，真挚

② dispirited [dis'piritid] *a.*
沮丧的，消沉的

③ befall [bi'fɔːl] *v.* 降临

④ ail [eil] *v.* 使受病痛，使
苦恼

不在焉，我还是打定主意离开了。他也不十分挽留，
但我和他握手分别时，他却握得比以往更亲热。

　　事后大概一个月我都没见过勒格朗，一天他的
随从朱庇特来到查尔斯顿找我。我从未见过这个善
良的老黑人如此沮丧，使我不由得担心我的老朋友
可能大祸临头了。

　　"欸，老朱，"我说，"怎么了？你家少爷还好吗？"

　　"哎呀，说实发吧，小爷，他可不肿么好。"

　　"不好？真替他难受。他有什么可抱怨的呢？"

　　"嗨，奏是啊！——他从来沙都不包怨——但他
实在病得灰常重。"

　　"病重，朱庇特？——你为什么不直说？他卧病
在床了吗？"

　　"昧，那倒昧有！——他哪也昧卧倒——坏奏坏
在这儿了——我真的灰常替可怜的威尔小爷旦心。"

　　"朱庇特，我真想弄明白你说的什么。你说你家
主人病了，他没告诉你什么病吗？"

　　"哎，小爷，为这事儿发火可翻不着——威尔小
爷根本昧说他肿么了——可他为啥低着头，耷拉脑
袋，端着肩膀，脸色鬼白，走来走去？这还不算，他
还老是解密麻——"

　　"解什么，朱庇特？"

　　"在石板上用数字解密麻——那么奇怪的数字我
可匆昧见过。告诉你，事情越来越科怕。我得不错
眼珠地看住他别耍花样。内天，太阳没出来他就给
我溜走了，出去一大天。我都准备好一根大棒子打算
他一回来就胖揍一顿——但我镇傻，瞎不去手——
他的气色灰常不好。"

　　"呃？——什么？——啊，哦！——总之一句话，
我觉得你还是别对这个可怜的家伙太严厉了——别

too severe with the poor fellow — don't **flog**① him, Jupiter — he can't very well stand it — but can you form no idea of what has **occasioned**② this illness, or rather this change of conduct? Has anything unpleasant happened since I saw you?"

"No, massa, dey aint bin noffin unpleasant since den — 'twas fore den I'm feared — 'twas de berry day you was dare."

"How? what do you mean?"

"Why, massa, I mean de bug — dare now."

"The what?"

"De bug, — I'm berry sartain dat Massa Will bin bit somewhere bout de head by dat goole-bug."

"And what cause have you, Jupiter, for such a **supposition**③?"

"Claws enuff, massa, and mouth too. I nebber did see sick a deuced bug — he kick and he bite ebery ting what cum near him. Massa Will cotch him fuss, but had for to let him go gin mighty quick, I tell you — den was de time he must ha got de bite. I didn't like de look oh de bug mouff, myself, no how, so I would n't take hold ob him wid my finger, but I cotch him wid a piece ob paper dat I found. I rap him up in de paper and stuff piece ob it in he mouff — dat was de way."

"And you think, then, that your master was really bitten by the beetle, and that the bite made him sick?"

"I do n't tink noffin about it — I nose it. What make him dream bout de goole so much, if taint cause he bit by de goole-bug? Ise heerd bout dem goole-bugs fore dis."

"But how do you know he dreams about gold?"

"How I know? why cause he talk about it in he sleep — dat's how I nose."

"Well, Jup, perhaps you are right; but to what fortunate circumstance am I to attribute the honor of a visit from you to-day?"

"What de matter, massa?"

① flog [flɔg] *v.* 鞭打，鞭答

② occasion [əˈkeiʒən] *v.* 引起，惹起

③ supposition [ˌsʌpəˈziʃən] *n.* 推测

揍他，朱庇特——他也不经揍——话说回来，你能想到他这病是怎么来的吗？或者说他举止怪异是什么时候开始的？自从我们上次见面后有什么不好的事情发生吗？"

"没有，小爷，那以后昧啥不愉快地四儿——我怀疑在内以前奏出四儿了——奏在你去的内天。"

"怎么会呢？你什么意思？"

"哎，小爷，我的意思是内虫子——就是这个。"

"那什么？"

"内虫子——我灰常缺定威尔小爷被内金甲虫在脑门上咬了。"

"朱庇特，你凭什么有这想法呢？"

"呢么多爪子，小爷，还有嘴。我匆来昧见过内种鬼虫子——一有东西靠近它，它就又蹬又咬。威尔小爷当时爪住它了，但很快又放它走了，我跟你说——肯定就在内时候被咬的。我不喜欢内虫子嘴的样儿，所以我不用手拿它，但我找到一张纸，垫着纸我把它爪起来，在它嘴里塞了点纸，然后用纸把它抱起来——就内样。"

"这么说，依你看，你家主人真被甲虫给咬了，因此才得了病？"

"我想不到别的——我奏知道是这样。如果昧被内金甲虫咬一口，他咋奏都想着金子？以前我奏停说过介种金甲虫。"

"可你怎么知道他做梦都想着金子？"

"我咋知道？我知道是因为他说梦话提到——所以我奏直道了。"

"好吧，老朱，或许你没错；但是我今天为什么如此荣幸能得你的大驾光临？"

"咋滴啦，小爷？"

"Did you bring any message from Mr. Legrand?"

"No, massa, I bring dis here pissel;" and here Jupiter handed me a note which ran thus:

MY DEAR —

Why have I not seen you for so long a time? I hope you have not been so foolish as to take offence at any little ***brusquerie***① of mine; but no, that is improbable. Since I saw you I have had great cause for anxiety. I have something to tell you, yet scarcely know how to tell it, or whether I should tell it at all.

I have not been quite well for some days past, and poor old Jup annoys me, almost beyond endurance, by his well-meant attentions. Would you believe it? — he had prepared a huge stick, the other day, with which to **chastise**② me for giving him the slip, and spending the day, ***solus***③, among the hills on the main land. I **verily**④ believe that my ill looks alone saved me a flogging.

I have made no addition to my cabinet since we met.

If you can, in any way, make it convenient, come over with Jupiter. *Do* come. I wish to see you to-*night*, upon business of importance. I assure you that it is of the *highest* importance.

Ever yours, WILLIAM LEGRAND.

There was something in the tone of this note which gave me great uneasiness. Its whole style differed materially from that of Legrand. What could he be dreaming of? What new **crotchet**⑤ possessed his excitable brain? What "business of the highest importance" could he possibly have to transact? Jupiter's account of him **boded**⑥ no good. I **dreaded**⑦ lest the continued pressure of misfortune had, at length, fairly unsettled the reason of my friend. Without a moment's hesitation, therefore, I prepared to accompany the negro.

Upon reaching the **wharf**⑧, I noticed a scythe and three **spades**⑨, all

"勒格朗先生让你带什么口信了吗？"

"没有，小爷，我带来一个小条。"说着，朱庇特递给我一张字条，上面写着：

××仁兄：

为何许久不见来访？万望不要因我粗鲁冒犯而气急一时；不，你不会这样。自从上次见面我就焦虑不堪。我有话要告知于你，却又不知从何说起，也不知是否该说。

前些天我感觉不大舒服，可怜的老朱用他那善意的关心烦得我几乎忍无可忍。你信吗？——有一天他居然准备了一根大棒子要教训我，只因为我趁他不防备一个人跑到大陆的山里待了一天。我敢说，肯定是我这副病容让我逃过一顿毒打。

自从上次见面后，我的柜子里也没添什么新标本。

如果你方便，无论如何请随朱庇特来一趟吧。一定来。我想今晚就见到你，有要事相商。向你保证，是至关重要的头等大事。

威廉·勒格朗　拜启

字条上的语气令我惴惴不安。整体风格与勒格朗的文笔大相径庭。他在梦想着什么？他那异常活跃的头脑中又钻出什么新的怪念头了？他要办什么"至关重要的头等大事"呢？朱庇特对他情况的描述可不是什么好征兆。我惧怕我的朋友在那接连不断的祸事重压之下最终崩溃。因此我一刻也没迟疑就准备跟这个黑人走一趟。

到了码头，我看到我们要乘的船底部放着一把

① brusquerie [ˌbrʌskə'riː] n. 〈法〉粗率，无礼

② chastise [tʃæs'taiz] v. 惩罚

③ solus ['səuləs] a. 〈拉〉单独的，独自的

④ verily [verəli] ad. 确实，的确

⑤ crotchet ['krɔtʃit] n. 奇想，怪想

⑥ bode [bəud] v. 预示

⑦ dread [dred] v. 害怕，担心

⑧ wharf [hwɔːf] n. 码头

⑨ scythe [saið] n. 长柄大镰刀

apparently new, lying in the bottom of the boat in which we were to **embark**①.

"What is the meaning of all this, Jup?" I inquired.

"Him syfe, massa, and spade."

"Very true; but what are they doing here?"

"Him de syfe and de spade what Massa Will sis pon my buying for him in de town, and de debbils own lot of money I had to gib for em."

"But what, in the name of all that is mysterious, is your 'Massa Will' going to do with scythes and spades?"

"Dat's more dan I know, and debbil take me if I don't blieve 'tis more dan he know, too. But it's all cum ob do bug."

Finding that no satisfaction was to be obtained of Jupiter, whose whole intellect seemed to be absorbed by "de bug," I now stepped into the boat and made sail. With a fair and strong breeze we soon ran into the little **cove**② to the northward of Fort Moultrie, and a walk of some two miles brought us to the hut. It was about three in the afternoon when we arrived. Legrand had been awaiting us in eager expectation. He grasped my hand with a nervous empressement which alarmed me and strengthened the suspicions already entertained. His **countenance**③ was pale even to **ghastliness**④, and his **deep-set**⑤ eyes glared with unnatural lustre. After some inquiries respecting his health, I asked him, not knowing what better to say, if he had yet obtained the scarabæus from Lieutenant G—.

"Oh, yes," he replied, coloring violently, "I got it from him the next morning. Nothing should tempt me to part with that scarabæus. Do you know that Jupiter is quite right about it?"

"In what way?" I asked, with a sad **foreboding**⑥ at heart.

"In supposing it to be a bug of real gold." He said this with an air of profound seriousness, and I felt inexpressibly shocked.

"This bug is to make my fortune," he continued, with a **triumphant**⑦ smile, "to **reinstate**⑧ me in my family possessions. Is it any wonder, then, that I prize it? Since Fortune has thought fit to **bestow**⑨ it upon me, I have only to use it

① embark [im'bɑ:k] v. 上船

② cove [kəuv] n. 小湾，小海湾

③ countenance ['kauntənəns] n. 面容

④ ghastliness ['gɑ:stlinis] n. 可怕

⑤ deep-set 深陷的

⑥ foreboding [fɔ:'bəudiŋ] n. 预感

⑦ triumphant [trai'ʌmfənt] a. 成功的，胜利的

⑧ reinstate [.ri:in'steit] v. 使恢复

⑨ bestow [bi'stəu] v. 授予

长镰刀和三把铲子，显然都是新的。

"老朱，这是干什么用的？"我询问道。

"他的镰刀和铲子，小爷。"

"没错。可是放在这儿干什么？"

"还不是威尔小爷，费得让我在镇上给他买镰刀铲子。见鬼了，花了一大把钱才搞到。"

"真让人摸不着头脑，你家'威尔小爷'究竟要拿镰刀和铲子做什么用？"

"内我可不晓得，我相信，见鬼，他也不晓得。但内豆是内虫子闹的。"

朱庇特的脑子都被"内虫子"吸走了，估计我从他口中也得不到满意的答复，于是我们就登船出发了。乘着强劲的风，我们很快就驶进穆特里城堡北边的海湾，又走了大约两英里，我们来到小屋。到时已经下午三点了。勒格朗一直在焦灼地等着我们。他紧张又热情地攥住我的手，吓了我一跳，也更加深了我早先的疑惑。他的脸色惨白得吓人，深陷的眼睛透出异样的光芒。询问了一下他的身体状况后，我也没什么别的可说了，于是我就问他有没有从 G 中尉那儿拿回金龟子。

"哦，拿回来了，"他答道，顿时血色上涌，"第二天早上我就拿回来了。无论如何我也不再把那金龟子放手。你知道吗？朱庇特说对了。"

"说对了什么？"我问道，心中升起一种不祥的预感。

"他不是说这虫子是真金的嘛。"说这话时他的脸上带有一种毋庸置疑的严肃，我不由得大惊失色。

"这虫子会让我发财，"他带着胜利的微笑接着说，"我要靠它重振家业。这么一来，我如此看重它应该不为过吧？既然命运把它赐予我，我就得好好

properly and I shall arrive at the gold of which it is the index. Jupiter; bring me that scarabæus!"

"What! de bug, massa? I'd rudder not go fer trubble dat bug — you mus git him for your own self." Hereupon Legrand arose, with a grave and stately air, and brought me the beetle from a glass case in which it was enclosed. It was a beautiful scarabæus, and, at that time, unknown to naturalists — of course a great prize in a scientific point of view. There were two round, black spots near one extremity of the back, and a long one near the other. The scales were exceedingly hard and **glossy**①, with all the appearance of **burnished**② gold. The weight of the insect was very remarkable, and, taking all things into consideration, I could hardly blame Jupiter for his opinion respecting it; but what to make of Legrand's **concordance**③ with that opinion, I could not, for the life of me, tell.

"I sent for you," said he, in a **grandiloquent**④ tone, when I had completed my examination of the beetle, "I sent for you, that I might have your counsel and assistance in furthering the views of Fate and of the bug" —

"My dear Legrand," I cried, interrupting him, "you are certainly unwell, and had better use some little precautions. You shall go to bed, and I will remain with you a few days, until you get over this. You are **feverish**⑤ and" —

"Feel my pulse," said he.

I felt it, and, to say the truth, found not the slightest indication of fever.

"But you may be ill and yet have no fever. Allow me this once to prescribe for you. In the first place, go to bed. In the next" —

"You are mistaken," he **interposed**⑥, "I am as well as I can expect to be under the excitement which I suffer. If you really wish me well, you will relieve this excitement."

"And how is this to be done?"

"Very easily. Jupiter and myself are going upon an expedition into the hills, upon the main land, and, in this expedition we shall need the aid of some person in whom we can **confide**⑦. You are the only one we can trust. Whether we succeed or fail, the excitement which you now perceive in me will be

利用它，它会指引我找到宝藏。朱庇特，把那金龟子拿来。"

"啥？内虫子，小爷？我科不想招惹内虫子——你害是自己拿去吧。"于是勒格朗严肃又庄重地站起身，把装在玻璃盒子里的甲壳虫递给了我。这金龟子可真美。那时这种甲虫还不为博物学家所知晓——从科学的角度看，的确是个重大收获。在甲虫背部的一端有两个黑色的圆点，另一端有一个稍长的圆点。甲壳又硬又光滑，浑像磨光的金子。这虫子还十分沉重。综合这些特点来看，我还真不能怪朱庇特对它有那样的看法；可勒格朗怎么也有同样的想法，我可真是做梦都想不出。

"我找你来，"等我彻底检查完这甲壳虫，他语气夸张地说，"我找你来，就是希望听听你的高见，希望你能帮我探寻命运和这虫子的奥妙……"

"我的勒格朗呀，"我打断他的话，惊呼道，"你真是病得不轻，还是当心身体为妙。你还是卧床休养，让我在这儿照顾你一些时日，等你好了再走。你一定是发烧呢，还……"

"摸摸我的脉搏。"他说。

我摸了摸他的脉，说实话，还真没有发烧的迹象。

"但是你得的也许是不发烧的病。就这一次，让我给你开点药吧。先躺下，然后……"

"是你错了，"他又打断我的话，"我现在身体好得不能再好啦，只是心情激动得无以平复。你若真的希望我康健，就先帮我消了这激动的心情吧。"

"要我怎么帮你？"

"说起来也容易。我和朱庇特要进到大陆的山里去探险，期间我们需要靠得住的人帮忙。你是我们唯一能够信任的人。事后无论成败，你在我身上所

① glossy ['glɔsi] *a.* 光滑的，有光泽的
② burnished ['bə:niʃt] *a.* 铮亮的，光洁的
③ concordance [kən'kɔ:dəns] *n.* 一致
④ grandiloquent [græn'diləkwənt] *a.* 夸张的
⑤ feverish ['fi:vəriʃ] *a.* 发热的
⑥ interpose [ˌintə'pəuz] *v.* 插话
⑦ confide [kən'faid] *v.* 信赖，委托

equally allayed."

"I am anxious to **oblige**① you in any way," I replied; "but do you mean to say that this **infernal**② beetle has any connection with your expedition into the hills?"

"It has."

"Then, Legrand, I can become a party to no such absurd proceeding."

"I am sorry — very sorry — for we shall have to try it by ourselves."

"Try it by yourselves! The man is surely mad! — but stay! — how long do you propose to be absent?"

"Probably all night. We shall start immediately, and be back, at all events, by sunrise."

"And will you promise me, upon your honor, that when this freak of yours is over, and the bug business (good God!) settled to your satisfaction, you will then return home and follow my advice implicitly, as that of your physician?"

"Yes; I promise; and now let us be off, for we have no time to lose."

With a heavy heart I accompanied my friend. We started about four o'clock — Legrand, Jupiter, the dog, and myself. Jupiter had with him the scythe and spades — the whole of which he insisted upon carrying — more through fear, it seemed to me, of trusting either of the implements within reach of his master, than from any excess of industry or **complaisance**③. His demeanor was **dogged**④ in the extreme, and "dat deuced bug" were the sole words which escaped his lips during the journey. For my own part, I had charge of a couple of dark lanterns, while Legrand contented himself with the scarabæus, which he carried attached to the end of a bit of whip-cord; twirling it to and fro, with the air of a **conjuror**⑤, as he went. When I observed this last, plain evidence of my friend's **aberration**⑥ of mind, I could scarcely refrain from tears. I thought it best, however, to humor his fancy, at least for the present, or until I could adopt some more energetic measures with a chance of success. In the mean time I **endeavored**⑦, but all in vain, to sound him in regard to the object of the expedition. Having succeeded in inducing me to accompany him, he seemed

见的这份激动都会得以平复。"

"我愿意尽我所能为你,"我答道,"但你说这次山中探险和这可恶的甲虫有关联?"

"有关联啊。"

"那,勒格朗,我可不想参与到这荒唐事中来。"

"很遗憾——太遗憾了——那我们只能自己去了。"

"你们自己去!这家伙绝对是疯了!欸,等等!你们打算去多久?"

"可能得一整晚。我们现在即刻动身,怎么也得到日出了才能回来。"

"那么请你答应我,以你的名誉担保,等你这股疯劲儿过去,那虫子的事情(我的老天爷!)令你满意地解决了,你就立刻回来,我做你的医生,我说什么你就得做什么。行不?"

"好,我答应你。现在我们就出发,刻不容缓。"

我虽闷闷不乐,却还是跟着我的朋友走了。我们四点钟出发——勒格朗、朱庇特、那条狗,还有我。朱庇特扛着长镰刀和铲子——他坚持都让他扛着——依我看,他看起来是过分卖力献殷勤,实则是怕他的主人随手抄起哪件家什来。他这副样子真是倔到家了,一路上只咕哝着"这见鬼的虫子"。我负责提着两盏遮光灯,而勒格朗则把金龟子拴在鞭绳的一端,一边走一边像变戏法似的把它转来转去。这明显就是神经错乱的表现。看到他这样,我险些忍不住流下眼泪。但是在想出更有把握的治愈良策之前,我想就目前来看只能先迎合他的幻想。一路上我拼命地向他询问此番探险的目的,结果都白费了口舌。既已哄骗我跟他一起来,他就不愿在次要的话题上

① oblige [ə'blaidʒ] v. 帮助
② infernal [in'fə:nəl] a. 可憎的,可恨的

③ complaisance [kəm'pleizəns] n. 殷勤,彬彬有礼
④ dogged ['dɔgid] a. 顽固的

⑤ conjuror ['kʌndʒərə] n. 魔术师
⑥ aberration [,æbə'reiʃən] n. 失常

⑦ endeavor [in'devə] v. 努力,尽力

unwilling to hold conversation upon any topic of minor importance, and to all my questions **vouchsafed**① no other reply than "we shall see!"

We crossed the creek at the head of the island by means of a skiff; and, **ascending**② the high grounds on the shore of the main land, proceeded in a northwesterly direction, through a tract of country excessively wild and **desolate**③, where no trace of a human footstep was to be seen. Legrand led the way with decision; pausing only for an instant, here and there, to consult what appeared to be certain landmarks of his own **contrivance**④ upon a former occasion.

In this manner we journeyed for about two hours, and the sun was just setting when we entered a region infinitely more dreary than any yet seen. It was a species of table land, near the summit of an almost inaccessible hill, densely wooded from base to **pinnacle**⑤, and **interspersed**⑥ with huge **crags**⑦ that appeared to lie loosely upon the soil, and in many cases were prevented from **precipitating**⑧ themselves into the valleys below, merely by the support of the trees against which they reclined. Deep **ravines**⑨, in various directions, gave an air of still sterner **solemnity**⑩ to the scene.

The natural platform to which we had **clambered**⑪ was thickly overgrown with **brambles**⑫, through which we soon discovered that it would have been impossible to force our way but for the scythe; and Jupiter, by direction of his master, proceeded to clear for us a path to the foot of an enormously tall tulip-tree, which stood, with some eight or ten oaks, upon the level, and far surpassed them all, and all other trees which I had then ever seen, in the beauty of its **foliage**⑬ and form, in the wide spread of its branches, and in the general majesty of its appearance. When we reached this tree, Legrand turned to Jupiter, and asked him if he thought he could climb it. The old man seemed a little **staggered**⑭ by the question, and for some moments made no reply. At length he approached the huge trunk, walked slowly around it, and examined it with minute attention. When he had completed his scrutiny, he merely said,

"Yes, massa, Jup climb any tree he ebber see in he life."

"Then up with you as soon as possible, for it will soon be too dark to see

① vouchsafe [vautʃ'seif] *v.*
给予

② ascend [ə'send] *v.* 攀登，
上升

③ desolate ['desələt] *a.* 荒
凉的

④ contrivance
[kən'traivəns] *n.* 计谋

⑤ pinnacle ['pinəkl] *n.* 山
峰

⑥ intersperse [,intə'spə:s] *v.*
散布

⑦ crag [kræg] *n.* 峭壁，悬
崖

⑧ precipitate [pri'sipitit] *v.*
猛地落下

⑨ ravine [rə'vi:n] *n.* 沟壑，
深谷

⑩ solemnity [sə'lemnəti] *n.*
庄严，严肃

⑪ clamber ['klæmbə] *v.* 攀
登，爬上

⑫ bramble ['bræmbl] *n.* 荆
棘

⑬ foliage ['fəuliidʒ] *n.* 叶
子（总称）

⑭ staggered ['stægəd] *a.* 吃
惊的

多费唇舌，不管我问什么，他都只是敷衍地回答："到
了就知道了！"

我们乘着小艇渡过小岛那头的小溪；上岸后登上
大陆的高地，一路往西北走，穿过了无人烟的荒芜
地带。勒格朗果断地在前边带路，时不时地停下来
查看某些记号，显然是他以前来的时候做好的标记。

我们就这样走了大约两个小时，太阳刚刚西沉，
面前呈现出一片空前阴森的景象。这是一片台地，旁
边是一座几乎高不可攀的山峰，从山脚到山顶都密密
地长满树。到处都是大块陡峭的岩石，好似浮在土上，
只因有下面树的倚靠才没滚下山谷。四处延伸的深
谷又给这景色平添了一份阴森肃穆。

我们爬上来的这片天然平台布满了厚密的荆棘，
不久我们就发现要想穿过去，不用长镰刀砍出一条
路还真不行；朱庇特在他主人的指引下，为我们砍出
一条路来，一直通到一棵参天百合树脚下。这棵百
合树四周长着八到十棵橡树，但是都不及它高。这
棵树的树叶葱郁，形态美丽，枝丫四散伸展，整体
看来特别雄伟，在各方面都超过了我见过的所有其
他的树。走到树跟前，勒格朗转向朱庇特，问他能
不能爬上去。这老头听到这要求似乎有些吃惊，好
半天也没说话。最后他走到巨大的树干面前，绕着
它慢慢踱步，并仔细地端详一番。研究完后，他就
说了一句："好嘞，小爷，老朱我这辈子见过的树都
能爬得上。"

"那就快爬吧，不然一会儿天黑了我们就找不到
想要的东西了。"

what we are about."

"How far mus go up, massa?" inquired Jupiter.

"Get up the main trunk first, and then I will tell you which way to go — and here — stop! take this beetle with you."

"De bug, Massa Will! — de goole bug!" cried the negro, drawing back in **dismay**① — "what for mus tote de bug way up de tree? — d-n if I do!"

"If you are afraid, Jup, a great big negro like you, to take hold of a harmless little dead beetle, why you can carry it up by this string — but, if you do not take it up with you in some way, I shall be under the necessity of breaking your head with this **shovel**②."

"What de matter now, massa?" said Jup, evidently shamed into **compliance**③; "always want for to raise fuss wid old nigger. Was only funnin any how. Me feered de bug! what I keer for de bug?" Here he took cautiously hold of the extreme end of the string, and, maintaining the insect as far from his person as circumstances would permit, prepared to ascend the tree.

In youth, the tulip-tree, or Liriodendron Tulipferum, the most magnificent of American foresters, has a trunk peculiarly smooth, and often rises to a great height without lateral branches; but, in its riper age, the bark becomes **gnarled**④ and uneven, while many short limbs make their appearance on the stem. Thus the difficulty of ascension, in the present case, lay more in **semblance**⑤ than in reality. Embracing the huge cylinder, as closely as possible, with his arms and knees, seizing with his hands some projections, and resting his naked toes upon others, Jupiter, after one or two narrow escapes from falling, at length **wriggled**⑥ himself into the first great fork, and seemed to consider the whole business as virtually accomplished. The risk of the achievement was, in fact, now over, although the climber was some sixty or seventy feet from the ground.

"Which way mus go now, Massa Will?" he asked.

"Keep up the largest branch — the one on this side," said Legrand. The negro obeyed him promptly, and apparently with but little trouble; ascending higher and higher, until no **glimpse**⑦ of his **squat**⑧ figure could be obtained through the dense

① dismay [dis'mei] n. 诧异；惊愕

② shovel ['ʃʌvəl] n. 铁铲

③ compliance [kəm'plaiəns] n. 顺从，服从

④ gnarl [nɑ:l] v. 长木瘤

⑤ semblance ['sembləns] n. 假象

⑥ wriggle ['rigl] v. 蠕动，扭动

⑦ glimpse [glimps] n. 一瞥，一看

⑧ squat [skwɔt] a. 矮胖的

"歹爬多高，小爷？"朱庇特问。

"先爬上树干，然后我会告诉你往哪里爬——嘿——慢着！带上甲虫。"

"内虫子，威尔少爷！——内金甲虫！"这老黑人错愕地后退几步惊呼道——"干吗费要呆虫子爬树？——死也不干！"

"老朱，如果像你这么大个头的黑人还害怕用手捏一只完全无害的小死甲虫，那你用这根绳子提着它上去吧——但是如果你不想办法把它带上去，看我不用铁锹砸烂你的脑袋。"

"你说煞呢，小爷？"老朱说道，很显然他羞愧得只好照做，"总亘老黑奴大呼小叫。我不过是在凯玩笑。我害怕内虫子！内虫子酸个啥？"说着他就小心翼翼地捏住绳子的最那头，让那虫子离他要多远有多远，准备爬树。

这种百合树，又称岭南鹅掌楸，是美洲森林中最雄伟的树。这种树在幼年时树干极其光滑，往往长到很高也没有横向枝丫；但是成熟后，树皮就开始变得粗糙，还会生出许多节瘤，树干上也长出许多短枝。因此看起来难爬，实则不难。只见朱庇特手臂和双膝尽量贴紧树身，双手攀住树上的节瘤，光着的脚趾也踩在树干凸起的地方，有一两回几乎摔下来，但最终还是咕扭着爬到了第一个大树杈上，看样子他以为自己大功告成了呢。虽然已经爬到离地六七十英尺[1]，但实际上危险已经解除了。

"威尔小爷，现在望哪爬？"他问。

"爬到最大的那根树枝上——在这边这根，"勒格朗说道。那黑人马上遵照他的指令，显然不费吹灰之力就越爬越高，直到浓密的树叶将他那粗壮的

1　18 到 21 米。

foliage which enveloped it. Presently his voice was heard in a sort of **halloo**①.

"How much fudder is got for go?"

"How high up are you?" asked Legrand.

"Ebber so fur," replied the negro; "can see de sky fru de top ob de tree."

"Never mind the sky, but attend to what I say. Look down the trunk and count the limbs below you on this side. How many limbs have you passed?"

"One, two, tree, four, fibe — I done pass fibe big limb, massa, pon dis side."

"Then go one limb higher."

In a few minutes the voice was heard again, announcing that the seventh limb was attained.

"Now, Jup," cried Legrand, evidently much excited, "I want you to work your way out upon that limb as far as you can. If you see anything strange, let me know." By this time what little doubt I might have entertained of my poor friend's **insanity**②, was put finally at rest. I had no alternative but to conclude him stricken with **lunacy**③, and I became seriously anxious about getting him home. While I was **pondering**④ upon what was best to be done, Jupiter's voice was again heard.

"Mos feerd for to ventur pon dis limb berry far — tis dead limb putty much all de way."

"Did you say it was a dead limb, Jupiter?" cried Legrand in a quavering voice.

"Yes, massa, him dead as de door-nail — done up for sartain — done departed dis here life."

"What in the name of heaven shall I do?" asked Legrand, seemingly in the greatest distress. "Do!" said I, glad of an opportunity to interpose a word, "why come home and go to bed. Come now! — that's a fine fellow. It's getting late, and, besides, you remember your promise."

"Jupiter," cried he, without heeding me in the least, "do you hear me?"

① halloo [hə'lu:] *n.* 高呼

身形包裹得看不见影子。紧接着就传来他的喊叫声。

"害得爬夺高？"

"你爬到哪了？"勒格朗问。

"高得不得了，"那黑人答道，"从树顶能看到天啦。"

"别看天啦，照我说的，从这边往下看，数一数你爬过多少树枝。"

"一、二、三、四、补——小爷，介边我爬过了补个树枝。"

"那就再往上爬一根。"

几分钟过后，喊声又响起，宣告爬上了第七根树枝。

"现在，老朱，"勒格朗显然非常兴奋地喊道，"我要你顺着那根树枝往外爬，能爬多远就爬多远。看到有不寻常的东西就告诉我。"原先我还不确定这位可怜的仁兄是否有些精神失常，现如今终于搞清楚了，除了彻底疯掉已经别无他解。这让我非常焦虑，一心想把他弄回家去。正当我思忖最佳方案时，朱庇特的声音再次响起。

② insanity [in'sænəti] *n.* 精神错乱

③ lunacy ['lu:nəsi] *n.* 精神失常

④ ponder ['pɔndə] *v.* 仔细考虑

"忒吓人啦，不敢再望前爬啦——介根树枝豆死光了。"

"你说那是一根枯枝，朱庇特？"勒格朗用颤抖的声音喊道。

"是啊，小爷，死得像门钉一样——巧巧实实死了——死透啦。"

"老天呀，这可如何是好？"勒格朗问道，似乎一下子无比沮丧。"这么办！"我说，庆幸自己找到了机会插句话，"回家躺床上休息。现在就走！——听话吧。天快黑了，而且你可还记得答应过我的话吧。"

"朱庇特，"他喊道，完全把我的话当成耳旁风，"听到了吗？"

"Yes, Massa Will, hear you ebber so plain."

"Try the wood well, then, with your knife, and see if you think it very **rotten**①."

"Him rotten, massa, sure nuff," replied the negro in a few moments, "but not so berry rotten as mought be. Mought ventur out leetle way pon de limb by myself, dat's true."

"By yourself! — what do you mean?"

"Why I mean de bug. 'Tis berry hebby bug. Spose I drop him down fuss, and den de limb won't break wid just de weight ob one nigger."

"You infernal **scoundrel**②!" cried Legrand, apparently much relieved, "what do you mean by telling me such nonsense as that? As sure as you drop that beetle I'll break your neck. Look here, Jupiter, do you hear me?"

"Yes, massa, needn't hollo at poor nigger dat style."

"Well! now listen! — if you will **venture**③ out on the limb as far as you think safe, and not let go the beetle, I'll make you a present of a silver dollar as soon as you get down."

"I'm gwine, Massa Will — deed I is," replied the negro very **promptly**④ — "mos out to the eend now."

"Out to the end!" here fairly screamed Legrand, "do you say you are out to the end of that limb?"

"Soon be to de eend, massa, — o-o-o-o-oh! Lor-gol-a-marcy! what is dis here pon de tree?"

"Well!" cried Legrand, highly delighted, "what is it?"

"Why taint noffin but a skull — somebody bin lef him head up de tree, and de crows done gobble ebery bit ob de meat off."

"A skull, you say! — very well! — how is it **fastened**⑤ to the limb? — what holds it on?"

"Sure nuff, massa; mus look. Why dis berry curous sarcumstance, pon my word — dare's a great big nail in de skull, what fastens ob it on to de tree."

"Well now, Jupiter, do exactly as I tell you — do you hear?"

① rotten ['rɔtən] *a.* 腐烂的

"听见了，威尔小爷，听得补能再清楚啦。"

"你用刀试试木头，看看是不是烂透了。"

"他烂了，小爷，绝对的，"过了几分钟，那黑人答道，"烂了可是没太烂透。要是我自己一个人害能在介树枝上爬远点儿，说真个。"

"你一个人！——你在说什么啊？"

"哎呀，我是说介虫子。它忒重了。要四我把它丢下去，那介树枝单爬着我一个黑人就补能断。"

② scoundrel ['skaundrəl] *n.* 恶棍，无赖

"你这可恶的坏蛋！"勒格朗喊道，显然不再担心了，"你说那么多废话干什么？你要真把甲虫丢下来，我肯定扭断你的脖子。看着吧，朱庇特，听见了吗？"

"是，小爷，何必跟我这可怜的黑人那么搭喊搭叫地。"

③ venture ['ventʃə] *v.* 冒险

"好了，听着！——如果你能在那树枝上尽量往前爬，爬到你觉得不能往前爬了为止，不把甲虫丢下，那么你下来我就给你一枚银币。"

④ promptly ['prɔmptli] *ad.* 迅速地

"我爬啦，威尔小爷——介不爬着呢嘛，"那黑人立刻回答道——"现在快到树勺啦。"

"爬到树梢去！"勒格朗几乎嘶喊道，"你说你爬到树梢了没？"

"马上到树勺啦，小爷，——啊——啊呀！上帝老天爷！介树上是啥啊？"

"喂！"勒格朗兴高采烈地喊道，"是什么？"

"唉，昧啥，不过是个头颅骨——不定谁把头留在介树上了，乌鸦把肉豆吃光了。"

⑤ fasten ['fɑːsən] *v.* 使固定

"你说一个头颅骨！——太好啦！它是怎么固定在树枝上的？——用什么拴住的？"

"昧错，小爷；我得瞧瞧。说真个，介可太奇怪了——介头颅骨上又个大钉子，把它钉在介树上了。"

"好，现在，朱庇特，我怎么说，你怎么做——

"Yes, massa."

"Pay attention, then! — find the left eye of the skull."

"Hum! hoo! dat's good! why dare aint no eye lef at all."

"Curse your stupidity! do you know your right hand from your left?"

"Yes, I nose dat — nose all bout dat — tis my lef hand what I chops de wood wid."

"To be sure! you are left-handed; and your left eye is on the same side as your left hand. Now, I suppose, you can find the left eye of the skull, or the place where the left eye has been. Have you found it?"

Here was a long pause. At length the negro asked,

"Is de lef eye of de skull pon de same side as de lef hand of de skull, too? — cause de skull aint got not a bit ob a hand at all — nebber mind! I got de lef eye now — here de lef eye! what mus do wid it?"

"Let the beetle drop through it, as far as the string will reach — but be careful and not let go your hold of the string."

"All dat done, Massa Will; mighty easy ting for to put de bug fru de hole — look out for him dare below!"

During this **colloquy**① no portion of Jupiter's person could be seen; but the beetle, which he had suffered to descend, was now visible at the end of the string, and **glistened**②, like a globe of burnished gold, in the last rays of the setting sun, some of which still faintly **illumined**③ the **eminence**④ upon which we stood. The scarabæus hung quite clear of any branches, and, if allowed to fall, would have fallen at our feet. Legrand immediately took the scythe, and cleared with it a circular space, three or four yards in **diameter**⑤, just beneath the insect, and, having accomplished this, ordered Jupiter to let go the string and come down from the tree.

Driving a peg, with great **nicety**⑥, into the ground, at the precise spot where the beetle fell, my friend now produced from his pocket a tape measure. Fastening one end of this at that point of the trunk, of the tree which was nearest the peg, he **unrolled**⑦ it till it reached the peg, and thence farther unrolled it, in

听到了吗？"

"听到了，小爷。"

"那好，注意听好了！——找到头颅骨的左眼。"

"嗯！吼吼！好极了！介也昧剩下眼睛啊。"

"你个蠢东西！你能分清左右手吗？"

"能，分地出——内还是几道地——我用左手劈柴。"

"可不是嘛！你是个左撇子；你的左眼就和你左手在一边。我想你现在能找到头颅骨的左眼了吧，或者原先长左眼的那个洞。找到了吗？"

许久也没动静，过了半晌那黑人才问道："内头颅骨的左眼也和它的左手在一边不？——介头颅骨也昧有手啊——昧事啦！我找到左眼啦——在介呢！该咋办？"

"把那甲壳虫从左眼里垂下来，用绳子尽量往下放——但一定小心别松手。"

"得嘞，威尔小爷；把虫子从洞里放下去忒容易个四了——在下面看好喽！"

说了这么多话，自始至终也没见到朱庇特的身影；太阳的最后一抹余晖微弱地照在我们所在的高地上，只见朱庇特用绳子吊下的甲虫被最后一点日光照得像磨光的金球一样光亮。那金龟子并没有碰到任何树杈，若掉下来，就会落在我们脚边。勒格朗马上操起长镰刀就在那虫子正下方清理出一块三四英尺[1]直径的圆形区域，清理好后，命令朱庇特放开绳子，爬下树。

就在甲虫掉落的那个点，我的朋友在地上精准地打下一个木桩。他从口袋里拿出一个卷尺，将一头固定在离木桩最近的树干上，然后把卷尺展开，拉

① colloquy [ˈkɔləkwi] *n.* 交谈，对话

② glisten [ˈglisən] *v.* 闪光

③ illumine [iˈl(j)u:min] *v.* 照明

④ eminence [ˈeminəns] *n.* 山丘，高地

⑤ diameter [daiˈæmitə] *n.* 直径

⑥ nicety [ˈnaisiti] *n.* 精密，细节

⑦ unroll [ˌʌnˈrəul] *v.* 展开

1　0.9 米到 1.2 米。

the direction already established by the two points of the tree and the peg, for the distance of fifty feet — Jupiter clearing away the brambles with the scythe. At the spot thus attained a second peg was driven, and about this, as a centre, a rude circle, about four feet in diameter, described. Taking now a spade himself, and giving one to Jupiter and one to me, Legrand begged us to set about digging as quickly as possible.

To speak the truth, I had no especial **relish**① for such amusement at any time, and, at that particular moment, would most willingly have declined it; for the night was coming on, and I felt much **fatigued**② with the exercise already taken; but I saw no mode of escape, and was fearful of disturbing my poor friend's **equanimity**③ by a refusal. Could I have depended, indeed, upon Jupiter's aid, I would have had no hesitation in attempting to get the **lunatic**④ home by force; but I was too well assured of the old negro's disposition, to hope that he would assist me, under any circumstances, in a personal contest with his master. I made no doubt that the latter had been infected with some of the **innumerable**⑤ Southern superstitions about money buried, and that his phantasy had received confirmation by the finding of the scarabæus, or, perhaps, by Jupiter's obstinacy in maintaining it to be "a bug of real gold." A mind disposed to lunacy would readily be led away by such suggestions — especially if **chiming in with**⑥ favorite preconceived ideas — and then I called to mind the poor fellow's speech about the beetle's being "the index of his fortune." Upon the whole, I was sadly vexed and puzzled, but, at length, I concluded to make a virtue of necessity — to dig with a good will, and thus the sooner to convince the visionary, by **ocular**⑦ demonstration, of the fallacy of the opinions he entertained.

The lanterns having been lit, we all fell to work with a zeal worthy a more rational cause; and, as the glare fell upon our persons and implements, I could not help thinking how **picturesque**⑧ a group we composed, and how strange and suspicious our labors must have appeared to any **interloper**⑨ who, by chance, might have **stumbled upon**⑩ our **whereabouts**⑪.

We dug very steadily for two hours. Little was said; and our chief

① relish ['relɪʃ] n. 兴趣，
乐趣

② fatigued [fə'tiːgd] a. 疲
乏的

③ equanimity
[.iːkwə'niməti] n. 平静，
镇定

④ lunatic ['luːnətik] n. 疯
子，疯人

⑤ innumerable
[i'njuːmərəbl] a. 无数的，
不计其数的

⑥ chime in with 与……协
调一致

⑦ ocular ['ɔkjulə] a. 眼睛
的，视觉的

⑧ picturesque [.piktʃə'resk]
a. 如画的

⑨ interloper ['intələupə] n.
闯入者

⑩ stumble upon 偶然发现

⑪ whereabouts
[weərə'bauts] n. 行踪

到木桩，朝树和木桩连线的方向继续放卷尺，又拉了五十英尺[1]——朱庇特用长镰刀将荆棘丛清理干净。就在这点，勒格朗又钉了一根木桩。以此为圆心粗略画了一个大概四英尺[2]直径的圆。勒格朗自己拿把铁锹，给我和朱庇特各一把，然后央求我们快挖。

说实话，我从来都不喜欢这种消遣，就在当时我很想婉言拒绝；天色不早了，我已经折腾得筋疲力尽；但看样子我是逃不过的了，我害怕我一拒绝，这位可怜的仁兄又受刺激。如果能指望朱庇特帮忙，我早就想法将这疯子拖回家了；但是我太了解这老黑人的脾气了，在任何情况下都别指望他能帮我跟他家少爷争一场。我断定勒格朗听信了那些形形色色的南方迷信，说是地下埋藏着宝藏，而他的这些幻想在找到金龟子的那一刻被他当真了，或许，也是因为朱庇特固执地坚信那是一个"纯金的虫子"，他才信以为真。神经错乱的人轻易就会被这些谣言所蛊惑——尤其是这些谣言刚好和心里的想法相吻合时，最容易上当——于是我想起这位可怜的仁兄曾说到这个甲壳虫能"指引他找到宝藏"。想到这些，我心乱如麻，苦不堪言，但我最终决定，既然非干不可——索性认真挖，眼见为实，让这位空想家尽早承认他是在异想天开。

两盏灯都点上了，我们投入到工作中，这份热情真应该放到正经事上；灯光洒在我们身上，也照在工具上，我不由得遐想，这真是一幅奇异如画的场景啊。如果有人无意中闯入我们的工地，那看起来得多么怪异，多么可疑啊。

我们一刻不停地挖了两个小时，谁也没怎么吭

1　约 15.2 米。
2　约 1.2 米。

embarrassment lay in the **yelpings**① of the dog, who took exceeding interest in our proceedings. He, at length, became so **obstreperous**② that we grew fearful of his giving the alarm to some **stragglers**③ in the **vicinity**④; — or, rather, this was the apprehension of Legrand; — for myself, I should have **rejoiced**⑤ at any interruption which might have enabled me to get the wanderer home. The noise was, at length, very effectually silenced by Jupiter, who, getting out of the hole with a dogged air of deliberation, tied the brute's mouth up with one of his suspenders, and then returned, with a grave **chuckle**⑥, to his task.

When the time mentioned had **expired**⑦, we had reached a depth of five feet, and yet no signs of any treasure became **manifest**⑧. A general pause **ensued**⑨, and I began to hope that the **farce**⑩ was at an end. Legrand, however, although evidently much **disconcerted**⑪, wiped his brow thoughtfully and **recommenced**⑫. We had **excavated**⑬ the entire circle of four feet diameter, and now we slightly enlarged the limit, and went to the farther depth of two feet. Still nothing appeared. The gold-seeker, whom I sincerely pitied, at length **clambered**⑭ from the pit, with the bitterest disappointment **imprinted**⑮ upon every feature, and proceeded, slowly and reluctantly, to put on his coat, which he had thrown off at the beginning of his labor. In the mean time I made no remark. Jupiter, at a signal from his master, began to gather up his tools. This done, and the dog having been **unmuzzled**⑯, we turned in profound silence towards home.

We had taken, perhaps, a dozen steps in this direction, when, with a loud **oath**⑰, Legrand strode up to Jupiter, and seized him by the collar. The astonished negro opened his eyes and mouth to the fullest extent, let fall the spades, and fell upon his knees.

"You scoundrel," said Legrand, hissing out the syllables from between his **clenched**⑱ teeth — "you infernal black villain! — speak, I tell you! — answer me this instant, without **prevarication**⑲! — which — which is your left eye?"

"Oh, my golly, Massa Will! aint dis here my lef eye for sartain?" roared the terrified Jupiter, placing his hand upon his right organ of vision, and holding it

① yelp [jelp] v. 狗吠

② obstreperous [əb'strepərəs] a. 喧闹的，喧哗的

③ straggler ['stræglə] n. 流浪者

④ vicinity [vi'sinəti] n. 附近，临近

⑤ rejoice [ri'dʒɔis] v. 欣喜，感到高兴

⑥ chuckle ['tʃʌkl] n. 轻笑，窃笑

⑦ expire [ik'spaiə] v. 期满

⑧ manifest ['mænifest] a. 明显的

⑨ ensue [in'sju:] v. 继而发生

⑩ farce [fɑ:s] n. 闹剧

⑪ disconcerted [ˌdiskən'sə:tid] a. 不安的，窘迫的

⑫ recommence [ˌri:kə'mens] v. 重新开始

⑬ excavate ['ekskəˌveit] v. 挖掘

⑭ clamber ['klæmbə] v. 攀登，爬上

⑮ imprint [im'print] v. 压印，使带有……的特征

⑯ unmuzzle [ˌʌn'mʌzl] v. 给（狗）取掉笼罩

⑰ oath [əuθ] n. 诅咒，咒骂

⑱ clench [klentʃ] v. 咬紧（牙齿）

⑲ prevarication [priˌværi'keiʃən] n. 支吾，搪塞

声，只是那狗对我们干的活产生了莫大的兴趣，时不时地叫几声，让我们一阵一阵地惊恐。最后它实在是叫得太响，我们都担心它会引来附近的路人——或者，不如说勒格朗才这么想——而我巴不得有人闯进来，好让我把这个空想家弄回家。最后朱庇特狠下心来爬出土坑，用吊裤带把这畜生的嘴给绑了起来，总算消灭了这狗叫声，然后他阴笑了两声回来继续挖土。

刚才说的两个小时过去了，我们挖了五英尺[1]深，没有任何宝藏的迹象。大家都停下手里的活，我开始希望这场闹剧就此结束。然而勒格朗尽管已经尽显窘态，仍若有所思地抹了抹额角继续挖起来。我们已经把这四英尺[2]直径的圆形地带都挖了个遍，还向外多挖了一些，又挖深两英尺[3]。仍然一无所获。我由衷同情的那淘金人终于从坑里爬上来，带着满脸痛苦的失望，慢吞吞地极不情愿地穿上一开始干活时扔在一旁的外套。我一言不发，朱庇特一看到他家主人的举动，也开始收拾工具。收拾完，解开狗嘴上的吊裤带，我们默默地打道回府了。

我们往回大概走了有十几步，勒格朗突然大骂一声冲向朱庇特，薅住他的脖领。那黑人吓得瞪大了眼睛张大了嘴，扔掉了铲子，扑通跪在地上。

"你这坏蛋，"勒格朗咬牙切齿地一字一字地说道——"你这天杀的黑鬼！——说，我让你说！——马上给我说，别支支吾吾地！——哪只——哪只是你的左眼？"

"哎呀，天哪，威尔小爷！介不就是我的左眼吗？"吓坏了的朱庇特赶紧喊道，一边喊一边把手放

---

1 约 1.5 米。

2 约 1.2 米。

3 约 0.6 米。

there with a desperate **pertinacity**①, as if in immediate dread of his master's attempt at a gouge.

"I thought so! — I knew it! hurrah!" **vociferated**② Legrand, letting the negro go, and executing a series of **curvets**③ and **caracols**④, much to the astonishment of his **valet**⑤, who, arising from his knees, looked, **mutely**⑥, from his master to myself, and then from myself to his master.

"Come! we must go back," said the latter, "the game's not up yet;" and he again led the way to the tulip-tree.

"Jupiter," said he, when we reached its foot, "come here! was the skull nailed to the limb with the face outwards, or with the face to the limb?"

"De face was out, massa, so dat de crows could get at de eyes good, widout any trouble."

"Well, then, was it this eye or that through which you dropped the beetle?" — here Legrand touched each of Jupiter's eyes.

"Twas dis eye, massa — de lef eye — jis as you tell me," and here it was his right eye that the negro indicated.

"That will do — must try it again."

Here my friend, about whose madness I now saw, or fancied that I saw, certain indications of method, removed the peg which marked the spot where the beetle fell, to a spot about three inches to the westward of its former position. Taking, now, the tape measure from the nearest point of the trunk to the peg, as before, and continuing the extension in a straight line to the distance of fifty feet, a spot was indicated, removed, by several yards, from the point at which we had been digging.

Around the new position a circle, somewhat larger than in the former instance, was now described, and we again set to work with the spades. I was dreadfully weary, but, scarcely understanding what had occasioned the change in my thoughts, I felt no longer any great aversion from the labor imposed. I had become most unaccountably interested — nay, even excited. Perhaps there was something, amid all the extravagant demeanor of Legrand — some air of

① pertinacity [ˌpəːtiˈnæsiti]
   n. 顽固，执拗

② vociferate [vəuˈsifəreit]
   v. 怒吼

③ curvet [ˈkəːvit] n. 腾跃

④ caracol [ˈkærəkɔl] n. 半
   旋转

⑤ valet [ˈvælit] n. 贴身男
   仆

⑥ mutely [ˈmjutli]] ad. 沉
   默地

在他的右眼上，捂得紧紧的，好像生怕他家主人要把它挖掉一样。

"我就说嘛！——我早料到了！啊哈！"勒格朗大声嚷着，松开那黑人，径自蹦跳了一阵，又打了个旋。他那侍从吓得瞠目结舌，默默地站起身，看看他家主人又看看我，看看我又看看他家主人。

"快，我们得回去，"勒格朗说，"好戏还没完呢。"他边说边把我们领回到百合树下。

"朱庇特，"我们走到树下时他说，"过来！那个头颅骨是面对着树枝还是背对着树枝被钉在那儿的？"

"内脸是朝外的，小爷，内样乌鸦才把眼睛吃得精光，一点儿不费劲儿。"

"那，你是从这只还是那只眼睛把甲虫吊下来的？"——说着，勒格朗指了指朱庇特的两只眼睛。

"介只眼睛，小爷——奏是左眼——是你告诉我的。"而那黑人指的却是右眼。

"那就对了——必须重来一次。"

我这才搞懂，或者我自以为弄清楚了，原来我这位朋友癫狂之中做事还不乏条理。他把原先吊下甲虫的那个木桩拔出来，向西挪动了大概三英尺[1]，再把卷尺从离树干最近的那点拉到木桩，沿直线继续拉出五十英尺[2]远，定下一点，这点距离我们原先挖的那点相差好几码[3]。

在新定的那点，画了一个比原来稍大一些的圆圈，然后我们又开始挖起来。我已疲惫不堪，但一种说不清的感觉却在内心深处产生了波动，现在我对挖坑这苦差事并不感到那么抗拒了。我不知怎的变

1　约 0.9 米。

2　约 15.2 米。

3　1 码约等于 0.9144 米。

forethought[①], or of deliberation, which impressed me. I dug eagerly, and now and then caught myself actually looking, with something that very much resembled expectation, for the fancied treasure, the vision of which had **demented**[②] my unfortunate companion. At a period when such **vagaries**[③] of thought most fully possessed me, and when we had been at work perhaps an hour and a half, we were again interrupted by the violent howlings of the dog. His uneasiness, in the first instance, had been, evidently, but the result of playfulness or **caprice**[④], but he now assumed a bitter and serious tone. Upon Jupiter's again attempting to muzzle him, he made **furious**[⑤] resistance, and, leaping into the hole, tore up the mould **frantically**[⑥] with his claws. In a few seconds he had uncovered a mass of human bones, forming two complete skeletons, **intermingled**[⑦] with several buttons of metal, and what appeared to be the dust of decayed woollen. One or two strokes of a spade upturned the blade of a large Spanish knife, and, as we dug farther, three or four loose pieces of gold and silver coin came to light.

At sight of these the joy of Jupiter could scarcely be restrained, but the countenance of his master wore an air of extreme disappointment. He urged us, however, to continue our **exertions**[⑧], and the words were hardly uttered when I stumbled and fell forward, having caught the toe of my boot in a large ring of iron that lay half buried in the loose earth.

We now worked in earnest, and never did I pass ten minutes of more intense excitement. During this interval we had fairly unearthed an **oblong**[⑨] chest of wood, which, from its perfect preservation and wonderful hardness, had plainly been subjected to some mineralizing process — perhaps that of the Bi-chloride of Mercury. This box was three feet and a half long, three feet broad, and two and a half feet deep. It was firmly secured by bands of **wrought**[⑩] iron, riveted, and forming a kind of open **trelliswork**[⑪] over the whole. On each side of the chest, near the top, were three rings of iron — six in all — by means of which a firm hold could be obtained by six persons. Our utmost united endeavors served only to disturb the coffer very slightly in its bed. We at once saw the impossibility of removing so great a weight. Luckily, the sole fastenings of the lid consisted of

① forethought ['fɔːθɔːt] *n.* 深谋远虑，先见

② dement [di'ment] *v.* 使发狂

③ vagary ['veigəri] *n.* 异常行为

④ caprice [kə'priːs] *n.* 任性，反复无常

⑤ furious ['fjuəriəs] *a.* 激烈的

⑥ frantically ['fræntikəli] *ad.* 狂暴地

⑦ intermingle [.intə'miŋgl] *v.* 使掺和

⑧ exertion [ig'zəːʃən] *n.* 努力

⑨ oblong ['ɔblɔŋ] *a.* 长方形的

⑩ wrought [rɔːt] *a.* 锻造的，加工的

⑪ trelliswork ['treliswəːk] *n.* 格子细工

得饶有兴趣——不对，是兴奋起来。或许勒格朗夸张的行为中有什么打动了我——他的先见之明，或者说深谋远虑令我动容。我铆足劲儿继续挖，有时发现自己其实是带着某种类似期待的心情去寻找那个想象中的宝藏，而我那不幸的朋友却着实对那幻想中的宝藏着了魔。我们奋力挖了一个半小时左右，我满脑子都充斥着这些怪异的想法，突然我们又被那狗的嚎叫声打断了。上次挖坑时，它显然是因为淘气任性而表现得很不安，而现在它的嚎叫又尖利又严肃。朱庇特又想把它的嘴拴住，它奋力反抗，跳进坑里，疯狂地扒开烂泥，不一会儿就扒出一堆人骨。这是两具完整的骷髅，其中夹杂着几枚金属扣子，还有烂成灰的绒呢。又挖了两铲子，挖出了一把西班牙大刀，我们接着挖，便发现有三四枚金币银币散落在那里。

看到这些，朱庇特再也抑制不住内心的欣喜，但他主人却显得极其失望。他催我们接着干，话音未落，我的脚尖就被半埋在浮土里的一个大铁环给钩住了，往前栽了个跟头。

这下我们干得起劲儿了，我这辈子从没像接下来的十分钟那么兴奋过。期间，我们顺利地出土了一只长方形的木箱，箱子保存完好，质地坚硬，显然做过矿化处理——可能是氯化汞防腐处理。这箱子有三英尺半[1]长，三英尺[2]宽，二英尺半[3]高。四周结结实实缠着几条铸铁用铆钉钉住，将箱子分成一格一格的。在箱子两侧靠近箱盖的位置各有三个铁环——总共六个——这样六个人就可以抓着把手抬箱子。我们三个联合起来使出吃奶的劲儿才让宝箱

1　约1米。

2　约0.91米。

3　约0.76米。

two sliding bolts. These we drew back — trembling and **panting**[①] with anxiety. In an instant, a treasure of incalculable value lay gleaming before us. As the rays of the lanterns fell within the pit, there flashed upwards a glow and a glare, from a confused heap of gold and of jewels, that absolutely dazzled our eyes.

I shall not pretend to describe the feelings with which I gazed. Amazement was, of course, predominant. Legrand appeared exhausted with excitement, and spoke very few words. Jupiter's countenance wore, for some minutes, as deadly a **pallor**[②] as it is possible, in nature of things, for any negro's **visage**[③] to assume. He seemed stupified — **thunderstricken**[④]. Presently he fell upon his knees in the pit, and, burying his naked arms up to the elbows in gold, let them there remain, as if enjoying the luxury of a bath. At length, with a deep sigh, he **exclaimed**[⑤], as if in a **soliloquy**[⑥],

"And dis all cum ob de goole-bug! de putty goole bug! de poor little goole-bug, what I boosed in dat sabage kind ob style! Aint you shamed ob yourself, nigger? — answer me dat!"

It became necessary, at last, that I should arouse both master and valet to the **expediency**[⑦] of removing the treasure. It was growing late, and it **behooved**[⑧] us to make exertion, that we might get every thing housed before daylight. It was difficult to say what should be done, and much time was spent in deliberation — so confused were the ideas of all. We, finally, lightened the box by removing two thirds of its contents, when we were enabled, with some trouble, to raise it from the hole. The articles taken out were deposited among the brambles, and the dog left to guard them, with strict orders from Jupiter neither, upon any pretence, to stir from the spot, nor to open his mouth until our return. We then hurriedly made for home with the chest; reaching the hut in safety, but after excessive toil, at one o'clock in the morning. Worn out as we were, it was not in human nature to do more immediately. We rested until two, and had supper; starting for the hills immediately afterwards, armed with three stout sacks, which, by good luck, were upon the premises. A little before four we arrived at the pit, divided the remainder of the **booty**[⑨], as equally as might be,

① pant [pænt] v. 气喘，喘息

② pallor ['pælə] n.（尤指因恐惧或疾病所引起的脸色等的）苍白

③ visage ['vizidʒ] n. 面貌，容貌

④ thunderstricken ['θʌndə,strikən] a. 惊愕的，惊呆的

⑤ exclaim [ik'skleim] v. 呼喊，惊叫

⑥ soliloquy [sə'liləkwi] n. 自言自语

⑦ expediency [ik'spi:diənsi] n. 权宜之计

⑧ behoove [bi'hu:v] v. 理应

在地基中松动了一点点。我们马上意识到这么重的箱子我们是不可能抬动的。所幸箱盖上的封锁处只有两个活动栓。我们颤抖而焦急地喘着气，拉开这两个栓。一瞬间，价值连城的财宝就在我们面前闪闪发光。当灯光射进坑里，成堆的金银珠宝发射出的璀璨光辉闪得我们眼花缭乱。

看到此番景象的心情我简直无法描述，当然最主要的就是惊奇。勒格朗兴奋到没了力气，不怎么说话了。朱庇特一时间脸色惨白，当然了，一个普通黑人的脸能有多白，他的脸就有多白。他好像惊呆了——呆若木鸡。他跪在坑里，赤裸的手臂伸进财宝堆，一动不动，似乎在享受一场财富的沐浴。临了，他深深叹息，又似自言自语地说道："介豆亏了内金甲虫！内好看的金甲虫！内可怜的小金甲虫，我还使脏话骂它！也布害臊，乃个黑鬼？说话呀！"

最后还得我提醒这主仆二人想个办法把财宝搬走。夜色越来越深了，我们得努努力在天亮前把所有财宝都搬回家。一时间也想不出什么好办法，左思右想了大半天——所有办法都觉得行不通。最后，我们把财宝搬出三分之二，让箱子变轻，即便这样还是费了好大功夫才把箱子从洞里抬出来。拿出来的那些东西都掩藏在荆棘丛中，把狗留下看着。朱庇特严厉叮嘱了一番，让它无论如何都不准离开半步，更不许张嘴乱叫，一直等到我们回来。于是我们赶忙抬着箱子往家赶，等费尽了周身力气终于安全到家时，已经是凌晨一点钟了。我们已经累得瘫软在地，再马上出发太不近人情了。我们休息到两点钟，吃了点饭，刚巧屋里有三个结实的麻袋，于是我们拿上麻袋就立刻向山里出发了。快到四点钟，我们回到坑边，把剩下的战利品尽量平均地分成三份，也没再把坑填回去，就

⑨ booty ['bu:ti] n. 战利品

among us, and, leaving the holes unfilled, again set out for the hut, at which, for the second time, we deposited our golden burthens, just as the first faint streaks of the dawn gleamed from over the tree-tops in the East.

We were now thoroughly broken down; but the intense excitement of the time denied us **repose**①. After an **unquiet**② slumber of some three or four hours' duration, we arose, as if by **preconcert**③, to make examination of our treasure.

The chest had been full to the brim, and we spent the whole day, and the greater part of the next night, in a scrutiny of its contents. There had been nothing like order or arrangement. Every thing had been **heaped**④ in **promiscuously**⑤. Having assorted all with care, we found ourselves possessed of even vaster wealth than we had at first supposed. In coin there was rather more than four hundred and fifty thousand dollars — estimating the value of the pieces, as accurately as we could, by the tables of the period. There was not a particle of silver. All was gold of antique date and of great variety — French, Spanish, and German money, with a few English **guineas**⑥, and some counters, of which we had never seen specimens before. There were several very large and heavy coins, so worn that we could make nothing of their **inscriptions**⑦. There was no American money. The value of the jewels we found more difficulty in estimating. There were diamonds — some of them exceedingly large and fine — a hundred and ten in all, and not one of them small; eighteen rubies of remarkable brilliancy; — three hundred and ten **emeralds**⑧, all very beautiful; and twenty-one **sapphires**⑨, with an **opal**⑩. These stones had all been broken from their settings and thrown loose in the chest. The settings themselves, which we picked out from among the other gold, appeared to have been beaten up with hammers, as if to prevent identification. Besides all this, there was a vast quantity of solid gold ornaments; — nearly two hundred massive finger and earrings; — rich chains — thirty of these, if I remember; — eighty-three very large and heavy **crucifixes**⑪; — five gold **censers**⑫ of great value; — a **prodigious**⑬ golden punch bowl, ornamented with richly chased vine-leaves and Bacchanalian figures; with two sword-handles exquisitely **embossed**⑭,

① repose [ri'pəuz] *n.* 休息
② unquiet [ˌʌn'kwaiət] *a.*
焦虑的，不安的
③ preconcert [ˌpri:kən'sə:t]
n. 预先的安排
④ heap [hi:p] *v.* 堆积
⑤ promiscuously
[prəu'miskjuəsli] *ad.* 混
杂地，杂乱地

⑥ guinea ['gini] *n.* 几尼
（英国旧时的一种金币
或货币单位，合 1.05 英
镑）
⑦ inscription [in'skripʃən]
n. （硬币、奖章等上的）
镌刻文字
⑧ emerald ['emərəld] *n.* 翡
翠
⑨ sapphire ['sæfaiə] *n.* 蓝
宝石
⑩ opal ['əupəl] *n.* 蛋白石
⑪ crucifix ['kru:sifiks] *n.* 十
字架
⑫ censer ['sensə] *n.* 香炉
⑬ prodigious [prə'didʒəs] *a.*
巨大的，惊人的
⑭ emboss [im'bɔs] *v.* 在
（表面）上浮雕图案

返回了小屋。当我们把第二次扛回来的财宝藏好时，太阳已经透过树梢从东方照射出第一道朦胧的曙光。

这回我们可彻底累垮了，但是当时极度的兴奋令谁也无法入睡。辗转反侧地迷瞪了大概三四个小时，我们都起床了，好像事先约定好一般，开始清点宝藏。

满满一箱多得快溢出来的财宝花了我们整个白天和大半个晚上才清点完毕。原来的财宝放得既没有顺序也没有分类，全都杂乱地堆在一起。经过仔细分类，我们发现财宝比我们最初预想的要多得多。我们尽可能准确地按照当时的兑换价格估算了价值，硬币大概值四十五万美元，一枚银币也没有，都是古代的金币，种类繁多——法国的、西班牙的、德国的、一些英国旧时的金几尼，还有一些样式我们从没见过的筹码。有几枚沉甸甸的大硬币，磨得几乎看不见表面的图样了。没有美国的货币。珠宝的价值更难估算了。总共一百一十颗钻石，没有一颗是小的——其中有些个头特大质地又晶莹剔透；十八颗璀璨的红宝石；三百一十颗都极其精美的绿宝石；二十一颗蓝宝石；还有一颗蛋白石。这些宝石都是从嵌托上抠下来的，分散地撒在箱子里。我们在其他金器中找到的那些嵌托都已经被锤子砸扁，好像怕被认出来。除了这些，还有无数的纯金饰品——近两百个厚重的戒指和耳环；若没记错，昂贵的金链有三十条；八十三个又大又重的十字架；五只价值连城的金香炉；有一只硕大的金潘趣酒碗，精工雕琢着蜿蜒的葡萄藤叶以及酒神像；两个带有精致浮雕的剑柄，还有好多小物件我都记不得了。这

and many other smaller articles which I cannot recollect. The weight of these valuables exceeded three hundred and fifty pounds **avoirdupois**①; and in this estimate I have not included one hundred and ninety-seven superb gold watches; three of the number being worth each five hundred dollars, if one. Many of them were very old, and as time keepers valueless; the works having suffered, more or less, from corrosion — but all were richly jewelled and in cases of great worth. We estimated the entire contents of the chest, that night, at a million and a half of dollars; and upon the subsequent disposal of the **trinkets**② and jewels (a few being retained for our own use), it was found that we had greatly **undervalued**③ the treasure. When, at length, we had concluded our examination, and the intense excitement of the time had, in some measure, **subsided**④, Legrand, who saw that I was dying with impatience for a solution of this most extraordinary riddle, entered into a full detail of all the circumstances connected with it.

"You remember;" said he, "the night when I handed you the rough sketch I had made of the scarabæus. You recollect also, that I became quite vexed at you for insisting that my drawing resembled a death's-head. When you first made this assertion I thought you were jesting; but afterwards I called to mind the **peculiar**⑤ spots on the back of the insect, and admitted to myself that your remark had some little foundation in fact. Still, the **sneer**⑥ at my **graphic**⑦ powers irritated me — for I am considered a good artist — and, therefore, when you handed me the scrap of **parchment**⑧, I was about to crumple it up and throw it angrily into the fire."

"The scrap of paper, you mean," said I.

"No; it had much of the appearance of paper, and at first I supposed it to be such, but when I came to draw upon it, I discovered it, at once, to be a piece of very thin parchment. It was quite dirty, you remember. Well, as I was in the very act of crumpling it up, my glance fell upon the sketch at which you had been looking, and you may imagine my astonishment when I perceived, in fact, the figure of a death's-head just where, it seemed to me, I had made the drawing of the beetle. For a moment I was too much amazed to think with accuracy. I knew

① avoirdupois [ˌævədə'pɔiz] *n.* 常衡（质量制度，用于金银、药物以外的一般物品，区别于金衡、药衡）

② trinket ['triŋkit] *n.* 小装饰品

③ undervalue [ˌʌndə'vælju:] *v.* 低估……的价值

④ subside [səb'said] *v.* 平息，减弱

⑤ peculiar [pi'kju:ljə] *a.* 奇怪的，奇异的

⑥ sneer [sniə] *n.* 嘲笑，冷笑

⑦ graphic ['græfik] *a.* 绘画的，书画的

⑧ parchemnt ['pɑ:tʃmənt] *n.* 羊皮纸

些贵重物品加起来总重量超过三百五十常衡磅。就这，我还没把一百九十七块上等金表算在内；其中三块每块都值五百美元。好多表都已经有年头了，作为计时器一文不值；零件多少有点朽坏了——但都镶满珠宝，配有昂贵的表壳。那晚，我们估计整箱财物共值一百五十万美元。后来在我们变卖这些珠宝首饰时（有些没卖，我们自己留用了）才发现我们最初的估值太低了。最后清点完毕，当时的兴奋劲头相对消退了几分，勒格朗看我急不可耐地想知道这最离奇的谜语的谜底，就把这事的原委细细向我道来。

"你记得，"他说，"那天晚上我递给你一张我画的金龟子的草图。你还能回忆起吧，你说我的画像骷髅头时，我非常生气。起初你这么说的时候，我以为你在开玩笑呢；后来我忆起那昆虫背部的几个特别的黑点，这才承认你的话也不无依据。但你嘲笑我的绘画能力还是让我心里很气——别人都说我是出色的艺术家呢——所以当你把那片羊皮纸递给我的时候，我打算把它揉成团，一气之下扔到火堆里。"

"你指的是那张纸片吧。"我说。

"不；看着非常像纸，一开始我也把它当纸，但我在上面画画时，马上就感觉到那是一张非常薄的羊皮。它很脏，你记得吧。欸，就在我把它揉成团时，我往你看过的那个草图上瞄了一眼，你都想象不到我当时多惊奇，事实上我看到在我画甲壳虫的那个位置，真的有一个骷髅头。当时我惊奇得都无法理智思考了。我明明画得和这骷髅头细节上相差甚远——纵然大体轮廓有几分相似。于是我马上拿着蜡烛走到屋那头继续仔细地

that my design was very different in detail from this — although there was a certain similarity in general outline. Presently I took a candle, and seating myself at the other end of the room, proceeded to scrutinize the parchment more closely. Upon turning it over, I saw my own sketch upon the reverse, just as I had made it. My first idea, now, was mere surprise at the really remarkable similarity of outline — at the singular coincidence involved in the fact, that unknown to me, there should have been a skull upon the other side of the parchment, immediately beneath my figure of the scarabæus, and that this skull, not only in outline, but in size, should so closely resemble my drawing. I say the **singularity**① of this coincidence absolutely stupified me for a time. This is the usual effect of such coincidences. The mind struggles to establish a connexion — a sequence of cause and effect — and, being unable to do so, suffers a species of temporary **paralysis**②. But, when I recovered from this **stupor**③, there dawned upon me gradually a **conviction**④ which **startled**⑤ me even far more than the coincidence. I began distinctly, positively, to remember that there had been no drawing upon the parchment when I made my sketch of the scarabæus. I became perfectly certain of this; for I recollected turning up first one side and then the other, in search of the cleanest spot. Had the skull been then there, of course I could not have failed to notice it. Here was indeed a mystery which I felt it impossible to explain; but, even at that early moment, there seemed to **glimmer**⑥, faintly, within the most remote and secret chambers of my intellect, a glow-worm-like conception of that truth which last night's adventure brought to so magnificent a demonstration. I arose at once, and putting the parchment securely away, **dismissed**⑦ all farther reflection until I should be alone.

"When you had gone, and when Jupiter was fast asleep, I betook myself to a more **methodical**⑧ investigation of the affair. In the first place I considered the manner in which the parchment had come into my possession. The spot where we discovered the scarabaeus was on the coast of the main land, about a mile eastward of the island, and but a short distance above high water mark. Upon my taking hold of it, it gave me a sharp bite, which caused me to let it drop.

查看那片羊皮纸。我把它翻过来，看到我的画还原模原样地在那儿。我的第一个念头就是惊讶，因为它们的轮廓实在太相似了，这真是个惊人的巧合——我竟不知道在羊皮纸的反面赫然画着一个骷髅头，而且就在我画的金龟子图案的正下方，它不论大小还是轮廓都和我画的金龟子几乎一样。刚说到遇到这等惊人的巧合，我一时也缓不过神来。遇到这等巧合，谁都会这样。绞尽脑汁思索个中关联——前因后果的关系——但又苦于想不出，一时间思想卡壳了。但当我从这恍惚中逐渐清醒，我想明白了一个事实，这事远比那巧合更令我震惊。我十分清晰，十分确定地记得我在羊皮纸上画金龟子的时候，那里根本没有画。这点我完全可以肯定；因为我仍记得为了找到最干净的地方画画，我翻看了一面又看了另一面。若当时就有一个骷髅头，我当然不可能没注意到。这真是个难以解开的谜团；但其实早在那时候，我头脑最幽深隐蔽的地方似乎就微弱地闪烁着如萤火虫般真相的光辉，昨晚的探险就是有力的证明。我当即站起身，把羊皮纸放在安全的地方，打算等我自己一个人的时候再接着思考这件事。

"等你走了，朱庇特也睡熟了，我就按条理把这件事情研究了一番。首先我思考的是这块羊皮纸是怎么到我手里来的。我们是在小岛往东一英里的内陆海岸，距离满潮标不远处发现那只金龟子的。刚抓到它时就被它狠狠咬了一口，我一下就把它丢下了。朱庇特一向办事谨慎，在抓那虫子之前，眼看

① singularity [ˌsiŋgju'læriti] *n.* 奇怪，异常

② paralysis [pə'rælisis] *n.* 麻痹，无力

③ stupor ['stju:pə] *n.* 恍惚

④ conviction [kən'vikʃən] *n.* 确信

⑤ startle ['stɑ:tl] *v.* 使震惊

⑥ glimmer ['glimə] *v.* 发出微光

⑦ dismiss [dis'mis] *v.* 不予理会，不予考虑

⑧ methodical [mi'θɔdikəl] *a.* 有条理的

Jupiter, with his accustomed caution, before seizing the insect, which had flown towards him, looked about him for a leaf, or something of that nature, by which to take hold of it. It was at this moment that his eyes, and mine also, fell upon the scrap of parchment, which I then supposed to be paper. It was lying half buried in the sand, a corner sticking up. Near the spot where we found it, I observed the remnants of the hull of what appeared to have been a ship's long boat. The **wreck**① seemed to have been there for a very great while; for the resemblance to boat timbers could scarcely be traced.

"Well, Jupiter picked up the parchment, wrapped the beetle in it, and gave it to me. Soon afterwards we turned to go home, and on the way met Lieutenant G-. I showed him the insect, and he begged me to let him take it to the fort. Upon my consenting, he **thrust**② it forthwith into his waistcoat pocket, without the parchment in which it had been wrapped, and which I had continued to hold in my hand during his inspection. Perhaps he dreaded my changing my mind, and thought it best to make sure of the prize at once — you know how enthusiastic he is on all subjects connected with Natural History. At the same time, without being conscious of it, I must have deposited the parchment in my own pocket.

"You remember that when I went to the table, for the purpose of making a sketch of the beetle, I found no paper where it was usually kept. I looked in the drawer, and found none there. I searched my pockets, hoping to find an old letter, when my hand fell upon the parchment. I thus detail the precise mode in which it came into my possession; for the circumstances impressed me with peculiar force.

"No doubt you will think me fanciful — but I had already established a kind of connexion. I had put together two links of a great chain. There was a boat lying upon a sea-coast, and not far from the boat was a parchment — not a paper — with a skull depicted upon it. You will, of course, ask 'where is the connexion?' I reply that the skull, or death's-head, is the well-known **emblem**③ of the pirate. The flag of the death's head is **hoisted**④ in all engagements.

"I have said that the scrap was parchment, and not paper. Parchment

虫子朝他飞去，就开始找叶子之类的东西，好拿来
逮虫子。就在这时我们两人目光同时落在了那片羊
皮纸上，当时我还以为是一张纸。那张羊皮半埋在
沙子里，一角翘起。在找到羊皮纸的地方不远处，
我看到船的残骸，看样子像是大船上的舢板。那残
骸已经在那儿许久了，木板烂得已经快要看不出船
的样子。

① wreck [rek] *n.* 残骸

　　"就这样，朱庇特捡起那块羊皮，包起甲壳虫，
递给我。不久我们就往回走了，回家的路上遇到了 G
中尉。我把那虫子拿给他看，他就央求我要把虫子
带回城堡。我刚答应，他就把那虫子塞进坎肩口袋里，
并没有拿包虫子的那张羊皮纸，因为他看虫子时，
羊皮纸一直在我手里拿着。或许他是怕我改变主意，
想着最好马上把这战利品拿到手——你也知道凡是
跟博物学沾边的东西他都格外热衷。那时我肯定是
顺手就把那块羊皮塞到我自己的口袋里了。

② thrust [θrʌst] *v.* 猛塞

　　"你还记得吧，我走到桌边，要画一张那甲壳虫
的简图，平常放纸的地方都找不到纸。抽屉里也没有。
我就掏了掏口袋，希望能找到一封旧信，这时我的
手就刚好摸到了那块羊皮。我能如此详尽地把它落
到我手中的过程解释完整，就是因为这件事在我脑
海中留下了异常深刻的印象。

　　"无疑，你肯定以为我在异想天开——但我真的
已经弄清其中的关联了。我把一条长链的两头连在了
一起。海岸边有一艘船，船不远处有一块羊皮——不
是普通的纸——上面画着骷髅头。当然，你会问'关
联在哪呢？'告诉你，就在于骷髅头，或者说是头颅
骨，是众所周知的海盗的象征。他们与其他船只交
战时总会升起骷髅旗。

③ emblem ['embləm] *n.* 象
　征，标志
④ hoist [hɔist] *v.* 升起，吊
　起

　　"我说过了，那是一块羊皮纸，不是普通的纸。

is durable — almost **imperishable**①. Matters of little moment are rarely consigned to parchment; since, for the mere ordinary purposes of drawing or writing, it is not nearly so well adapted as paper. This reflection suggested some meaning — some **relevancy**② — in the death's-head. I did not fail to observe, also, the form of the parchment. Although one of its corners had been, by some accident, destroyed, it could be seen that the original form was oblong. It was just such a slip, indeed, as might have been chosen for a **memorandum**③ — for a record of something to be long remembered and carefully preserved."

"But," I interposed, "you say that the skull was not upon the parchment when you made the drawing of the beetle. How then do you trace any connexion between the boat and the skull — since this latter, according to your own admission, must have been designed (God only knows how or by whom) at some period subsequent to your sketching the scarabæus?"

"Ah, hereupon turns the whole mystery; although the secret, at this point, I had comparatively little difficulty in solving. My steps were sure, and could afford but a single result. I reasoned, for example, thus: When I drew the scarabæus, there was no skull apparent upon the parchment. When I had completed the drawing I gave it to you, and observed you narrowly until you returned it. You, therefore, did not design the skull, and no one else was present to do it. Then it was not done by human agency. And nevertheless it was done.

"At this stage of my reflections I endeavored to remember, and did remember, with entire distinctness, every incident which occurred about the period in question. The weather was chilly (oh rare and happy accident!), and a fire was blazing upon the hearth. I was heated with exercise and sat near the table. You, however, had drawn a chair close to the chimney. Just as I placed the parchment in your hand, and as you were in the act of inspecting it, Wolf, the Newfoundland, entered, and leaped upon your shoulders. With your left hand you caressed him and kept him off, while your right, holding the parchment, was permitted to fall **listlessly**④ between your knees, and in close **proximity**⑤ to the fire. At one moment I thought the blaze had caught it, and was about to caution

① imperishable [im'periʃəbl] *a.* 不会腐烂的

② relevancy ['reləvənsi:] *n.* 关联

③ memorandum [,memə'rændəm] *n.* 备忘录

④ listlessly ['listlisli] *ad.* 无精打采地

⑤ proximity [prɔk'simiti] *n.* 接近

羊皮可以长久保存——几乎不烂。小事小情的可不大会记在羊皮上，因为光是为了平常写字画画还不如用纸呢。这样想来，这骷髅头还真是有些深意——有些关联啦。我也没忽略羊皮纸的形状。尽管有一角被无意中弄坏，还是能看得出原来是长方形的。备忘录——永世不忘的记录，仔细保存的事情——很可能会选用这样的羊皮纸条。

　　"可是，"我打断他的话，"你说在你画甲壳虫的时候，那头颅骨并不在羊皮纸上啊。那你是怎么把船和头颅骨牵扯到一起的呢？——你也承认，头颅骨是在你画了金龟子之后的一段时间才画上去的（天知道是谁画的，怎么画的）。"

　　"哈，这就是整件事的神秘之处；不过到了这一步，我解开这个谜团已经不难了。我每一步的推论都有理有据，最终只能得到一个结论。比如，我是这么推论的：当我画金龟子的时候，羊皮上没有显示出头颅骨。当我画完把画交给你的时候，一直到你把画还给我，我都密切地注视着你。因此，并不是你把头颅骨画上去的，当时在场的也没人那么做。所以这就不是人力而为的。尽管如此，头颅骨还是出现了。

　　"推理到这步，我就试图回想，把这段时间整件事情的每个细节都清清楚楚想了一遍。当时天气寒冷（哎呀，真是个难得又幸运的巧合！），壁炉里燃着旺火。我刚从外边回来，走得热了，就坐在桌子旁边。而你把椅子拖到火炉边坐着。就在我把羊皮纸交到你手上，你正打算仔细查看的时候，武夫，我的纽芬兰大狗跑进来扑到你的肩上。你用左手抚摸它，把它哄走，这时你的右手捏着那块羊皮纸就懒懒地垂在两膝间，恰好离火炉很近。当时我还以

you, but, before I could speak, you had withdrawn it, and were engaged in its examination. When I considered all these particulars, I doubted not for a moment that heat had been the agent in bringing to light, upon the parchment, the skull which I saw designed upon it. You are well aware that chemical preparations exist, and have existed time out of mind, by means of which it is possible to write upon either paper or **vellum**①, so that the characters shall become visible only when subjected to the action of fire. Zaffre, digested in aqua regia, and **diluted**② with four times its weight of water, is sometimes employed; a green tint results. The regulus of **cobalt**③, **dissolved**④ in spirit of **nitre**⑤, gives a red. These colors disappear at longer or shorter intervals after the material written upon cools, but again become apparent upon the re-application of heat.

"I now scrutinized the death's-head with care. Its outer edges — the edges of the drawing nearest the edge of the vellum — were far more distinct than the others. It was clear that the action of the **caloric**⑥ had been imperfect or unequal. I immediately kindled a fire, and subjected every portion of the parchment to a glowing heat. At first, the only effect was the strengthening of the faint lines in the skull; but, upon persevering in the experiment, there became visible, at the corner of the slip, **diagonally**⑦ opposite to the spot in which the death's-head was **delineated**⑧, the figure of what I at first supposed to be a goat. A closer scrutiny, however, satisfied me that it was intended for a kid."

"Ha! ha!" said I, "to be sure I have no right to laugh at you — a million and a half of money is too serious a matter for **mirth**⑨ — but you are not about to establish a third link in your chain — you will not find any especial connexion between your pirates and a goat — pirates, you know, have nothing to do with goats; they **appertain**⑩ to the farming interest."

"But I have just said that the figure was not that of a goat."

"Well, a kid then — pretty much the same thing."

"Pretty much, but not altogether," said Legrand. "You may have heard of one Captain Kidd. I at once looked upon the figure of the animal as a kind of punning or **hieroglyphical**⑪ signature. I say signature; because its position

① vellum ['veləm] *n.* 上等皮纸

② dilute [dai'lju:t] *v.* 冲淡，稀释

③ cobalt ['kəubɔ:lt] *n.* 钴

④ dissolve [di'zɔlv] *v.* 使溶解

⑤ nitre ['naitə] *n.* 硝石

⑥ caloric [kə'lɔrik] *n.* 热（量）

⑦ diagonally [dai'ægənəli] *ad.* 对角地，斜对地

⑧ delineate [di'linieit] *v.* 画出（或勾画出）……的轮廓

⑨ mirth [mə:θ] *n.* 欢乐，欢笑

⑩ appertain [ˌæpə'tein] *v.* 属于，和……有关

⑪ hieroglyphical [ˌhaiərəu'glifikəl] *a.* 似象形文字的，难辨认的

为火苗会烧到它，正要提醒你，但还没开口，你就把它拿起来开始仔细查看。考虑完所有的细节，我当即断定是热力使我所看到的那个头颅骨在羊皮纸上显现出来的。你也知道，自古以来就有一种化学药剂，用这种试剂在纸上或皮纸上书写，字迹只在受热的情况下才显现出来。有人曾用过氧化钴溶解到王水中，再用四倍于其质量的水稀释后调出绿色溶液。钴渣溶解在硝酸溶液里会调出红色溶液。用这些溶液无论写在什么上，只要冷却，或时间长点，或时间短点，颜色就会消失，但是再次遇热就会显出字来。

"于是我把骷髅头仔细检查一遍。骷髅头的外圈——就是靠近羊皮纸边缘的那圈——比其他地方颜色都浅。显然是由于受热不够或者不均。我马上燃起火，让羊皮的每部分都受到火烤。最开始，只是原来头颅骨不明显的地方更突出了；但随着不断的加热，在这片纸的一角，斜对着画出骷髅头的地方，呈现出一个图形。开始我还以为是山羊，但仔细研究了一番后，我可以确定那是一只羔羊。"

"哈！哈！"我说，"我肯定无权嘲笑你——一百五十万块钱可不是闹着玩儿的——但你现在不是要在你的证据链条中安排第三个环节吧——你这海盗和山羊之间总不见得有什么特殊的关联吧——你也知道，海盗和山羊可扯不到一块；山羊只跟畜牧业有关。"

"但我说了，那图案可不是山羊。"

"对，那是羔羊——差不多一样。"

"差不多，但不能混为一谈，"勒格朗说道。"你可能听说有个基德[1]船长吧。我马上就想到把这动物的形状看成是某种双关字或者象形字签名。我说是签

1　"基德"与英文单词 kid（羔羊）谐音。

upon the vellum suggested this idea. The death's-head at the corner diagonally opposite, had, in the same manner, the air of a stamp, or seal. But I was sorely put out by the absence of all else — of the body to my imagined instrument — of the text for my context."

"I presume you expected to find a letter between the stamp and the signature."

"Something of that kind. The fact is, I felt irresistibly impressed with a **presentiment**① of some vast good fortune **impending**②. I can scarcely say why. Perhaps, after all, it was rather a desire than an actual belief; — but do you know that Jupiter's silly words, about the bug being of solid gold, had a remarkable effect upon my fancy? And then the series of accidents and coincidences — these were so very extraordinary. Do you observe how mere an accident it was that these events should have occurred upon the sole day of all the year in which it has been, or may be, sufficiently cool for fire, and that without the fire, or without the intervention of the dog at the precise moment in which he appeared, I should never have become aware of the death's-head, and so never the possessor of the treasure?"

"But **proceed**③ — I am all impatience."

"Well; you have heard, of course, the many stories current — the thousand **vague**④ rumors **afloat**⑤ about money buried, somewhere upon the Atlantic coast, by Kidd and his associates. These rumors must have had some foundation in fact. And that the rumors have existed so long and so continuous, could have resulted, it appeared to me, only from the circumstance of the buried treasure still remaining **entombed**⑥. Had Kidd concealed his **plunder**⑦ for a time, and afterwards **reclaimed**⑧ it, the rumors would scarcely have reached us in their present unvarying form. You will observe that the stories told are all about money-seekers, not about money-finders. Had the pirate recovered his money, there the affair would have dropped. It seemed to me that some accident — say the loss of a memorandum indicating its locality — had **deprived**⑨ him of the means of recovering it, and that this accident had become known to his followers,

名，是因为它在羊皮纸上出现的位置刚好是签名的位置。斜对角的那个骷髅头同样有某种印记或者封签的意味。但除此之外别无其他——没有我想象中文件的正文——没有能让我设定情境的原文文字。"

"我想你是指望在印记和签名之间找到信吧。"

"是这个意思。其实我不禁发自内心地产生一种预感，我就要发大财了。我说不出缘由。或许，毕竟，还没有信以为真，只是但愿如此罢了——可你看不正是朱庇特说那虫子是金甲虫的傻话让我异想天开了吗？紧接着又是一连串的意外和巧合——一切都太离奇了。你看，所有的事情都凑到一天了，多巧！一年里偏偏就那天出奇的冷，偏偏那天生起火来，偏偏那一刻狗进屋来干扰了你，若不是狗在彼时彼刻出现，我也就看不到那骷髅头，更不会享有这些宝藏啦！"

"快往下讲——我都等不及啦。"

"好；你应该也听说过很多流传的故事——千百种捕风捉影的谣言，说基德和他的手下在大西洋沿岸某处埋了钱财。想来这些谣言也是有事实依据的。传了那么久，还一直不断，依我看只有一种可能，就是那些埋藏的财宝仍未被发掘。如果基德把抢来的财宝藏起来，后来又取走，那么传入我们耳朵里的谣言就不至于像现在这样遵循一个不变的规律了。你要注意到这点，所有的故事讲的都是寻宝的事，并没有人找到宝藏。若是海盗取回了钱财，那寻宝的事也就尘埃落定了。依我看，应该是出了意外——比方说丢失了备忘录找不到藏宝地了——他没法找到那些钱财了。他的手下原本是不该知道有隐藏宝藏这档子事的，而这个意外却被他们知道

① presentiment
[pri'zentimənt] *n.* 预感
② impending [im'pendiŋ] *a.*
即将发生的，迫近的

③ proceed [prəu'si:d] *v.* 继
续进行
④ vague [veig] *a.* 含糊的
⑤ afloat [ə'fləut] *a.* (消息、
谣言等) 流传着的

⑥ entomb [in'tu:m] *v.* 埋葬
⑦ plunder ['plʌndə] *n.* 掠夺
的财物

⑧ reclaim [ri'kleim] *v.* 拿
回，收回
⑨ deprive [di'praiv] *v.* 使丧
失，剥夺

who otherwise might never have heard that treasure had been concealed at all, and who, busying themselves in vain, because unguided attempts, to regain it, had given first birth, and then universal currency, to the reports which are now so common. Have you ever heard of any important treasure being unearthed along the coast?"

"Never."

"But that Kidd's accumulations were immense, is well known. I took it for granted, therefore, that the earth still held them; and you will scarcely be surprised when I tell you that I felt a hope, nearly amounting to certainty, that the parchment so strangely found, involved a lost record of the place of deposit."

"But how did you proceed?"

"I held the vellum again to the fire, after increasing the heat; but nothing appeared. I now thought it possible that the coating of dirt might have something to do with the failure; so I carefully **rinsed**[①] the parchment by pouring warm water over it, and, having done this, I placed it in a tin pan, with the skull downwards, and put the pan upon a **furnace**[②] of lighted **charcoal**[③]. In a few minutes, the pan having become thoroughly heated, I removed the slip, and, to my inexpressible joy, found it spotted, in several places, with what appeared to be figures arranged in lines. Again I placed it in the pan, and suffered it to remain another minute. Upon taking it off, the whole was just as you see it now." Here Legrand, having re-heated the parchment, submitted it to my inspection. The following characters were rudely traced, in a red tint, between the death's-head and the goat:

"53‡‡†305))6*;4826)4‡)4‡);806*;48†8¶60))85;1‡);:‡
8†83(88)5†;46(;88*96*?;8)*‡(;485);5*†2:*‡(;4956*
2(5*—4)8¶8*;4069285);)6†8)4‡‡;1(‡9;48081;8:8‡1;4
8†85;4)485†528806*81(‡9;48;(88;4(‡?34;48)4‡;161;:
188;‡?;"

了，这些手下就开始毫无根据地想发掘宝藏，但都无功而返，现在广为流传的谣言最开始就是这样传出来的。你听说过有人在大西洋沿岸发现大的宝藏了吗？"

"从没听说过。"

"众所周知，基德积累的财富多得数不清。我敢肯定它们仍被埋在地下；因此我这么跟你说，你一定不会太吃惊——我希望，而且几乎可以肯定，那离奇发现的羊皮纸上就记录着遗失的藏宝地点。"

"然后你是怎么做的呢？"

"我把火生旺，又把羊皮纸放在火上烤；但是什么也没有出现。我就觉得可能是表面的那层土在碍事；于是我用温水小心翼翼地冲洗羊皮，之后，把它放进平底锅，头颅骨一面朝下，把锅放在燃着的炭火上面烤。过了几分钟，锅就烧烫了，我再拿起那羊皮一看，真是喜出望外，我发现有几处显现出一行行像是字的东西。我把羊皮又放回锅里，又让它烤了一分钟。这次拿出来上面的字就全出来了，给你看。"勒格朗说到这就把重新烤过的羊皮递给我看。在骷髅头和山羊之间，用潦草的红色笔迹写着如下的符号：

"53‡‡†305))6*;4826)4‡)4‡);806*;48†8¶60))85;1‡);:‡ *8†83(88)5*†;46(;88*96*?;8)*‡(;485);5*†2:*‡(;4956* 2(5*—4)8¶8*;4069285);)6†8)4‡‡;1(‡9;48081;8:8‡1;4 8†85;4)485†528806*81(‡9;48;(88;4(‡?34;48)4‡;161;: 188;‡?;"

① rinse [rins] *v.* 冲洗
② furnace ['fə:nis] *n.* 炉子，火炉
③ charcoal ['tʃɑ:kəul] *n.* 木炭

"But," said I, returning him the slip, "I am as much in the dark as ever. Were all the jewels of Golconda awaiting me upon my solution of this **enigma**①, I am quite sure that I should be unable to earn them."

"And yet," said Legrand, "the solution is by no means so difficult as you might be lead to imagine from the first **hasty**② inspection of the characters. These characters, as any one might readily guess, form a **cipher**③ — that is to say, they convey a meaning; but then, from what is known of Kidd, I could not suppose him capable of constructing any of the more **abstruse**④ **cryptographs**⑤. I made up my mind, at once, that this was of a simple species — such, however, as would appear, to the **crude**⑥ intellect of the sailor, absolutely **insoluble**⑦ without the key."

"And you really solved it?"

"Readily; I have solved others of an abstruseness ten thousand times greater. Circumstances, and a certain bias of mind, have led me to take interest in such riddles, and it may well be doubted whether human **ingenuity**⑧ can construct an enigma of the kind which human ingenuity may not, by proper application, resolve. In fact, having once established connected and **legible**⑨ characters, I scarcely gave a thought to the mere difficulty of developing their import.

"In the present case — indeed in all cases of secret writing — the first question regards the language of the cipher; for the principles of solution, so far, especially, as the more simple ciphers are concerned, depend upon, and are varied by, the genius of the particular idiom. In general, there is no alternative but experiment (directed by probabilities) of every tongue known to him who attempts the solution, until the true one be attained. But, with the cipher now before us, all difficulty was removed by the signature. The pun upon the word 'Kidd' is **appreciable**⑩ in no other language than the English. But for this consideration I should have begun my attempts with the Spanish and French, as the tongues in which a secret of this kind would most naturally have been

① enigma [i'nigmə] *n*. 谜

② hasty ['heisti] *a*. 急促的，匆忙的

③ cipher ['saifə] *n*. 密码

④ abstruse [æb'stru:s] *a*. 深奥的，难懂的

⑤ cryptograph ['kriptəugrɑ:f] *n*. 密文

⑥ crude [kru:d] *a*. 粗鲁的，不精明的

⑦ insoluble [in'sɔljubl] *a*. 不能解决的

⑧ ingenuity [,indʒi'nju:əti] *n*. 机灵，机智

⑨ legible ['ledʒəbl] *a*.（字迹）可以辨认的，易读的

⑩ appreciable [ə'pri:ʃiəbl] *a*. 明显的

"可是，"我把羊皮还给他说，"我还是搞不懂。就算解了这哑谜便有堆成山的珠宝等着我，我也是肯定没办法弄到手。"

"可是，"勒格朗说，"这谜并不难解，只是你乍一看这些符号就被迷惑了。谁都会轻易猜到，这些符号形成了一组密码——也就是说它们都是有含义的；据我对基德的了解，我觉得他也造不出什么深奥的密文。我马上料定这是一种简码——然而即使这样简单地写出来，对于头脑简单的水手来说，没有密钥也是绝对解不出来的。"

"你真的解开了？"

"轻而易举啊，比这难解一万倍的我都解开过。环境使然，也是天生喜好，我向来就对这些哑谜感兴趣。但凡是凭人类的聪明才智设下的哑谜，只要采用适当的方法，我不相信利用人类同样的聪明才智还有解不出的。事实上，只要符号清晰易读，互相关联，那我推出其中的含义也就不是什么难事了。

"就这份密码来看——诚然所有密文都一样——首要问题就是明确密码使用的语言；因为解谜的原则，尤其是较简单的密码，全取决于独特的熟语特征，也因这些熟语的变化而不同。通常，要解谜的人别无选择，只能用他所懂的语言逐一尝试（根据可能性决定先试哪种后试哪种），直到试对为止。但我们面前的这份密码，因为有了签名就可以省去这些麻烦。'基德'这个词除了在英语中，在其他语言中都没有双关意。若不是考虑到这点，我一开始就会用西班牙语和法文尝试了，因为一个活跃在南美洲北岸的海盗自然最有可能用这两种语言写出这种密码。

written by a pirate of the Spanish main. As it was, I assumed the cryptograph to be English.

"You observe there are no divisions between the words. Had there been divisions, the task would have been comparatively easy. In such case I should have **commenced**[①] with a **collation**[②] and analysis of the shorter words, and, had a word of a single letter occurred, as is most likely, (a or I, for example,) I should have considered the solution as assured. But, there being no division, my first step was to **ascertain**[③] the predominant letters, as well as the least frequent. Counting all, I constructed a table, thus:

Of the character 8 there are 33.

;	"	26.
4	"	19.
‡)	"	16.
*	"	13.
5	"	12.
6	"	11.
† 1	"	8.
0	"	6.
9 2	"	5.
: 3	"	4.
?	"	3.
¶	"	2.
-.	"	1.

"Now, in English, the letter which most frequently occurs is e. Afterwards, succession runs thus: *a o i d h n r s t u y c f g l m w b k p q x z*. E predominates so remarkably that an individual sentence of any length is rarely seen, in which it is not the **prevailing**[④] character.

"Here, then, we leave, in the very beginning, the **groundwork**[⑤] for something more than a mere guess. The general use which may be made of the table is obvious — but, in this particular cipher, we shall only very partially

就这样，我相信这密码是英文。

"你看，这些符号之间没有空格。如果有空格，事情就会相对简单些。在这种情况下，我开始核对分析较短的词，如果有单字母的词——很可能会有（比如 a 或者 I）——那我保证就能揭开谜底了。但没有空格，我的第一步就是查出使用最多的字符和使用最少的字符。全部统计完，我列了这么一张表格：

8 符号有 33 个。

;	26 个	† 和 1	分别 8 个
4	19 个	0	6 个
‡ 和)	分别 16 个	9 和 2	分别 5 个
*	13 个	: 和 3	分别 4 个
5	12 个	?	3 个
6	11 个	¶	2 个
		-.	1 个

"那么，在英语中，出现频率最高的字母是 e。接下来依次是：a、o、i、d、h、n、r、s、t、u、y、c、f、g、l、m、w、b、k、p、q、x、z。字母 e 被使用的次数最多，一个单句无论多长，主要字母都是 e。

"现在可以说，我们已经在最开始为后面打下了基础，再破译密码就不仅仅是靠猜测了。这个表格的用途很明显——但在解这份密码时，我们只需要依靠表格很小的一部分。我们发现这份密码里出现最多的符号是 8，那我们就首先假设 8 就代表着普通

① commence [kə'mens] v. 开始，着手
② collation [kɔ'leiʃən] n. 核对，整理
③ ascertain [ˌæsə'tein] v. 确定，弄清

④ prevailing [pri'veiliŋ] a. 占主导地位的
⑤ groundwork ['graundwə:k] n. 基础

require its aid. As our predominant character is 8, we will commence by assuming it as the *e* of the natural alphabet. To verify the supposition, let us observe if the 8 be seen often in couples — for *e* is doubled with great frequency in English — in such words, for example, as 'meet,' 'fleet,' 'speed,' 'seen,' 'been,' 'agree,' &c. In the present instance we see it doubled no less than five times, although the cryptograph is brief.

"Let us assume 8, then, as *e*. Now, of all *words* in the language, 'the' is most usual; let us see, therefore, whether there are not repetitions of any three characters, in the same order of **collocation**①, the last of them being 8. If we discover repetitions of such letters, so arranged, they will most probably represent the word 'the.' Upon inspection, we find no less than seven such arrangements, the characters being ;48. We may, therefore, assume that ; represents *t*, 4 represents *h*, and 8 represents *e* — the last being now well confirmed. Thus a great step has been taken.

"But, having established a single word, we are enabled to establish a vastly important point; that is to say, several commencements and **terminations**② of other words. Let us refer, for example, to the last instance but one, in which the combination ;48 occurs — not far from the end of the cipher. We know that the ; immediately ensuing is the commencement of a word, and, of the six characters succeeding this 'the,' we are **cognizant**③ of no less than five. Let us set these characters down, thus, by the letters we know them to represent, leaving a space for the unknown —

t eeth.

"Here we are enabled, at once, to **discard**④ the 'th,' as forming no portion of the word commencing with the first t; since, by experiment of the entire alphabet for a letter adapted to the **vacancy**⑤, we perceive that no word can be formed of which this *th* can be a part. We are thus narrowed into

t ee,

and, going through the alphabet, if necessary, as before, we arrive at the word

英文字母中的 e。为了证实这个假设，让我们看看符号 8 是不是成双出现的——因为在英语中，字母 e 叠用的频率较高——例如在 meet、fleet、speed、seen、been、agree 等词汇中，e 都是叠用的。单看眼前这份密码，虽然简短，但是 8 成双出现的情况不下五次。

"那么就把 8 当成 e。再看，在所有的英语词中，the 这个词最常见；因此让我们看看这里有没有排列顺序相同的三个符号反复出现，并且第三个是 8。如果发现这样排列的字符重复出现，那么他们非常有可能代表 the 这个单词。检查一遍后，我们发现不少于七处，这三个字符是 ;48。据此，我们可以假定密码中的 ; 代表字母 t，4 代表字母 h，8 代表字母 e——最后那个字符解码肯定没错了。这样，我们就迈出了重要的一步。

"确定了一个单词，我们就能够确定极其重要的一点；也就是说，能够确定其他词开头和结尾的字母了。我们就拿倒数第二处 ;48 组合出现的地方来举例吧——此处离密码结尾不远。我们知道这组字符后边紧接着的 ; 就是一个词的开头，在这组字符代表的 the 后边紧接着的六个字符我们就认出不下五个。让我们把这些知道的有代表符号的字母列出来，不知道的先空下——t eeth。

"我们将字母表中的所有字母逐一放到这个空里，没有哪个字母能形成以 t 开头，以 th 结尾的词，因此我们就认为 th 不属于这个词把它去掉，把这个词缩短成 t ee 了。如果有必要，再用所有字母试一遍，我们能得到唯一可能的结果就是 tree 这个词。这样一来，我们就得出 (代表字母 r 这个结论，the tree 这两个词相邻。

"再从这几个词往后看一小段，我们又看到 ;48

① collocation
[ˌkɔləu'keiʃən] *n.* 排列

② termination
[ˌtə:mi'neiʃən] *n.* 结束

③ cognizant ['kɔgnizənt] *a.*
认知的，了解的

④ discard [dis'kɑ:d] *v.* 丢
弃，放弃

⑤ vacancy ['veikənsi] *n.* 空
白

'tree,' as the sole possible reading. We thus gain another letter, *r*, represented by (, with the words 'the tree' in **juxtaposition**①.

"Looking beyond these words, for a short distance, we again see the combination ;48, and employ it by way of *termination* to what immediately precedes. We have thus this arrangement:

the tree ;4(‡?34 the,

or, **substituting**② the natural letters, where known, it reads thus:

the tree thr‡?3h the.

"Now, if, in place of the unknown characters, we leave blank spaces, or substitute dots, we read thus:

the tree thr...h the,

when the word '*through*' makes itself evident at once. But this discovery gives us three new letters, *o*, *u* and *g*, represented by ‡, ? and 3.

"Looking now, narrowly, through the cipher for combinations of known characters, we find, not very far from the beginning, this arrangement,

83(88, or egree,

which, plainly, is the conclusion of the word 'degree,' and gives us another letter, *d*, represented by †.

"Four letters beyond the word 'degree,' we perceive the combination

;46(;88.

"Translating the known characters, and representing the unknown by dots, as before, we read thus:

th.rtee

an arrangement immediately suggestive of the word 'thirteen,' and again furnishing us with two new characters, *i* and *n*, represented by 6 and *.

"Referring, now, to the beginning of the cryptograph, we find the combination,

53‡‡†.

"Translating, as before, we obtain

.good,

这个字符组合，我们用它来确定先前那个词段的结尾。如此一来，我们就得出如下排列：the tree ;4(‡?34 the。把我们知道的符号用字母代替，就写成：the tree thr‡?3h the。

"如果我们把不知道的符号空着，或者用小点代替，就写成：the tree thr…h the。很明显，我们马上就能拼出 through 这个词。这个发现给我们提供了三个新的字母 o、u、g，分别由 ‡、?、3 这三个字符代表。

"现在从头到尾仔细地看一遍密码，寻找已经知道的能连在一起的字母，我们可以发现，在离开头不远处，有这样一个排列：83(88，可以拼成 egree，一看就知道是 degree 这个词。这又给我们提供了一个新字母 d，由符号 † 代表。

"degree 这个词往后数四个字符，我们可以看出这样一个组合：;46(;88。

"把已知的翻译成字母，未知的用小点表示，像刚才一样，我们可以写出 th.rtee 这样的组合。这样的排列马上就能猜出是 thirteen 这个词，这就给我们提供了另两个新字母 i 和 n，分别由 6 和 * 代表。

"现在我们来看密码的开头，找到 53‡‡† 这个组合。

"像前边那样翻译过来，得到 .good 这个词。因

① juxtaposition [ˌdʒʌkstəpə'ziʃən] n. 并置，并列

② substitute ['sʌbstitjuːt] v. 替代

which assures us that the first letter is *A*, and that the first two words are 'A good.'

"It is now time that we arrange our key, as far as discovered, in a **tabular**[1] form, to avoid confusion. It will stand thus:

5	*represents*	*a*
†	"	*d*
8	"	*e*
3	"	*g*
4	"	*h*
6	"	*i*
*	"	*n*
‡	"	*o*
(	"	*r*
;	"	*t*

"We have, therefore, no less than ten of the most important letters represented, and it will be unnecessary to proceed with the details of the solution. I have said enough to convince you that ciphers of this nature are readily **soluble**[2], and to give you some **insight**[3] into the **rationale**[4] of their development. But be assured that the specimen before us appertains to the very simplest species of cryptograph. It now only remains to give you the full translation of the characters upon the parchment, as **unriddled**[5]. Here it is:

'A good glass in the **bishop**[6]'s hostel in the devil's seat forty-one degrees and thirteen minutes northeast and by north main branch seventh limb east side shoot from the left eye of the death's-head a bee-line from the tree through the shot fifty feet out.'"

"But," said I, "the enigma seems still in as bad a condition as ever. How is it possible to **extort**[7] a meaning from all this **jargon**[8] about 'devil's seats,' 'death's heads,' and 'bishop's hotels?'"

此我们可以确定，第一个字母肯定是 A，开头两个字就是 A good。

"为了避免混乱，我们把已经发现的密钥列成一个表格，像这样：

5	等于	a	6	等于	i
†	等于	d	*	等于	n
8	等于	e	‡	等于	o
3	等于	g	(	等于	r
4	等于	h	;	等于	t

"这样我们就已经能认出十多个代表字母的符号了，至于解密的细节，我就不必多说了。我说了这么多就是为了让你知道像这类的密码很容易解开，并且你也深入了解解密过程的基本原理了。可以肯定的是，眼前这份密码属于最简单的那种。接下来，我就把羊皮纸上所有的符号翻译出来。请看：

'一面好镜子在毕晓普客栈魔椅四十一度十三分东北偏北主枝第七根枝丫东边从骷髅头左眼射击从树前引一最短线通过弹孔延伸五十英尺。'"

"但是，"我说，"这个字谜看起来还是令人费解。像'魔椅''骷髅头'，还有'毕晓普客栈'，这都是些隐语，怎么才能推敲出其中真正的意思呢？"

① tabular ['tæbjulə] *a.* 表格式的

② soluble ['sɔljubl] *a.* 可解决的

③ insight ['insait] *n.* 洞察，深刻见解

④ rationale [ˌræʃə'nɑ:li] *n.* 基本原理

⑤ unriddle [ˌʌn'ridl] *v.* 解决，解答

⑥ bishop ['biʃəp] *n.* 主教

⑦ extort [ik'stɔ:t] *v.* 牵强地推断出

⑧ jargon ['dʒɑ:gən] *n.*（难懂的）行话，术语

"I **confess**①," replied Legrand, "that the matter still wears a serious aspect, when regarded with a casual glance. My first endeavor was to divide the sentence into the natural division intended by the cryptographist."

"You mean, to **punctuate**② it?"

"Something of that kind."

"But how was it possible to effect this?"

"I reflected that it had been a point with the writer to run his words together without division, so as to increase the difficulty of solution. Now, a not over-acute man, in pursuing such an object would be nearly certain to **overdo**③ the matter. When, in the course of his composition, he arrived at a break in his subject which would naturally require a pause, or a point, he would be exceedingly **apt to**④ run his characters, at this place, more than usually close together. If you will observe the MS., in the present instance, you will easily detect five such cases of unusual crowding. Acting upon this hint, I made the division thus:

'A good glass in the bishop's hostel in the devil's seat — forty-one degrees and thirteen minutes — northeast and by north — main branch seventh limb east side — shoot from the left eye of the death's-head — a bee-line from the tree through the shot fifty feet out.'"

"Even this division," said I, "leaves me still in the dark."

"It left me also in the dark," replied Legrand, "for a few days; during which I made **diligent**⑤ inquiry, in the neighborhood of Sullivan's Island, for any building which went by the name of the 'Bishop's Hotel;' for, of course, I dropped the **obsolete**⑥ word 'hostel.' Gaining no information on the subject, I was on the point of extending my **sphere**⑦ of search, and proceeding in a more systematic manner, when, one morning, it entered into my head, quite suddenly, that this 'Bishop's Hostel' might have some reference to an old family, of the name of Bessop, which, time out of mind, had held possession of an ancient manor-house, about four miles to the northward of the Island. I accordingly went over to the **plantation**⑧, and re-instituted my inquiries among the older negroes of the place. At length one of the most aged of the women said that she

① confess [kən'fes] *v.* 承
认，坦白

② punctuate ['pʌŋktjueit] *v.*
加标点

③ overdo [,əuvə'du:] *v.*
把……做得过头

④ apt to 倾向于

⑤ diligent ['dilidʒənt] *a.* 勤
勉的

⑥ obsolete ['ɔbsəli:t] *a.* 老
式的

⑦ sphere [sfiə] *n.* 领域，范
围

⑧ plantation [plæn'teiʃən]
n. 大农场，种植园

"我承认，"勒格朗答道，"若是粗略一看，这些话还是有些难解。我就开始想办法把这句子按照加密者的原意分解成自然分句。"

"你是说加标点吧？"

"和加标点差不多。"

"可是怎么操作呢？"

"我考虑到写密码的人把这些词不分句地连在一起写就是为了增加解密的难度。试想一个头脑不太灵光的人越是想达到这个目的，就越会过犹不及。在这篇密码中，自然语句需要加标点或者停顿的地方，他就会让字符挨得更紧密，其实在这些地方就该分句了。你如果仔细观察我们手头的这份原稿，不难找到有五处字符靠得特别近。根据这一暗示，我就这样给这段话做了分句：'一面好镜子在毕晓普客栈魔椅——四十一度十三分——东北偏北——主枝第七根枝丫东边——从骷髅头左眼射击——从树前引一最短线通过弹孔延伸五十英尺。'"

"即使这么分，"我说，"我还是摸不着头脑。"

"我也是摸不着头脑，"勒格朗答道，"有好几天，我都在沙利文岛附近一带费尽心力地打听一座叫作'毕晓普旅店'的建筑；当然我没用'客栈'这种老叫法。在这方面打听不到什么有用的消息，我本打算以更加系统的方法进一步扩大调查范围。可是有一天早上，我突然想起这个'毕晓普客栈'或许和一个古老的贝索普家族有关联，很久以前，这个贝索普家族在沙利文岛往北约四英里的地方拥有一座古老的府邸。根据这个想法，我就去了那个庄园，向那里上了年纪的黑人们打听我想知道的事情。最后，其中一个年纪最大的老太太说她听说过一个叫作贝索普城堡的地方，可以领我去，但是这个地方既不

had heard of such a place as Bessop's Castle, and thought that she could guide me to it, but that it was not a castle nor a **tavern**[①], but a high rock.

"I offered to pay her well for her trouble, and, after some **demur**[②], she consented to accompany me to the spot. We found it without much difficulty, when, dismissing her, I proceeded to examine the place. The 'castle' consisted of an irregular **assemblage**[③] of cliffs and rocks — one of the latter being quite remarkable for its height as well as for its insulated and artificial appearance. I clambered to its **apex**[④], and then felt much at a loss as to what should be next done.

"While I was busied in reflection, my eyes fell upon a narrow **ledge**[⑤] in the eastern face of the rock, perhaps a yard below the summit upon which I stood. This ledge projected about eighteen inches, and was not more than a foot wide, while a **niche**[⑥] in the cliff just above it, gave it a rude resemblance to one of the hollow-backed chairs used by our ancestors. I made no doubt that here was the 'devil's seat' alluded to in the MS., and now I seemed to grasp the full secret of the riddle.

"The 'good glass,' I knew, could have reference to nothing but a telescope; for the word 'glass' is rarely employed in any other sense by seamen. Now here, I at once saw, was a telescope to be used, and a definite point of view, admitting no variation, from which to use it. Nor did I hesitate to believe that the phrases, "forty-one degrees and thirteen minutes,' and 'northeast and by north,' were intended as directions for the **levelling**[⑦] of the glass. Greatly excited by these discoveries, I hurried home, procured a telescope, and returned to the rock.

"I let myself down to the ledge, and found that it was impossible to retain a seat upon it except in one particular position. This fact confirmed my preconceived idea. I proceeded to use the glass. Of course, the 'forty-one degrees and thirteen minutes' could allude to nothing but elevation above the visible horizon, since the horizontal direction was clearly indicated by the words, 'northeast and by north.' This latter direction I at once established by means of a pocket-compass; then, pointing the glass as nearly at an angle of forty-one degrees of elevation

① tavern ['tævən] *n.* 酒吧，
小旅店
② demur [di'mə:] *n.* 反对

③ assemblage [ə'semblidʒ]
n. 组合

④ apex ['eipeks] *n.* 顶点，
尖端
⑤ ledge [ledʒ] *n.* 岩架

⑥ niche [nitʃ] *n.* （山坡或
峭壁上）天然凹陷处

⑦ level ['levəl] *v.* 瞄准，对
准

是城堡，也不是客店，而是一块高耸的岩石。

"我主动提出给她一大笔辛苦费，一番推辞后，
她还是答应收下钱，带我去那个地方。我们没怎么
费周折就找到了，把她打发走后，我继续查看这个
地点。这座'城堡'由许多错乱的峭壁和乱石组
成——其中一块大石高耸入云，巍然独立，如同假
山。我爬到那石头顶端，至于接下来该干什么则完
全没有头绪。

"正当我站在岩石顶端陷入思考时，无意中看见
这块石头的东面，距我站的岩石顶端向下大约一码
的地方有一个壁架。这个壁架突出约十八英寸[1]，不过
一英尺[2]宽，在它上方有一处凹陷，粗看就像我们老
辈人用过的凹背椅。我马上就想到这就是密码原文
中提到的'魔椅'，至此，似乎我已经完全掌握了这
字谜的破解之法了。

"'好镜子'我想只能指望远镜，因为除此之外
水手很少用'镜子'指别的东西。那么我马上就明白，
得用望远镜看一下，并且只能在固定的一点看，绝不
能换别的地方。我也不怀疑地确信'四十一度十三分'
和'东北偏北'这两个短语就是指望远镜所看的高
度和方向。有此发现，我兴奋不已，飞奔回家，弄
到一副望远镜，又回到岩石处。

"我往下爬到壁架，才发现只有一处位置能够坐
人。这也证实了我之前的假设。我用望远镜看了一下。
当然，'四十一度十三分'就是暗指水平仰角，而水
平偏转的方向就由'东北偏北'指示清楚了。我用
便携指南针马上就确定了偏转的方向，然后估摸着
把望远镜尽量精确地指向仰角四十一度。我小心翼

1　约0.46米。
2　约0.3米。

as I could do it by guess, I moved it cautiously up or down, until my attention was arrested by a circular **rift**① or opening in the foliage of a large tree that **overtopped**② its fellows in the distance. In the centre of this rift I perceived a white spot, but could not, at first, distinguish what it was. Adjusting the focus of the telescope, I again looked, and now made it out to be a human skull.

"Upon this discovery I was so **sanguine**③ as to consider the enigma solved; for the phrase 'main branch, seventh limb, east side,' could refer only to the position of the skull upon the tree, while 'shoot from the left eye of the death's-Head' admitted, also, of but one interpretation, in regard to a search for buried treasure. I perceived that the design was to drop a bullet from the left eye of the skull, and that a bee-line, or, in other words, a straight line, drawn from the nearest point of the trunk through 'the shot,' (or the spot where the bullet fell,) and thence extended to a distance of fifty feet, would indicate a definite point — and beneath this point I thought it at least possible that a deposit of value lay concealed."

"All this," I said, "is exceedingly clear, and, although **ingenious**④, still simple and **explicit**⑤. When you left the Bishop's Hotel, what then?"

"Why, having carefully taken the bearings of the tree, I turned homewards. The instant that I left 'the devil's seat,' however, the circular rift **vanished**⑥; nor could I get a glimpse of it afterwards, turn as I would. What seems to me the chief ingenuity in this whole business, is the fact (for repeated experiment has convinced me it is a fact) that the circular opening in question is visible from no other attainable point of view than that afforded by the narrow ledge upon the face of the rock.

"In this expedition to the 'Bishop's Hotel' I had been attended by Jupiter, who had, no doubt, observed, for some weeks past, the **abstraction**⑦ of my demeanor, and took especial care not to leave me alone. But, on the next day, getting up very early, I **contrived**⑧ to give him the slip, and went into the hills in search of the tree. After much **toil**⑨ I found it. When I came home at night my valet proposed to give me a flogging. With the rest of the adventure I believe you are as well acquainted as myself."

翼地把望远镜上下移动，直到最后，我注意到有一棵树比其他树都高，树叶间有个圆形缺口，或说是空隙。在缺口的中心，我看到一个白点，但一开始无法分辨是什么。调整好望远镜的焦距，我再一看，才看出来是个人头骨。

"据此发现，我可以十分乐观地认为谜底揭开了；因为'主枝，第七根枝丫，东边'那句就只能是指头颅骨在树上的位置，而就寻找地下宝藏的方法而言，'从骷髅头左眼射击'也只能有一种解读。我意识到，方法就是从头颅骨的左眼射下一枚子弹，从树身最近点到'弹孔'（即子弹落下的地方），画一条最短线，换句话说就是直线，再从弹孔处继续画五十英尺，就会指出一个确定的点——在这点下方，我猜，至少有地下藏宝的可能。

"一切都清楚了，"我说"虽然巧妙独特，却也简单明了。你离开毕晓普旅店之后呢？"

"这个嘛，仔细记下那棵树的方位，我就转身回家了。说来也怪，我一离开'魔椅'，那圆缺口就消失了；后来任我怎么调整望远镜也看不到分毫。依我看，整个解密过程中最精妙之处，就是这关键的圆缺口只能从那块巨石上伸出的狭窄壁架上的那一点才能看到（经过多次实验我可以确信的确如此）。

"这次的'毕晓普旅店'探险，有朱庇特陪着我呢，他肯定是在过去的几周里看到我举止反常，于是格外操心，不想让我一人前往。但是第二天，我起了大早，故意趁他不注意一个人溜出去，跑到山里去找那棵树。找到它真是颇费周折啊。那晚回到家，我的这位随从打算揍我一顿。接下来的历险，我想，你和我一样都了解了。"

① rift [rift] *n.* 裂缝，裂隙
② overtop [ˌəuvə'tɔp] *v.* 高于，超出

③ sanguine ['sæŋgwin] *a.* 自信的

④ ingenious [in'dʒi:njəs] *a.* 巧妙的
⑤ explicit [ik'splisit] *a.* 明确的
⑥ vanish ['væniʃ] *v.* 消失

⑦ abstraction [æb'strækʃən] *n.* 心不在焉

⑧ contrive [kən'traiv] *v.* 设计
⑨ toil [tɔil] *n.* 辛苦

"I suppose," said I, "you missed the spot, in the first attempt at digging, through Jupiter's stupidity in letting the bug fall through the right instead of through the left eye of the skull."

"Precisely. This mistake made a difference of about two inches and a half in the 'shot' — that is to say, in the position of the peg nearest the tree; and had the treasure been beneath the 'shot,' the error would have been of little moment; but 'the shot,' together with the nearest point of the tree, were merely two points for the establishment of a line of direction; of course the error, however **trivial**[1] in the beginning, increased as we proceeded with the line, and by the time we had gone fifty feet, threw us quite off the **scent**[2]. But for my deep-seated impressions that treasure was here somewhere actually buried, we might have had all our labor in vain."

"But your **grandiloquence**[3], and your conduct in swinging the beetle — how excessively odd! I was sure you were mad. And why did you insist upon letting fall the bug, instead of a bullet, from the skull?"

"Why, to be frank, I felt somewhat annoyed by your evident suspicions touching my **sanity**[4], and so resolved to punish you quietly, in my own way, by a little bit of sober **mystification**[5]. For this reason I swung the beetle, and for this reason I let it fall it from the tree. An observation of yours about its great weight suggested the latter idea."

"Yes, I perceive; and now there is only one point which puzzles me. What are we to make of the skeletons found in the hole?"

"That is a question I am no more able to answer than yourself. There seems, however, only one **plausible**[6] way of accounting for them — and yet it is dreadful to believe in such atrocity as my suggestion would imply. It is clear that Kidd — if Kidd indeed **secreted**[7] this treasure, which I doubt not — it is

"我想，"我说，"你第一次挖土的时候挖错了地方，都是因为朱庇特笨，把甲虫从头颅骨右眼而不是左眼穿下来了。"

"的确，这个失误使'弹孔'产生了约两英寸[1]的误差——也就是说，离树最近的那根木桩的位置就差了约两英寸；如果宝藏就在'弹孔'下方，那这点误差也没有太大影响；但是'弹孔'和树与之最近的点只是为了形成一条指明方向的直线；这一误差在最开始肯定是微不足道的，但是随着我们将线画长，一直画到距离'弹孔'，也就是木桩，五十英尺远的时候，就将我们误导甚远了。所谓失之毫厘，差之千里。若不是我深信宝藏就埋在那里某个地方，我们可能就一切徒劳了。"

"但是你还装神弄鬼，你还那样把那甲壳虫晃来晃去——真是古怪至极！我当时以为你真的疯了。而且你为什么不用子弹，而是用那虫子，从头颅骨穿下呢？"

"为什么？实话告诉你吧，当时你分明就是怀疑我神经不正常，我多少还是有点恼火的，所以决心用自己的办法暗地里惩罚你，故意一本正经地弄些玄虚。因此我才舞动那甲壳虫，我才把它从树上吊下。我也是听你说到那甲壳虫很重，才萌生了后面的那个念头。"

"哈，我懂了；现在我只有一点不明。我们挖的坑里那两副骷髅骨该怎么解释呢？"

"这个问题，我跟你一样无法回答。可似乎只有一种说法能解释清——但如果真像我猜测的那样，那其中可能包含的暴行可真是想想都令人毛骨悚然。如果基德的确埋藏了这宝藏——这点我从不怀疑——

1　约5厘米。

① trivial ['triviəl] a. 琐碎的，不重要的

② scent [sent] n. 踪迹，线索

③ grandiloquence [græn'diləkwəns] n. 夸张

④ sanity ['sænəti] n. 明智，理智

⑤ mystification [,mistifi'keiʃən] n. 骗局

⑥ plausible ['plɔ:zəble] a. 看似合理的

⑦ secrete ['sikri:t] v. 藏匿

clear that he must have had assistance in the labor. But this labor concluded, he may have thought it expedient to remove all participants in his secret. Perhaps a couple of blows with a **mattock**① were sufficient, while his **coadjutors**② were busy in the pit; perhaps it required a dozen — who shall tell?"

那么他显然需要帮手。但是等活干完了，他可能认为把牵到这秘密中的人都干掉更为周全。也许趁他们在挖坑时挥两锄头就解决了，也或许要砍十几下——没人知道。"

① mattock ['mætək] *n.* 鹤嘴锄
② coadjutor [kəu'ædʒutə] *n.* 助手

The Balloon-Hoax①

ASTOUNDING② NEWS!
BY EXPRESS VIA NORFOLK:

THE ATLANTIC CROSSED IN
THREE DAYS!

SIGNAL TRIUMPH

OF

MR. MONCK MASON'S
FLYING
MACHINE!!!

Arrival at Sullivan's Island, near Charlestown, S. C., of Mr. Mason, Mr. Robert
Holland, Mr. Henson, Mr. Harrison Ainsworth, and four others, in the

STEERING BALLOON
"VICTORIA,"
AFTER A PASSAGE OF
SEVENTY-FIVE HOURS

气球骗局

① hoax [həuks] *n*. 骗局
② astounding [ə'staundiŋ]
　 a. 令人震惊的

惊天新闻！

诺福克速递：

———————

三天

跨越大西洋！

———————

蒙克·梅森先生的

飞行器

取得重大胜利！

———————

梅森先生、罗伯特·霍兰德先生、恒森先生、
哈里森·安斯沃斯先生，以及四位同行者驾乘
转向气球
"维多利亚号"，
历时 75 小时
到达美国南卡罗来纳州查尔斯顿附近的沙利文岛，

FROM LAND TO LAND.

FULL PARTICULARS OF THE
VOYAGE!!!

[*The* **subjoined**① *jeu d'esprit with the preceding heading in
magnificent capitals, well interspersed with notes of admiration, was
originally published, as matter of fact, in the "New York Sun," a
daily newspaper, and therein fully* **subserved**② *the purpose of creating*
indigestible③ **aliment**④ *for the* **quidnuncs**⑤ *during the few hours
intervening between a couple of the Charleston mails. The rush for
the "sole paper which had the news," was something beyond even the
prodigious; and, in fact, if (as some assert) the "Victoria" did
not absolutely accomplish the voyage recorded, it will be difficult
to assign a reason why she should not have accomplished it.*]

The great problem is at length solved! The air, as well as the earth and the
ocean, has been **subdued**⑥ by science, and will become a common and convenient
highway for mankind. *The Atlantic has been actually crossed in a Balloon!* and
this too without difficulty — without any great apparent danger — with thorough
control of the machine — and in the **inconceivably**⑦ brief period of seventy-five
hours from shore to shore! By the energy of an agent at Charleston, S.C., we are
enabled to be the first to furnish the public with a detailed account of this most
extraordinary voyage, which was performed between Saturday, the 6th instant,
at 11, A.M., and 2, P.M., on Tuesday, the 9th instant, by Sir Everard Bringhurst;
Mr. Osborne, a nephew of Lord Bentinck's; Mr. Monck Mason and Mr. Robert
Holland, the well-known **aeronauts**⑧; Mr. Harrison Ainsworth, author of "Jack
Sheppard," &c.; and Mr. Henson, the projector of the late unsuccessful flying

完成跨洋陆对陆最短航线！

航行记录
全揭秘！

【这篇不知真假的新闻，加之巨大的黑体标题，充满溢美之词，最初以事实报道的形式刊登在每日发行的《纽约太阳报》上。在查尔斯顿两次邮递之间的几小时之间，这个消息充分实现了一个目的，那就是为那些爱道听途说的人们创造了晦涩难懂的字眼。争抢购买"独家报道"的人潮真是更甚海潮；其实，若如有些人断言，"维多利亚号"没有完全实现所记录的航程，那么也会很难找出它本不该完成航行的理由。】

重大难题终被攻克！继陆地和海洋之后，科学又征服了天空，天空将成为大众的便捷出行通道。气球跨越大西洋已成事实！不难——显然也不存在重大险情——完全通过操纵机器——岸对岸航行不可思议地仅历时 75 小时！经过查尔斯顿一名代理人的努力，我们成为向公众揭示这次卓越飞行详细记录的首家报纸。这次飞行从本月六日周六上午十一点开始，于本月九日周二下午两点完成，驾乘人员共八人，其中包括：埃弗拉德·布令赫斯特爵士、本汀克勋爵的外甥奥斯本先生、知名气球驾驶员蒙克·梅森先生和罗伯特·霍兰德先生、《杰克·谢帕德》等的作者哈里森·安斯沃斯先生、前期飞行失败的飞行器设计者恒森先生，还有两位来自乌尔维奇的海

① subjoin [ˌsəb'dʒɔin] v. 增补，添加

② subserve [səb'sə:v] v. 对……有帮助，促进

③ indigestible [ˌindi'dʒestəbl] a. 难消化的

④ aliment ['ælimənt] n. 食物

⑤ quidnunc ['kwidnʌŋk] n. 爱说长道短的人

⑥ subdue [səb'dju:] v. 征服，制服

⑦ inconceivably [ˌinkən'sivəbli] ad. 不可思议地

⑧ aeronaut ['ɛeərənɔ:t] n. 飞机（或飞船、气球）驾驶员

machine — with two seamen from Woolwich — in all, eight persons. The particulars furnished below may be relied on as authentic and accurate in every respect, as, with a slight exception, they are copied **verbatim**① from the joint diaries of Mr. Monck Mason and Mr. Harrison Ainsworth, to whose politeness our agent is also indebted for much verbal information respecting the balloon itself, its construction, and other matters of interest. The only alteration in the MS. received, has been made for the purpose of throwing the hurried account of our agent, Mr. Forsyth, into a connected and intelligible form.

"THE BALLOON.

"Two very decided failures, of late — those of Mr. Henson and Sir George Cayley — had much weakened the public interest in the subject of **aerial**② navigation. Mr. Henson's scheme (which at first was considered very feasible even by men of science,) was founded upon the principle of an inclined plane, started from an **eminence**③ by an **extrinsic**④ force, applied and continued by the revolution of impinging **vanes**⑤, in form and number resembling the vanes of a **windmill**⑥. But, in all the experiments made with models at the Adelaide Gallery, it was found that the operation of these fans not only did not **propel**⑦ the machine, but actually **impeded**⑧ its flight. The only propelling force it ever exhibited, was the mere **impetus**⑨ acquired from the descent of the inclined plane; and this impetus carried the machine farther when the vanes were at rest, than when they were in motion — a fact which sufficiently demonstrates their **inutility**⑩; and in the absence of the propelling, which was also the *sustaining* power, the whole fabric would necessarily descend. This consideration led Sir George Cayley to think only of adapting a **propeller**⑪ to some machine having of itself an independent power of support — in a word, to a balloon; the idea, however, being novel, or original, with Sir George, only so far as regards the mode of its application to practice. He exhibited a model of his invention at the Polytechnic Institution. The propelling principle, or power, was here, also, applied to interrupted surfaces, or vanes, put in revolution. These vanes were four in number, but were found entirely **ineffectual**⑫ in moving the balloon, or in aiding

员。以下公布的细节，除些许例外，均真实精确地转录自蒙克·梅森先生和哈里森·安斯沃斯先生共同撰写的飞行日志，这两位还礼貌地向我们的代理人口头讲述了气球本身构造等大家颇感兴趣的信息。对所收到的新闻手稿做出的仅有改动也是为了使代理人福赛斯先生匆忙赶出的稿件变得连贯易懂。

"气球构造

"之前两次注定的失败——恒森先生和乔治·凯雷爵士实验失败——大大削减了公众对航空学的兴趣。恒森先生的设计（起初很多科学家都认为可行）是建立在斜面飞行原理之上的，飞行器从高地靠外力起飞，依靠连接叶片的持续旋转继续前进，这些连接叶片的数量和形状都与风车类似。但在阿德莱德展览场用模型进行的所有实验都表明，这些连接叶片的运行不仅不能推进飞行器，事实上还对飞行器产生了阻力。实验中展示出的推进力仅来自该斜面飞行器下降时产生的加速度；在叶片不运转时，这种加速度要比叶片运转时将飞行器推进得更远——这一事实足以证明这些叶片是无用的；卸掉叶片，同时也是卸掉了抬升力，之后，飞行器的整体结构必然会坠落。出于这种考虑，乔治·凯雷爵士只有想到将这个推进器应用在本身就具有上升力的飞行器上——简言之，就是气球；然而乔治爵士这新颖或原创的想法只需应用到实际中检验了。他将新发明的模型在工业学院展示。展示中，其推进原理，即推进力，仍然是通过被隔开的叶片旋转而获得。叶片有四个，但被证实完全不能有效推进气球，也不能增加气球的升力。整个计划就这样彻底

① verbatim [vəˈbeitim] *ad.*
逐字地

② aerial [ˈɛəriəl] *a.* 航空的，空中的

③ eminence [ˈeminəns] *n.*
高处

④ extrinsic [ekˈstrinsik] *a.*
外在的

⑤ vane [vein] *n.* 轮叶

⑥ windmill [ˈwindmil] *n.*
风车

⑦ propel [prəuˈpel] *v.* 推动，推进

⑧ impede [imˈpiːd] *v.* 阻碍

⑨ impetus [ˈimpitəs] *n.* 动力

⑩ inutility [ˌinjuːˈtiləti] *n.*
无用，无益

⑪ propeller [prəuˈpelə] *n.*
（飞机或轮船的）螺旋桨，推进器

⑫ ineffectual [ˌiniˈfektʃuəl]
a. 无效的，不起作用的

its ascending power. The whole project was thus a complete failure.

"It was at this juncture that Mr. Monck Mason (whose voyage from Dover to Weilburg in the balloon, "Nassau," occasioned so much excitement in 1837,) conceived the idea of employing the principle of the **Archimedean**[①] screw for the purpose of **propulsion**[②] through the air — rightly attributing the failure of Mr. Henson's scheme, and of Sir George Cayley's, to the interruption of surface in the independent vanes. He made the first public experiment at Willis's Rooms, but afterward removed his model to the Adelaide Gallery.

"Like Sir George Cayley's balloon, his own was an **ellipsoid**[③]. Its length was thirteen feet six inches — height, six feet eight inches. It contained about three hundred and twenty cubic feet of gas, which, if pure hydrogen, would support twenty-one pounds upon its first inflation, before the gas has time to **deteriorate**[④] or escape. The weight of the whole machine and **apparatus**[⑤] was seventeen pounds — leaving about four pounds to spare. Beneath the centre of the balloon, was a frame of light wood, about nine feet long, and rigged on to the balloon itself with a network in the **customary**[⑥] manner. From this framework was suspended a **wicker**[⑦] basket or car.

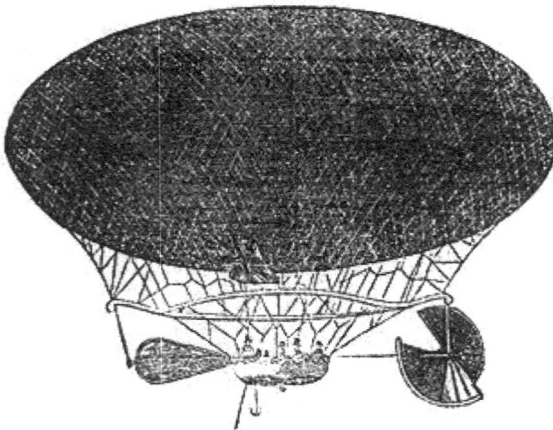

THE MODEL OF THE VICTORIA

失败了。

"就在此时，蒙克·梅森先生（1837 年他乘'拿骚号'气球从多佛至威尔堡的航行曾轰动一时）萌生了一个构想，将阿基米德螺旋泵原理应用到飞行器上，产生空气推力。他正确地认识到，恒森先生和乔治·凯雷爵士二人设计的败笔在于叶片是独立的并且表面断开。他的首次公开实验是在威利斯工作室，但后来将模型带到了阿德莱德展览场。

"如乔治·凯雷爵士的设计一样，梅森先生的飞行器也是椭圆形的。长 13 英尺 6 英寸，高 6 英尺 8 英寸，可充气 320 立方英尺，在充满纯氢并且不损耗泄漏的情况下，首次充气浮力为 21 磅。整个飞行器加上所携带的设备共 17 磅——也就是剩余 4 磅的浮力。在气球中心的正下方，有一个由轻质木头做成的框架，约 9 英尺长，按照常规方式用绳网与气球相连。在这框架下悬挂着一个枝条编成的吊篮，或者叫车厢。

① Archimedean [ˌɑːkiˈmiːdiən] *a*. 阿基米德的

② propulsion [prəuˈpʌlʃən] *n*. 推进，推进力

③ ellipsoid [iˈlipsɔid] *n*. 椭圆体

④ deteriorate [diˈtiəriəreit] *v*. 磨损，质量下降

⑤ apparatus [ˌæpəˈreitəs] *n*. 装置

⑥ customary [ˈkʌstəˌməri] *a*. 习惯的，通常的

⑦ wicker [ˈwikə] *n*. 柳条

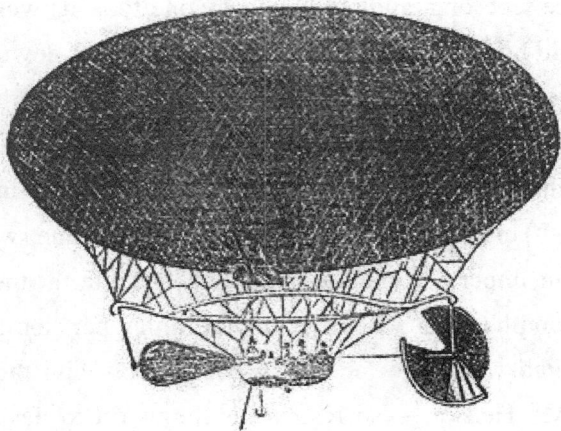

"维多利亚号"模型图

"The screw consists of an axis of hollow **brass**[1] tube, eighteen inches in length, through which, upon a **semi-spiral**[2] inclined at fifteen degrees, pass a series of steel wire radii, two feet long, and thus projecting a foot on either side. These radii are connected at the outer extremities by two bands of flattened wire — the whole in this manner forming the framework of the screw, which is completed by a covering of oiled silk cut into gores, and tightened so as to present a tolerably uniform surface. At each end of its axis this screw is supported by pillars of hollow brass tube descending from the hoop. In the lower ends of these tubes are holes in which the **pivots**[3] of the axis revolve. From the end of the axis which is next the car, proceeds a **shaft**[4] of steel, connecting the screw with the **pinion**[5] of a piece of spring machinery fixed in the car. By the operation of this spring, the screw is made to revolve with great rapidity, communicating a progressive motion to the whole. By means of the **rudder**[6], the machine was readily turned in any direction. The spring was of great power, compared with its dimensions, being capable of raising forty-five pounds upon a barrel of four inches diameter, after the first turn, and gradually increasing as it was wound up. It weighed, altogether, eight pounds six **ounces**[7]. The rudder was a light frame of cane covered with silk, shaped somewhat like a battle-door, and was about three feet long, and at the widest, one foot. Its weight was about two ounces. It could be turned *flat*, and directed upwards or downwards, as well as to the right or left; and thus enabled the æronaut to transfer the resistance of the air which in an inclined position it must generate in its passage, to any side upon which he might desire to act; thus determining the balloon in the opposite direction.

"This model (which, through want of time, we have necessarily described in an imperfect manner,) was put in action at the Adelaide Gallery, where it accomplished a **velocity**[8] of five miles per hour; although, strange to say, it excited very little interest in comparison with the previous complex machine of Mr. Henson — so resolute is the world to **despise**[9] anything which carries with it an air of simplicity. To accomplish the great **desideratum**[10] of ærial navigation, it was very generally supposed that some exceedingly complicated

① brass [brɑːs] *a.* 黄铜的
② semi-spiral 半螺旋形

③ pivot ['pivət] *n.* 枢轴，支点
④ shaft [ʃɑːft] *n.* 轴
⑤ pinion ['pinjən] *n.* 小齿轮
⑥ rudder ['rʌdə] *n.* 方向舵
⑦ ounce [auns] *n.* 盎司
⑧ velocity [vi'lɔsəti] *n.* 速度
⑨ despise [di'spaiz] *v.* 轻视，蔑视
⑩ desideratum [di‚zidə'reitəm] *n.* 想得到的东西

　　"那螺旋泵的轴是一根 18 英寸长的空心铜管，一连串 2 英尺长的钢线穿过空心铜管形成一个 15 度倾斜的半螺旋形，两边各 1 英尺。这些钢线的外缘由两根压扁的金属线相连——这就构成了螺旋泵的框架。将三角形的油绸蒙在螺旋杆框架上绷紧，形成基本完整连贯的表面，这才算基本完成。螺旋泵轴的两端由气球下方的框架伸出两根空铜管支撑。螺旋泵的轴心就从这两根铜管靠近末端的小洞穿过。靠近吊篮的那头安有一个钢柄，把螺旋泵轴与固定在吊篮里的带有发条装置的齿轮连接起来。启动发条装置，螺旋泵随即开始快速旋转，给整个飞行器带来推动力。再利用飞行舵，气球就能够轻易地调整方向了。发条装置体积虽小，直径只有 4 英寸，产生的动力却很大，拧一圈就可以产生 45 磅的推进力，拧的圈数越多，发条产生的力就越大。发条装置总重 8 磅 6 盎司。飞行舵是用绸布包裹起来的一个轻质藤条框，形状像板羽球球板，长约 3 英尺，最宽的地方约 1 英尺，重约 2 盎司。它可以转平，可以转向上下左右四个方向；这样，气球驾驶员就可以利用飞行舵将空气以一定角度通过气球表面必然产生的阻力导向任意方向；这样，气球飞行器就会向相反方向飞行。

　　"这个模型（由于时间仓促，我们的描述不尽完美）在阿德莱德展览场演示的时候达到了时速 5 英里；然而说来奇怪，相比之前恒森先生复杂的飞行器，它并没有激起公众太大的兴趣——看来这世界是铁了心鄙视一切看起来简单的东西。若要实现空中航行的伟大愿望，人们认为必须将非常深奥的动

application must be made of some unusually profound principle in dynamics.

"So well satisfied, however, was Mr. Mason of the ultimate success of his invention, that he determined to construct immediately, if possible, a balloon of sufficient capacity to test the question by a voyage of some extent — the original design being to cross the British Channel, as before, in the Nassau balloon. To carry out his views, he solicited and obtained the **patronage**[①] of Sir Everard Bringhurst and Mr. Osborne, two gentlemen well known for scientific acquirement, and especially for the interest they have exhibited in the progress of **aerostation**[②]. The project, at the desire of Mr. Osborne, was kept a profound secret from the public — the only persons entrusted with the design being those actually engaged in the construction of the machine, which was built (under the superintendence of Mr. Mason, Mr. Holland, Sir Everard Bringhurst, and Mr. Osborne,) at the seat of the latter gentleman near Penstruthal, in Wales. Mr. Henson, accompanied by his friend Mr. Ainsworth, was admitted to a private view of the balloon, on Saturday last — when the two gentlemen made final arrangements to be included in the adventure. We are not informed for what reason the two seamen were also included in the party — but, in the course of a day or two, we shall put our readers in possession of the minutest **particulars**[③] respecting this extraordinary voyage.

"The balloon is composed of silk, varnished with the liquid gum **caoutchouc**[④]. It is of vast dimensions, containing more than 40,000 cubic feet of gas; but as coal gas was employed in place of the more expensive and inconvenient hydrogen, the supporting power of the machine, when fully inflated, and immediately after inflation, is not more than about 2500 pounds. The coal gas is not only much less costly, but is easily procured and managed.

"For its introduction into common use for purposes of aerostation, we are indebted to Mr. Charles Green. Up to his discovery, the process of inflation was not only exceedingly expensive, but uncertain. Two, and even three days, have frequently been wasted in **futile**[⑤] attempts to procure a sufficiency of hydrogen to fill a balloon, from which it had great tendency to escape, owing to its extreme

力学原理应用到复杂得超乎寻常的飞行器上才行。

"梅森先生对他发明的最终成功表示非常满意，于是他决定，若可能，就立即建造一个容量足够大的气球，通过较长距离的航行来证实他的成功——最初计划是像以前'拿骚号'气球那样，飞越英吉利海峡。为实现他的理想，他向埃弗拉德·布令赫斯特爵士和奥斯本先生两位绅士请求资助并得到了他们的支持，他们都以热爱科学而闻名，对浮空学的发展尤其感兴趣。按照奥斯本先生的要求，这项工程对公众是完全保密的——设计只透露给实际参与建造飞行器的人（工程由梅森先生、霍兰德先生、埃弗拉德·布令赫斯特爵士和奥斯本先生监督），并且，飞行器就在奥斯本先生位于威尔士彭斯特拉索附近的宅第进行建造。上周六，恒森先生在朋友安斯沃斯先生的陪伴下被允许秘密查看了建好的气球——当时这两位绅士就赶在最后安排了参与这次冒险的事宜。对于两位海员也参与进来的原因，我们不得而知——但在接下来的一两天里，我们将让读者掌握本次旷世飞行的最详尽细节的第一手资料。

"气球主体由涂了橡胶的丝绸包裹制成，尺寸巨大，可容 4 万多立方英尺的气体；但并没有填充昂贵而使用不便的氢气，而是使用了煤气，因此，即使全部充满，在刚起飞时，飞行器的上升力也不超过 2500 磅。但之所以选择填充煤气，不仅因为它便宜，更因为它易获得、易处理。

"煤气被广泛应用于航空业，我们得感谢查尔斯·格林先生。在他这一发现以前，给气球充气极其昂贵，且氢气又不稳定，经常两三天也不能获得充够一个气球的氢气，又因为氢气密度小、活性强，与周围的空气融合性强，因此它极易泄漏。煤气就

① patronage ['pætrənidʒ] n. 赞助，支持

② aerostation [ˌɛərəu'steiʃən] n. 浮空学

③ particular [pə'tikjulə] n. 细节，详情

④ caoutchouc ['kautʃuk] n. 生橡胶

⑤ futile ['fju:tail] a. 无用的，无益的

subtlety①, and its **affinity**② for the surrounding atmosphere. In a balloon sufficiently perfect to retain its contents of coal-gas unaltered, in quantity or amount, for six months, an equal quantity of hydrogen could not be maintained in equal purity for six weeks.

"The supporting power being estimated at 2500 pounds, and the united weights of the party amounting only to about 1200, there was left a **surplus**③ of 1300, of which again 1200 was exhausted by **ballast**④, arranged in bags of different sizes, with their respective weights marked upon them — by **cordage**⑤, **barometers**⑥, telescopes, barrels containing provision for a fortnight, water-casks⑦, cloaks, carpet-bags, and various other indispensable matters, including a coffee-warmer, contrived for warming coffee by means of slack-lime, so as to **dispense**⑧ altogether with fire, if it should be judged prudent to do so. All these articles, with the exception of the ballast, and a few trifles, were suspended from the hoop overhead. The car is much smaller and lighter, in proportion, than the one appended to the model. It is formed of a light wicker, and is wonderfully strong, for so frail looking a machine. Its rim is about four feet deep. The rudder is also very much larger, in proportion, than that of the model; and the screw is considerably smaller. The balloon is furnished besides with a **grapnel**⑨, and a guide-rope; which latter is of the most indispensable importance. A few words, in explanation, will here be necessary for such of our readers as are not **conversant**⑩ with the details of aerostation.

"As soon as the balloon quits the earth, it is subjected to the influence of many circumstances tending to create a difference in its weight; augmenting or diminishing its ascending power. For example, there may be a deposition of **dew**⑪ upon the silk, to the extent, even, of several hundred pounds; ballast has then to be thrown out, or the machine may descend. This ballast being discarded, and a clear sunshine **evaporating**⑫ the dew, and at the same time expanding the gas in the silk, the whole will again rapidly ascend. To check this **ascent**⑬, the only recourse is, (or rather *was*, until Mr. Green's invention of the guide-rope,) the permission of the escape of gas from the valve; but, in the loss of gas, is a

① subtlety ['sʌtlti] *n.* 细微，精细

② affinity [ə'finəti] *n.* 亲和性

③ surplus ['sə:pləs] *n.* 剩余

④ ballast ['bæləst] *n.* 压载物

⑤ cordage ['kɔ:didʒ] *n.* 绳索

⑥ barometer [bə'rɔmitə] *n.* 气压表

⑦ cask [kɑ:sk] *n.* 桶

⑧ dispense [dis'pens] *v.* 分配，分发

⑨ grapnel ['græpnəl] *n.* 抓钩

⑩ conversant [kən'və:sənt] *a.* 熟悉的，精通的

⑪ dew [dju:] *n.* 露水

⑫ evaporate [i'væpəreit] *v.* 蒸发

⑬ ascent [ə'sent] *n.* 上升，升高

不同了，一个完好的气球充满的煤气可以六个月都不改变纯度和体积，同样体积的氢气用不了六周就不具有原本的纯度了。

"上升力约 2500 磅，飞行器整体重量约 1200 磅，剩余 1300 磅，其中 1200 磅由压载物补充，它们装在大小不同的袋子里，上面标记了重量——其余物品还有绳索、气压计、望远镜、装有足够两周生活用品的桶、水桶、斗篷、毛毡，以及其他的路上必需品，其中包括用熟石灰加热的咖啡保温炉，使用熟石灰是为了完全杜绝火源，一切安排都经过慎重考虑。除了压载物之外的一切物品都挂在吊篮上方的系索框上。吊篮的比例要比模型上的小得多也轻得多，深 4 英尺，由柳条编筐制成，安在这个看起来十分脆弱的飞行器上显得格外结实。方向舵从比例上看却比模型上大得多，而螺旋泵相对较小。飞行器还配有锚钩和调节绳；后者具有不可或缺的重要性。在这里有必要多说几句，向不太了解飞行器航行细节的读者们作些解释。

"飞行器一旦离开地面，就会受到许多外界因素的影响，重量发生改变；其上升力也会有增减变化。例如，气球外层的绸布表面堆积的露水甚至会达到几百磅重；这样一来就要丢下压载物，否则飞行器就会下降。丢弃了压载物后，阳光将露水蒸发，同时，绸布气球中的气体体积也扩大了，飞行器整体就会迅速上升。为了平衡这股上升力，唯一的办法（或者说，过去唯一的办法，因为后来格林先生发明了调节绳）就是打开阀门泄出一些气体；但是，气球中气体的流失也就相对应地减少了上升力；因此，造得

proportionate① general loss of ascending power; so that, in a comparatively brief period, the best-constructed balloon must necessarily **exhaust**② all its resources, and come to the earth. This was the great **obstacle**③ to voyages of length.

"The guide-rope **remedies**④ the difficulty in the simplest manner conceivable. It is merely a very long rope which is suffered to trail from the car, and the effect of which is to prevent the balloon from changing its level in any material degree. If, for example, there should be a deposition of moisture upon the silk, and the machine begins to descend in consequence, there will be no necessity for discharging ballast to remedy the increase of weight, for it is remedied, or **counteracted**⑤, in an exactly just proportion, by the deposit on the ground of just so much of the end of the rope as is necessary. If, on the other hand, any circumstances should cause undue **levity**⑥, and consequent ascent, this levity is immediately counteracted by the additional weight of rope upraised from the earth. Thus, the balloon can neither ascend or descend, except within very narrow limits, and its resources, either in gas or ballast, remain comparatively unimpaired. When passing over an expanse of water, it becomes necessary to employ small **kegs**⑦ of copper or wood, filled with liquid ballast of a lighter nature than water. These float, and serve all the purposes of a mere rope on land. Another most important office of the guide-rope, is to point out the *direction* of the balloon. The rope *drags*, either on land or sea, while the balloon is free; the latter, consequently, is always in advance, when any progress whatever is made: a comparison, therefore, by means of the compass, of the relative positions of the two objects, will always indicate the *course*. In the same way, the angle formed by the rope with the vertical axis of the machine, indicates the ***velocity***⑧. When there is *no* angle — in other words, when the rope hangs **perpendicularly**⑨, the whole **apparatus**⑩ is **stationary**⑪; but the larger the angle, that is to say, the farther the balloon precedes the end of the rope, the greater the velocity; and the converse.

"As the original design was to cross the British Channel, and **alight**⑫ as near Paris as possible, the voyagers had taken the **precaution**⑬ to prepare

① proportionate [prəu'pɔːʃənit] *a.* 成比例的，相称的

② exhaust [ig'zɔːst] *v.* 耗尽

③ obstacle ['ɔbstəkl] *n.* 障碍

④ remedy ['remidi] *v.* 补救，改善

⑤ counteract [ˌkauntə'rækt] *v.* 抵消，中和

⑥ levity ['levəti] *n.* 轻，浮力

⑦ keg [keg] *n.* 小桶

⑧ velocity [vi'lɔsəti] *n.* 速度

⑨ perpendicularly [ˌpəːpən'dikjuləli] *ad.* 垂直地，直立地

⑩ apparatus [ˌæpə'reitəs] *n.* 装置，设备

⑪ stationary ['steiʃənəri] *a.* 静止的

⑫ alight [ə'lait] *v.* 下来，飞落

⑬ precaution [pri'kɔːʃən] *n.* 预防措施

最好的飞行器在这样的情况下也会在相对较短的期间耗尽其能源，最终不得不落地。这就是阻碍气球长距离航行的最大障碍。

"调节绳用能想得到的最简单的办法解决了这一难题。它只是系在吊篮上的一根长绳，但它能令气球不产生剧烈的高度变化。例如，如果绸布上聚集了露水，飞行器开始下降，有了调节绳，就不用扔掉压载物来补偿增加的重量了，因为按照所需的长度将调节绳扔到地面，露水的重量就被补偿或者抵消了。在另外一种情况下，如果需要减小浮力，防止飞行器升得太高，那么也可以通过将调节绳收起来的办法用额外的重量来抵消浮力。这样，在气球里的气体和压载物相对无损耗的情况下，飞行器的上下浮动范围也不会太大。当飞行到宽阔水域上方时，将调节绳末端拴上一个铜桶或木桶，桶里装上密度小于水的液体压载物，它们会漂在水上，从而和调节绳抛在陆地上起到相同的作用。调节绳的另一个重要职责就是为飞行器指方向。无论在海洋还是陆地上空，只要飞行器在移动中，气球都自由地飞在前方，而调节绳会一直拖在后方，那么用指南针对照气球和调节绳的相对位置就可以确定航向了。同样的道理，调节绳与飞行器垂直轴形成的角度大小对应的是航速。当角度为零——换句话说，当调节绳垂直悬挂，整个飞行器就是静止的；角度越大，也就是说气球与调节绳尾端的距离越远，飞行速度越快，反之越慢。

"原来的计划是要穿越英吉利海峡，尽量靠近巴黎降落，航行者都提前准备好欧洲大陆各国的护照，

themselves with passports directed to all parts of the Continent, specifying the nature of the **expedition**①, as in the case of the Nassau voyage, and **entitling**② the adventurers to **exemption**③ from the usual formalities of office: unexpected events, however, rendered these passports **superfluous**④.

"The inflation was commenced very quietly at daybreak, on Saturday morning, the 6th instant, in the Court-Yard of Weal-Vor House, Mr. Osborne's seat, about a mile from Penstruthal, in North Wales; and at 7 minutes past 11, every thing being ready for departure, the balloon was set free, rising gently but steadily, in a direction nearly South; no use being made, for the first half hour, of either the screw or the rudder. We proceed now with the journal, as **transcribed**⑤ by Mr. Forsyth from the joint MSS. of Mr. Monck Mason, and Mr. Ainsworth. The body of the journal, as given, is in the hand-writing of Mr. Mason, and a P. S. is appended, each day, by Mr. Ainsworth, who has in preparation, and will shortly give the public a more minute, and no doubt, a thrillingly interesting account of the voyage.

"THE JOURNAL.

"*Saturday, April the 6th.* —

"Every preparation likely to embarrass us, having been made over night, we commenced the inflation this morning at daybreak; but owing to a thick fog, which **encumbered**⑥ the folds of the silk and rendered it unmanageable, we did not get through before nearly eleven o'clock. Cut loose, then, in high spirits, and rose gently but steadily, with a light breeze at North, which bore us in the direction of the British Channel. Found the ascending force greater than we had expected; and as we arose higher and so got clear of the cliffs, and more in the sun's rays, our ascent became very rapid. I did not wish, however, to lose gas at so early a period of the adventure, and so concluded to ascend for the present. We soon ran out our guide-rope; but even when we had raised it clear of the earth, we still went up very rapidly. The balloon was unusually steady, and looked beautifully. In about ten minutes after starting, the barometer indicated an **altitude**⑦ of 15,000 feet. The weather was remarkably

① expedition [,ekspi'diʃən] *n.* 远征

② entitle [in'taitl] *v.* 使有权利，使有资格

③ exemption [ig'zempʃən] *n.* 免除

④ superfluous [sju'pə:fluəs] *a.* 多余的，不必要的

⑤ transcribe [træn'skraib] *v.* 抄写

⑥ encumber [in'kʌmbə] *v.* 阻碍，妨碍

⑦ altitude ['æltitju:d] *n.* 高度，海拔

与'拿骚号'之行相同，本次飞行被注明是试航，因此给探险者们免除了常规的官方出入境手续；然而一些突发事件却令这些护照无用武之地了。

"本月六日周六早上，伴随着清晨第一缕阳光，气球开始充气了，就在奥斯本先生的住所威尔沃尔庄园的庭院进行，距离北威尔士彭斯特拉索一英里左右；11点过7分，准备好出发，气球被放开，缓缓平稳上升，方向接近正南方；飞行刚开始的半小时，都还没用到螺旋泵和方向舵。下面我们将向您展示的是由我们的代理人福赛斯先生摘录，蒙克·梅森先生和安斯沃斯先生联合执笔的飞行日记。每天飞行记录的主体由梅森先生手写，附记则由安斯沃斯先生完成；不久，安斯沃斯先生准备向公众展示一份更详尽的，无疑也必将是更激动人心，更有趣的航行记录。

"航行记录

"四月六日星期六——

"准备时期的一切麻烦都在前一天晚上解决了，我们在今天凌晨破晓时分就开始给气球充气；但由于浓雾使气球表面沾满水汽，很不好控制也不好打开，我们将近11点钟才准备妥当。我们兴高采烈地切断缆绳，气球平缓升空，徐徐吹来的北风刚好把我们吹向英吉利海峡。上升力比我们预期的强；我们升到高处避开了悬崖，接受到了更多的阳光照射，因此我们迅速上升。然而我并不想在开航初期就放掉气球里的气，所以决定先上升一段时间。但很快，我们就把调节绳全都收起；没有调节绳拖在地上的时候，我们仍然在迅速上升。气球飞行得异常平稳，看起来美极了。开航后十分钟，气压计显示我们已经到达海拔15000英尺。天气格外晴朗，下方的村

fine, and the view of the **subjacent**① country — a most romantic one when seen from any point, — was now especially **sublime**②. The **numerous**③ deep gorges presented the appearance of lakes, on account of the dense **vapors**④ with which they were filled, and the pinnacles and crags to the South East, piled in **inextricable**⑤ confusion, resembling nothing so much as the giant cities of eastern fable. We were rapidly approaching the mountains in the South; but our elevation was more than **sufficient**⑥ to enable us to pass them in safety. In a few minutes we soared over them in fine style; and Mr. Ainsworth, with the seamen, was surprised at their apparent want of altitude when viewed from the car, the tendency of great elevation in a balloon being to reduce inequalities of the surface below, to nearly a dead level.

At half-past eleven still proceeding nearly South, we obtained our first view of the Bristol Channel; and, in fifteen minutes afterward, the line of breakers on the coast appeared immediately beneath us, and we were fairly out at sea. We now resolved to **let off**⑦ enough gas to bring our guide-rope, with the **buoys**⑧ **affixed**⑨, into the water. This was immediately done, and we commenced a gradual descent. In about twenty minutes our first buoy dipped, and at the touch of the second soon afterwards, we remained stationary as to elevation. We were all now anxious to test the efficiency of the rudder and screw, and we put them both into **requisition**⑩ **forthwith**⑪, for the purpose of altering our direction more to the eastward, and in a line for Paris. By means of the rudder we instantly effected the necessary change of direction, and our course was brought nearly at right angles to that of the wind; when we set in motion the spring of the screw, and were **rejoiced**⑫ to find it propel us readily as desired. Upon this we gave nine hearty cheers, and dropped in the sea a bottle, **enclosing**⑬ a slip of parchment with a brief account of the principle of the invention.

Hardly, however, had we done with our rejoicings, when an **unforeseen**⑭ accident occurred which **discouraged**⑮ us in no little degree. The steel rod connecting the spring with the propeller was suddenly **jerked**⑯ out of place, at

① subjacent [ˌsʌb'dʒeisənt] *a.* 下方的

② sublime [sə'blaim] *a.* 雄伟的，壮丽的

③ numerous ['nju:mərəs] *a.* 许多的

④ vapor ['veipə] *n.* 蒸汽

⑤ inextricable [in'ekstrikəbl] *a.* 无法解脱的

⑥ sufficient [sə'fiʃənt] *a.* 足够的

⑦ let off 放出，排放

⑧ buoy [bɔi] *n.* 航标

⑨ affix [ə'fiks] *v.* 使固定

⑩ requisition [ˌrekwi'ziʃən] *n.* 征用

⑪ forthwith [fɔ:θ'wiθ] *ad.* 立刻，立即

⑫ rejoice [ri'dʒɔis] *v.* 高兴

⑬ enclose [in'kləuz] *v.* 装入

⑭ unforeseen [ˌʌnfɔ:'si:n] *a.* 未预料到的

⑮ discourage [dis'kʌridʒ] *v.* 使气馁

⑯ jerk [dʒə:k] *v.* 颠簸

庄——从任何角度看都十分浪漫——现在从这个角度看尤为壮观。无数深谷聚集了浓重的水汽，看起来像湖泊，东南方奇峰错叠、绵延起伏，宛若东方神话中的巨型城市。我们迅速飞向南方的山脉，但我们的海拔高度足以使我们在山峰上方安全通过。几分钟后，我们就优雅地从山顶上方滑过；安斯沃斯先生和那两位海员从吊篮看出去，不禁惊讶于俯视下的群山竟显得如此矮小。气球的升高压缩了地面上的高低起伏，几乎将崎岖的地表抹平。

十一点半，我们仍然接近向正南航行，途中我们首次俯瞰到布里斯托尔海峡；十五分钟后，浪花滚滚的海岸线出现在我们正下方，我们正式出海了。现在我们决定放掉足够的气体，好将系在调节绳上的浮标放到水中。我们马上打开气阀，开始缓缓下降，二十分钟后，我们投下第一个浮标，紧接着又投下第二个后，我们的高度平稳下来。现在我们都迫不及待地想测试一下方向舵和螺旋泵推进器的功效，于是，为了将我们的航向向东调整，与巴黎成一条直线，我们立即将这两样都启用。通过方向舵，我们马上就有效地对方向进行了必要调整，我们的航向与风向几乎成直角；当我们启动螺旋泵的发条，更是欣喜地发现它正如我们所愿能够推动气球前进。为此我们衷心地欢呼九声，向海里投下一个瓶子，里面封装了一张记录这项发明的简明原理的羊皮纸。

欢喜还未结束，一次不期而至的事故就大大削减了我们的锐气。在吊篮那头的连接螺旋桨和发条的钢条突然脱落（这是由于我们带的其中一个海员在吊篮里乱动，造成吊篮晃动），一下子脱离了螺杆

the car end, (by a swaying of the car through some movement of one of the two seamen we had taken up,) and in an instant hung dangling out of reach, from the pivot of the axis of the screw. While we were endeavoring to regain it, our attention being completely **absorbed**①, we became involved in a strong current of wind from the East, which bore us, with rapidly increasing force, towards the Atlantic. We soon found ourselves driving out to sea at the rate of not less, certainly, than fifty or sixty miles an hour, so that we came up with Cape Clear, at some forty miles to our North, before we had secured the rod, and had time to think what we were about. It was now that Mr. Ainsworth made an extraordinary, but to my fancy, a by no means unreasonable or **chimerical**② **proposition**③, in which he was instantly seconded by Mr. Holland — viz.: that we should take advantage of the strong **gale**④ which bore us on, and in place of beating back to Paris, make an attempt to reach the coast of North America. After slight reflection I gave a willing assent to this bold proposition, which (strange to say) met with objection from the two seamen only. As the stronger party, however, we **overruled**⑤ their fears, and kept resolutely upon our course. We steered due West; but as the trailing of the buoys materially impeded our progress, and we had the balloon abundantly at command, either for ascent or descent, we first threw out fifty pounds of ballast, and then wound up (by means of a windlass) so much of the rope as brought it quite clear of the sea. We perceived the effect of this **manoeuvre**⑥ immediately, in a vastly increased rate of progress; and, as the gale freshened, we flew with a velocity nearly inconceivable; the guide-rope flying out behind the car, like a streamer from a vessel. It is needless to say that a very short time **sufficed**⑦ us to lose sight of the coast.

We passed over **innumerable**⑧ vessels of all kinds, a few of which were endeavoring to beat up, but the most of them lying to. We occasioned the greatest excitement on board all — an excitement greatly relished by ourselves, and especially by our two men, who, now under the influence of a dram of Geneva, seemed resolved to give all scruple, or fear, to the wind. Many of the vessels fired signal guns; and in all we were **saluted**⑨ with loud cheers

① absorb [əb'sɔːb] v. 吸引

② chimerical [kai'miərikəl]
 a. 空想的，妄想的
③ proposition [,prɔpə'ziʃən]
 n. 提议，建议
④ gale [geil] n. 大风

⑤ overrule [,əuvə'ruːl] v. 否决

⑥ manoeuvre [mə'nuːvə] n.
 策略

⑦ suffice [sə'fais] v. 使满足
⑧ innumerable
 [i'njuːmərəbl] a. 无数的，数不清的

⑨ salute [sə'ljuːt] v. 致敬，欢迎

的轴，吊在吊篮外面。正当我们全神贯注地设法把它归位时，又被卷入了一股东风带来的湍流中，这股疾风以迅猛的力量将我们卷向大西洋方向。很快我们就发现我们正在大西洋上空以绝不低于每小时五六十英里的速度航行，因此我们还没来得及修理好那根钢条，也没有时间考虑该怎么办，就被刮向往北约四十英里处的科利尔角。就在这时，安斯沃斯先生作出了一个奇特的，但在我看来并非不合情理也并非不切实际的提议，这个提议马上就得到了霍兰德先生的肯定——我们应该利用卷入的这场暴风，与其逆风飞向巴黎，不如试试看能不能跨越大西洋飞抵北美海岸。经过少时考虑，我马上同意了这个大胆的提议，说来也怪，只有两个海员持反对意见。然而，少数服从多数，我们否决了他们的担忧，坚定地继续我们的飞行。我们转向正西；但是由于拖在后面的浮标给我们的前行造成了严重的阻力，气球的上升和下降都还完全在控制之中，我们先扔掉了五十磅的压载物，然后（用绞盘）卷起调节绳，使绳子刚好脱离海面。这一操作马上就起作用了，飞行器的速度在迅速提升；并且由于风力增强，我们的飞行速度也是快得无法想象；飞在吊篮后面的调节绳就像船上的长条旗一样飘了起来。不消多说，以这样的速度，我们转眼就看不到海岸了。

我们飞过数不清的各色船只，有些正在顶风前行，但大多数都停在那里。见到我们的飞行器，船上的人们都兴奋万分——我们也同样兴致高涨，特别是我们的两位海员，在喝了些杜松子酒后，似乎也让所有的顾虑或是恐惧随风吹散了。许多船只射出信号弹；人们都挥舞着帽子和手帕大声欢呼向我们致敬（我们听到的声音出奇清晰）。整个白天，我们都

(which we heard with surprising **distinctness**①) and the waving of caps and handkerchiefs. We kept on in this manner throughout the day, with no material incident, and, as the shades of night closed around us, we made a rough estimate of the distance **traversed**②. It could not have been less than five hundred miles, and was probably much more. The propeller was kept in constant operation, and, no doubt, aided our progress materially. As the sun went down, the gale **freshened**③ into an absolute **hurricane**④, and the ocean beneath was clearly visible on account of its **phosphorescence**⑤. The wind was from the East all night, and gave us the brightest **omen**⑥ of success. We suffered no little from cold, and the dampness of the atmosphere was most unpleasant; but the **ample**⑦ space in the car enabled us to lie down, and by means of cloaks and a few blankets, we did sufficiently well.

"P.S. (by Mr. Ainsworth.) The last nine hours have been unquestionably the most exciting of my life. I can conceive nothing more sublimating than the strange **peril**⑧ and novelty of an adventure such as this. May God grant that we succeed! I ask not success for mere safety to my insignificant person, but for the sake of human knowledge and — for the vastness of the triumph. And yet the feat is only so evidently **feasible**⑨ that the sole wonder is why men have scrupled to attempt it before. One single gale such as now **befriends**⑩ us — let such a **tempest**⑪ whirl forward a balloon for four or five days (these gales often last longer) and the voyager will be easily borne, in that period, from coast to coast. In view of such a gale the broad Atlantic becomes a mere lake. I am more struck, just now, with the supreme silence which reigns in the sea beneath us, notwithstanding its **agitation**⑫, than with any other phenomenon presenting itself. The waters give up no voice to the heavens. The immense flaming ocean **writhes**⑬ and is tortured uncomplainingly. The mountainous surges suggest the idea of innumerable dumb gigantic **fiends**⑭ struggling in **impotent**⑮ **agony**⑯. In a night such as is this to me, a man *lives* — lives a whole century of ordinary life — nor would I **forego**⑰ this **rapturous**⑱ delight for that of a whole century of ordinary existence.

① distinctness [dis'tiŋktnis] *n.* 清晰

② traverse [trə'vɜ:s] *v.* 经过

③ freshen ['freʃən] *v.* (风) 增强，变冷

④ hurricane ['hʌrikən] *n.* 飓风，暴风

⑤ phosphorescence [ˌfɔsfə'resəns] *n.* 磷光，磷光现象

⑥ omen ['əumən] *n.* 预兆

⑦ ample ['æmpl] *a.* 充足的

⑧ peril ['peril] *n.* 危险

⑨ feasible ['fi:zəbl] *a.* 可行的

⑩ befriend [bi'frend] *v.* 帮助

⑪ tempest ['tempist] *n.* 暴风雨

⑫ agitation [ˌædʒi'teiʃən] *n.* 动荡，骚动

⑬ writhe [raið] *v.* 翻滚

⑭ fiend [fi:nd] *n.* 恶魔

⑮ impotent ['impətənt] *a.* 无力的

⑯ agony ['ægəni] *n.* 痛苦

⑰ forego [fɔ:'gəu] *v.* 放弃

⑱ rapturous ['ræptʃərəs] *a.* 狂喜的，兴高采烈的

顺风航行着，没再遇到大的波折。当夜色将我们笼罩，我们大致估算了一下飞过的距离，可能已经达到了 500 英里，也可能更远。螺旋泵推进器持续运转无疑大大助力了我们的进程。当太阳完全落下，卷着我们的狂风变成了强劲的飓风，下方的海水泛着磷光，清晰可见。整晚都吹着东风，是对我们成功的最辉煌的预示。我们忍受着严寒，海上潮湿的空气令我们最无法忍受；但吊篮里足够我们躺的，盖着斗篷和毯子，这一夜我们过得尚可。

"附记（安斯沃斯先生执笔）：毫无疑问，刚刚过去的九个小时是我人生最激动的时刻。我想象不到还有什么能比这次惊险新奇的探险之旅更令人赞叹。愿上帝保佑我们成功！我祈求成功不仅仅是为了微不足道的个人的安全，更是为了人类的知识而祈祷——为了征服天空的伟大胜利而祈祷。这一壮举显然是可行的，但唯一令人疑惑的是为什么以前人们却踌躇不肯尝试。只需一阵像现在这样眷顾我们的暴风——就让这阵风卷送着我们的气球刮上四五天吧（像这样的暴风通常刮得更久），这几天，气球就可以带着我们的航行者从此岸飞到彼岸。在如此暴风的狂卷中，大西洋变得就像一个湖泊那样小。下面的大海湍流搅动，却又寂然无声，此时，再没有什么景象能像这无边的寂静一样打动我。沧海并未向天穹透露心迹。广袤激荡的海水翻滚着，好似无怨地忍受着无名的痛楚。海水如山般汹涌，仿佛无数沉默的巨魔在苦难中无力地挣扎。这样的夜晚对于我来说，可以证明我活过——胜过整个世纪庸庸碌碌地活着——即使用一百年平凡的存在来交换也不能让我放弃这一夜销魂的喜悦。

"*Sunday, the seventh.*

"[Mr. Mason's MS.] This morning the gale, by 10, had subsided to an eight or nine — knot breeze, (for a vessel at sea,) and bears us, perhaps, thirty miles per hour, or more. It has **veered**①, however, very considerably to the north; and now, at sundown, we are holding our course due west, principally by the screw and rudder, which answer their purposes to admiration. I regard the project as thoroughly successful, and the easy navigation of the air in any direction (not exactly in the teeth of a gale) as no longer problematical. We could not have made head against the strong wind of yesterday; but, by ascending, we might have got out of its influence, if requisite. Against a pretty stiff breeze, I feel convinced, we can make our way with the propeller. At noon, to-day, ascended to an elevation of nearly 25,000 feet, by discharging ballast. Did this to search for a more direct current, but found none so favorable as the one we are now in. We have an abundance of gas to take us across this small pond, even should the voyage last three weeks. I have not the slightest fear for the result. The difficulty has been strangely exaggerated and **misapprehended**②. I can choose my current, and should I find *all* currents against me, I can make very tolerable headway with the propeller. We have had no incidents worth recording. The night promises fair.

P.S. [By Mr. Ainsworth.] I have little to record, except the fact (to me quite a surprising one) that, at an elevation equal to that of Cotopaxi, I experienced neither very intense cold, nor headache, nor difficulty of breathing; neither, I find, did Mr. Mason, nor Mr. Holland, nor Sir Everard. Mr. Osborne complained of constriction of the chest — but this soon wore off. We have flown at a great rate during the day, and we must be more than half way across the Atlantic. We have passed over some twenty or thirty vessels of various kinds, and all seem to be delightfully astonished. Crossing the ocean in a balloon is not so difficult

"七日，星期日。

"［梅森先生的手稿］到今早十点，强风减弱为（对于海上航船来说的）八九节微风，我们的时速可能有 30 英里或更高。然而风向非常偏北；现在，在这日落时分，我们的航向保持在正西方向，这主要还得靠螺旋泵和方向舵，它们所起的作用真是令人赞叹。我认为这个飞行器的设计在各方面都是非常成功的，在空中朝任何方向飞行（只要不逆强风而行）已经不成问题。在像昨天那样的狂风中就无法逆风飞行；但若有必要，我们可以提升高度来避开暴风的影响。如果是强度一般的风，我确信利用推进器就可以逆风通过。今天中午，为了搜寻更顺直的气流，我们抛下压载物，使气球上升到接近 25000 英尺，但是没有哪股气流能像我们正处在其中的这股一样平顺。即便飞行持续三周，我们也有充盈的气体带着我们穿越这个小池塘。对于本次飞行的结果，我没有丝毫担忧。困难总是被异常夸大和曲解。我可以选择合适的气流帮助飞行，即便所有的气流都对我不利，我也可以利用推进器保持过得去的速度继续飞行。至此，我们还没有什么值得记录的事件。今夜会是个好天气。

"附记［安斯沃斯先生执笔］：没什么可记录的，但有一件事（让我很吃惊的一件事），那就是当我们升高到科多帕西火山 [1] 那样的高度时，我既没有经历严寒，也没有感到头痛，呼吸也还轻松；梅森先生、霍兰德先生、埃弗拉德爵士都没有感到上述不适，奥斯本先生感到一些胸闷——但很快症状就消失了。白天我们飞行的速度极快，肯定已经飞过大半个大西洋了。我们飞越过二三十艘不同类型的船，船上所有

① veer [viə] v. 转向

② misapprehend [mis,æpri'hend] v. 误会，误解

1　位于厄瓜多尔北部。

a feat after all. *Omne ignotum pro magnifico. Mem:* at 25,000 feet elevation the sky appears nearly black, and the stars are distinctly visible; while the sea does not seem **convex**[①] (as one might suppose) but absolutely and most **unequivocally**[②] **concave**[③].*

"*Monday, the 8th.*

"[Mr. Mason's MS.] This morning we had again some little trouble with the rod of the propeller, which must be entirely **remodelled**[④], for fear of serious accident — I mean the steel rod — not the vanes. The latter could not be improved. The wind has been blowing steadily and strongly from the north-east all day and so far fortune seems bent upon favoring us. Just before day, we were all somewhat alarmed at some odd noises and **concussions**[⑤] in the balloon, accompanied with the apparent rapid **subsidence**[⑥] of the whole machine. These phenomena were occasioned by the expansion of the gas, through increase of heat in the atmosphere, and the consequent **disruption**[⑦] of the minute particles of ice with which the network had become **encrusted**[⑧] during the night. Threw down several bottles to the vessels below. Saw one of them picked up by a large ship — seemingly one of the New York line packets. Endeavored to make out her name, but could not be sure of it. Mr. Osborne's telescope made it out something like "Atalanta." It is now 12, at night, and we are still going nearly west, at a rapid pace. The sea is peculiarly phosphorescent.

"P.S. [By Mr. Ainsworth.] It is now 2, A.M., and nearly calm, as well as I can judge — but it is very difficult to determine this point, since we move *with* the air so completely. I have not slept since quitting Wheal-Vor, but can stand it no longer, and must take a nap. We cannot be far from the American coast.

"*Tuesday, the 9th.*

"[Mr. Ainsworth's MS.] *One, P.M. We are in full view of the low coast*

人看起来都十分惊奇又欣喜。乘坐气球穿越海洋并不算是艰辛的壮举。拉丁语里有句话这么说：不了解的事情总是被夸大难度。随记：上升到 25000 英尺高空时，天空看上去几乎是黑色的，繁星清晰可见；海面看上去并不是凸起的（如一般人猜测的那样），却是毫无疑问地凹下去的。*

"八日，星期一。

"［梅森先生手稿］今早，那个螺旋桨的钢条又给我们造成一点小麻烦，担心会导致严重的事故，我们必须把它彻底改装——我指那个钢条——不是螺旋泵的叶片。叶片已经不能再改进了。一整天都刮着强劲有力的东北风，到目前为止，幸运之神似乎非常眷顾我们。就在今早天亮前，伴随着明显的急剧下降，气球产生的一些怪响和震荡令我们有些警醒。这一现象的发生是由于外界空气温度升高，气球中的气体膨胀，原本包裹气球的网绳在夜里结了冰碴，在气球膨胀时，这些细小的冰碴碎裂发出声音。我们向下面的船只投去几个瓶子。看到其中一个瓶子被一艘大船——看着好像是一艘驶往纽约的邮轮——捞起。我们试图分辨它的名字，但是不能确定。奥斯本先生用望远镜看到了"亚特兰大"的字样。现在是午夜 12 点，我们仍向接近正西的方向急速飞行。海面闪着奇异的磷光。

"附记［安斯沃斯先生执笔］：现在是凌晨 2 点，据我判断，风几乎停了——这点很难确定，因为我们一直是随风而动的。从威尔沃尔庄园启程以来我都没睡觉，但是现在我再也撑不住了，必须得打个盹儿。我们肯定离美国海岸不远了。

"九日，星期二。

"［安斯沃斯先生手稿］下午一点，我们将南卡

① convex ['kɔnveks] *a.* 凸面的，凸圆的
② unequivocally [ˌʌni'kwivəkəli] *ad.* 明确地
③ concave [kɔn'keiv] *a.* 凹的，凹面的
④ remodel [ˌri:'mɔdəl] *v.* 改造

⑤ concussion [kən'kʌʃən] *n.* 猛烈的摇动，振动
⑥ subsidence [səb'saidns] *n.* 下降，下沉
⑦ disruption [dis'rʌpʃən] *n.* 分裂，瓦解
⑧ encrusted [in'krʌstid] *a.* 形成硬壳的，结外壳的

of South Carolina. The great problem is accomplished. We have crossed the Atlantic — fairly and *easily* crossed it in a balloon! God be praised! Who shall say that anything is impossible hereafter?"

The Journal here **ceases**[1]. Some particulars of the descent were communicated, however, by Mr. Ainsworth to Mr. Forsyth. It was nearly dead calm when the voyagers first came in view of the coast, which was immediately recognized by both the seamen, and by Mr. Osborne. The latter gentleman having acquaintances at Fort Moultrie, it was immediately resolved to descend in its vicinity. The balloon was brought over the beach (the tide being out and the sand hard, smooth, and admirably adapted for a descent,) and the grapnel let go, which took firm hold at once. The **inhabitants**[2] of the island, and of the fort, **thronged**[3] out, of course, to see the balloon; but it was with the greatest difficulty that any one could be made to **credit**[4] the actual voyage — *the crossing of the Atlantic*. The grapnel caught at 2 P.M., precisely; and thus the whole voyage was completed in seventy-five hours; or rather less, counting from shore to shore. No serious accident occurred. No real danger was at any time apprehended. The balloon was exhausted and secured without trouble; and when the MS. from which this narrative is compiled was despatched from Charleston, the party were still at Fort Moultrie. Their farther intentions were not ascertained; but we can safely promise our readers some additional information either on Monday or in the course of the next day, at farthest.

This is unquestionably the most **stupendous**[5], the most interesting, and the most important undertaking, ever accomplished or even attempted by man. What magnificent events may ensue, it would be useless now to think of determining.

    * *Note.* — Mr. Ainsworth has not attempted to account for this phenomenon, which, however, is quite **susceptible**[6] of explanation. A line dropped from an elevation of 25,000 feet, perpendicularly to the surface of the earth (or sea), would form the **perpendicular**[7] of a right-angled triangle, of which the base would extend from the right angle to the

罗莱纳州的南部海岸尽收眼底。伟大的难题被攻克。我们飞越了大西洋——乘着气球轻松顺利地越过了大西洋！感谢上帝！以后谁还会说哪件事不可能吗？"

飞行日记到此终止。但是，安斯沃斯先生向福赛斯先生传达了降落时的一些细节。飞行者们第一眼看到海岸线的时候，风几乎完全静止了，先是两个海员，紧接着奥斯本先生立刻认出了这片海岸。奥斯本先生在莫特里堡有熟人，所以立即决定就在这附近降落。气球降到海滩上（潮水已经落下，沙滩结实又平坦，非常适合降落），抛下锚钩，马上就固定住了。岛上的居民和城堡里的人们自然都蜂拥而至参观气球；但是无论如何他们当中也没有人相信这次真实的飞行——穿越大西洋的飞行。锚钩固定的时间刚好是下午2点整；因此，整个航行在75小时内完成；如果用岸对岸的方法算，用时更短。没有发生严重事故，全程并没有遇到真正的危险。气球放气和收起的过程也没有什么麻烦；当这份手稿被编辑成描述性的报道并从查尔斯顿送出时，飞行人员还待在莫特里堡。他们的下一步打算还不确定；但我们可以向本报读者承诺周一，最晚不超过周二，将刊登补充信息。

此次飞行无疑是人类迄今为止所完成的，甚至是试图完成的最惊人、最有趣，也是最重要的壮举。至于接下来还会有什么重大事件，现在再怎么猜也猜不到。

* 注释：安斯沃斯先生并没有试图解释这种现象，其实这种现象也很容易解释。从25000英尺的高度投下一条垂直于地面（或海面）的直线，这条线就是一个直角三角形的一条直角边。底边则从直角一直延伸到地平线，斜边是

① cease [si:s] v. 停止

② inhabitant [in'hæbitənt] n. 居民
③ throng [θrɔŋ] v. 蜂拥而至，群集
④ credit ['kredit] v. 相信

⑤ stupendous [stju:'pendəs] a. 惊人的

⑥ susceptible [sə'septəbl] a. 能经受某事物，有某种能力
⑦ perpendicular [,pə:pən'dikjulə] n. 垂线

horizon, and the **hypothenuse**[①] from the horizon to the balloon. But the 25,000 feet of altitude is little or nothing, in comparison with the extent of the prospect. In other words, the base and hypothenuse of the supposed triangle would be so long when compared with the perpendicular, that the two former may be regarded as nearly parallel. In this manner the horizon of the æronaut would appear to be *on a level* with the car. But, as the point immediately beneath him seems, and is, at a great distance below him, it seems, of course, also, at a great distance below the horizon. Hence the impression of *concavity*[②]; and this impression must remain, until the elevation shall bear so great a proportion to the extent of prospect, that the apparent **parallelism**[③] of the base and hypothenuse disappears — when the earth's real **convexity**[④] must become apparent.

① hypothenuse
[hai'pɔθinjuːz] *n.* 斜边

② concavity [kɔn'kæviti] *n.*
凹面
③ parallelism
['pærəlelizəm] *n.* 平行
④ convexity [kən'veksiti] *n.*
凸面

气球到地平线之间的连线。但是 25000 英尺的海拔高度相对于视野所能及的距离来说简直是微乎其微，甚至可以忽略。换句话说，假想的直角三角形的斜边和底边，相对于垂直的这条直角边来说，简直太长了，以至于可以被看成是平行的。这样一来，飞行员所见的地平线看上去就和吊篮处于同一水平面了。但是他正下方的地面上（或海面上）那点看起来和他之间相距很远（也的确如此），当然看起来就像在地平线下方很远的地方。因此就产生了海面凹下去的印象；而这一凹陷印象会一直持续到上升的高度相对于视野的远度足够大，也就是直角底边和斜边不再像平行的两条直线——这时，地球的凸面才真正显示出来。（作者注）

The Spectacles

Many years ago, it was the fashion to **ridicule**① the idea of "love at first sight;" but those who think, not less than those who feel deeply, have always **advocated**② its existence. Modern discoveries, indeed, in what may be termed ethical **magnetism**③ or magnetoesthetics, render it probable that the most natural, and, consequently, the truest and most intense of the human affections are those which arise in the heart as if by electric **sympathy**④ — in a word, that the brightest and most enduring of the **psychal**⑤ **fetters**⑥ are those which are riveted by a glance. The **confession**⑦ I am about to make will add another to the already almost innumerable instances of the truth of the position.

My story requires that I should be somewhat **minute**⑧. I am still a very young man — not yet twenty-two years of age. My name, at present, is a very usual and rather **plebeian**⑨ one — Simpson. I say "at present;" for it is only lately that I have been so called — having legislatively adopted this surname within the last year in order to receive a large **inheritance**⑩ left me by a distant male relative, Adolphus Simpson, Esq. The **bequest**⑪ was conditioned upon my taking the name of the **testator**⑫, — the family, not the Christian name; my Christian name is Napoleon Bonaparte — or, more properly, these are my first and middle **appellations**⑬.

I assumed the name, Simpson, with some **reluctance**⑭, as in my true

眼镜

① ridicule ['ridikju:l] *v.* 嘲笑
② advocate ['ædvəkeit] *v.*
提倡，拥护
③ magnetism
['mægnitizəm] *n.* 吸引
力，磁力
④ sympathy ['simpəθi] *n.*
共鸣，同感
⑤ psychal ['psaikəl] *a.* 精
神的，心理的
⑥ fetter ['fetə] *n.* 束缚
⑦ confession [kən'feʃən] *n.*
表白
⑧ minute [mai'nju:t] *a.* 仔
细的，缜密的
⑨ plebeian [pli'bi:jən] *a.* 普
通的，平民的
⑩ inheritance [in'heritəns]
n. 继承
⑪ bequest [bi'kwest] *n.* 遗
产，遗赠
⑫ testator [te'steitə] *n.* 立遗
嘱者
⑬ appellation [æpə'leiʃən]
n. 称呼
⑭ reluctance [ri'lʌktəns] *n.*
不情愿

很多年前，谁说"一见钟情"，都会被别人嘲笑；但也有许多人鼓吹它的存在，多情易感者如是，理性思考者亦然。的确，现代有关所谓伦理吸引力，或者说感情磁场的发现说明，那种如心电感应一般发自内心的情感，也许是人类最自然、最真实、最强烈的情感，如同心电感应一般，是源自内心的——一句话，最闪耀持久的精神之锁就是在那一瞥间牢牢扣住了。接下来我要讲的故事就是无数真实的一见钟情的事例之一。

这个故事我必须讲得详细些。现在我还很年轻——不到二十一岁。眼下，我的名字既平凡又普通——辛普森。我说"眼下"，是因为以前我并不叫这个名字——就在前一年，为了继承一位叫阿道弗斯·辛普森的远房亲戚的一大笔遗产，我就依法接受了这个姓氏。因为得到这份遗赠的条件就是要改姓赠予人的姓氏——是姓，不是教名，我的教名是拿 破仑·波拿巴——更准确地说，这两个是我的第一和第二予名。

我其实还是不太情愿接受辛普森这个姓的，因

patronym①, Froissart, I felt a very **pardonable**② pride — believing that I could trace a descent from the **immortal**③ author of the "Chronicles." While on the subject of names, by the bye, I may mention a singular coincidence of sound attending the names of some of my immediate **predecessors**④. My father was a Monsieur Froissart, of Paris. His wife — my mother, whom he married at fifteen — was a Mademoiselle Croissart, eldest daughter of Croissart the banker, whose wife, again, being only sixteen when married, was the eldest daughter of one Victor Voissart. Monsieur Voissart, very singularly, had married a lady of similar name — a Mademoiselle Moissart. She, too, was quite a child when married; and her mother, also, Madame Moissart, was only fourteen when led to the **altar**⑤. These early marriages are usual in France. Here, however, are Moissart, Voissart, Croissart, and Froissart, all in the direct line of descent. My own name, though, as I say, became Simpson, by act of Legislature, and with so much **repugnance**⑥ on my part, that, at one period, I actually hesitated about accepting the legacy with the useless and annoying **proviso**⑦ attached.

As to personal **endowments**⑧, I am by no means **deficient**⑨. On the contrary, I believe that I am well made, and possess what nine tenths of the world would call a handsome face. In height I am five feet eleven. My hair is black and curling. My nose is sufficiently good. My eyes are large and gray; and although, in fact they are weak a very inconvenient degree, still no **defect**⑩ in this regard would be suspected from their appearance. The weakness itself, however, has always much annoyed me, and I have **resorted**⑪ to every remedy — short of wearing glasses. Being youthful and good-looking, I naturally dislike these, and have resolutely refused to employ them. I know nothing, indeed, which so **disfigures**⑫ the countenance of a young person, or so impresses every feature with an air of **demureness**⑬, if not altogether of sanctimoniousness and of age. An eyeglass, on the other hand, has a savor of **downright**⑭ **foppery**⑮ and affectation. I have hitherto managed as well as I could without either. But something too much of these

① patronym ['pætrənim] *n.*
源于父母的姓或名字

② pardonable ['pɑrdnəbl] *a.*
可原谅的

③ immortal [i'mɔːtəl] *a.* 不
朽的

④ predecessor ['priːdisesə]
n. 前辈

⑤ altar ['ɔːltə] *n.* 圣坛

⑥ repugnance [ri'pʌgnəns]
n. 反感，厌恶

⑦ proviso [prəu'vaizəu] *n.*
附带条件

⑧ endowment [in'daumənt]
n. 天资

⑨ deficient [di'fiʃənt] *a.* 不
足的，有缺陷的

⑩ defect ['diːfekt] *n.* 缺点，
缺陷

⑪ resort [ri'zɔːt] *v.* 采取
（手段或方法）

⑫ disfigure [dis'figə] *v.*
使……变丑，损毁……
的外形

⑬ demureness [di'mjuənis]
n. 故作庄重，假正经

⑭ downright ['daunrait] *a.*
十足的，完全的

⑮ foppery ['fɔpəri] *n.* 纨绔
习气

为我从父亲那里继承的姓是佛瓦萨尔，我有理由为
这个姓氏感到骄傲——我坚信，通过族谱追根溯源，
我有可能是创作《编年史》的不朽作家佛瓦萨尔的后
人呢。说到姓氏，顺便提一下，有个巧合，就是与我
有直系血亲的上几辈人姓氏的发音都惊人地相似。我
祖籍巴黎，父亲姓佛瓦萨尔。他的妻子——我的母亲，
在十五岁时嫁给我父亲——姓科瓦萨尔，是家里最大
的女儿；她的父亲科瓦萨尔是位银行家，这位银行家
的妻子，也就是我的外祖母，在年仅十六岁时嫁给
他，她是维克托·沃瓦萨尔的长女；而奇特的是，这
位沃瓦萨尔先生娶了一位相似姓氏的女士，也就是我
的曾外祖母莫瓦萨尔女士。我的曾外祖母莫瓦萨尔结
婚时年龄也很小；她的母亲莫瓦萨尔夫人步入婚礼殿
堂时年仅十四。早婚在当时的法国十分常见。就这样，
莫瓦萨尔、沃瓦萨尔、科瓦萨尔、佛瓦萨尔一脉相
承下来。然而我自己的名字却依法改为辛普森，我
一度十分抵触这个姓氏，实际上，我也曾犹豫是否
接受附加有这一无用又烦人的限制性条件的遗产。

至于个人的天生条件，我也绝不差。事实上，
我自认貌美，世上十人有九人都会说我面貌英俊。我
身高五英尺十一英寸 [1]，头发乌黑卷曲；鼻梁高挺，虽
然两眼弱视给生活带来很多不便，但是单从这双灰
色大眼睛的外表是看不出来任何缺陷的。然而视力
的缺陷却一直困扰着我，我曾求助各种手段——就
差没戴眼镜了。年轻俊朗的我自然是不喜欢眼镜的，
也完全拒绝戴那东西。事实上我是不想让它毁坏我
年轻的外表，也不想让别人认为我死气沉沉，一旦
戴上眼镜，看上去就会道貌岸然又老气横秋。另一
方面，单片眼镜本身则会给人一种纨绔做作的感觉。

1　约180.3厘米。

merely personal details, which, after all, are of little importance. I will content myself with saying, in addition, that my **temperament**① is sanguine, rash, **ardent**②, enthusiastic — and that all my life I have been a devoted admirer of the women.

One night last winter I entered a box at the P — Theatre, in company with a friend, Mr. Talbot. It was an opera night, and the bills presented a very rare attraction, so that the house was excessively crowded. We were in time, however, to obtain the front seats which had been reserved for us, and into which, with some little difficulty, we **elbowed**③ our way.

For two hours my companion, who was a musical fanatico, gave his **undivided**④ attention to the stage; and, in the meantime, I amused myself by observing the audience, which consisted, in chief part, of the very elite of the city. Having satisfied myself upon this point, I was about turning my eyes to the **prima donna**⑤, when they were arrested and riveted by a figure in one of the private boxes which had escaped my observation.

If I live a thousand years, I can never forget the intense emotion with which I regarded this figure. It was that of a female, the most exquisite I had ever **beheld**⑥. The face was so far turned toward the stage that, for some minutes, I could not obtain a view of it — but the form was **divine**⑦; no other word can sufficiently express its magnificent proportion — and even the term "divine" seems ridiculously **feeble**⑧ as I write it.

The magic of a lovely form in woman — the **necromancy**⑨ of female gracefulness — was always a power which I had found it impossible to **resist**⑩, but here was grace personified, **incarnate**⑪, the beau ideal of my wildest and most enthusiastic visions. The figure, almost all of which the construction of the box permitted to be seen, was somewhat above the medium height, and nearly approached, without positively reaching, the majestic. Its perfect fullness and tournure were delicious. The head of which only the back was visible, **rivalled**⑫ in outline that of the Greek Psyche, and was rather displayed than concealed by an elegant cap of gaze aerienne, which put me in mind of the ventum textilem

① temperament
['tempərəmənt] *n.* 性格，
性情

② ardent ['ɑːdənt] *a.* 热情
的，热心的

③ elbow ['elbəu] *v.* 用肘挤
开

④ undivided [ˌʌndi'vaidid]
a. 专心的

⑤ prima donna 女主角

⑥ behold [bi'həuld] *v.* 见到

⑦ divine [di'vain] *a.* 神圣
的，极好的

⑧ feeble ['fiːbl] *a.*（效果
等）不足的，微弱的

⑨ necromancy
['nekrəumænsi] *n.* 巫术，
妖术

⑩ resist [ri'zist] *v.* 抵抗

⑪ incarnate [in'kɑːnit] *a.* 化
身的

⑫ rival ['raivəl] *v.* 比得上

我至今一直就这样得过且过，哪种眼镜也没戴过。说了这么多都仅仅是个人细节，毕竟不那么重要。另外，我可以很得意地说，我性情自信乐观、率性洒脱、热烈多情——而且一向衷心爱慕女性。

去年冬天的一个晚上，我在朋友塔尔博特先生的陪同下进到了 P 剧院的包厢。那是一个歌剧之夜，戏目单异常吸引人，因此那晚的剧院里十分拥挤。我们到达剧院时费了好大力气才挤进早先订好的包厢里的前排座位。

我的这位朋友可是个音乐迷，两个小时目不转睛地盯着舞台；而我呢，则一边看戏一边观察看戏的人作为消遣，这些观众大部分可都是这城市里的上层人物。看够了观众，我正要把目光转向台上的女主角，却不由得被刚才没注意到的一个包厢里的一个身影所吸引，且再也不想把视线移开。

对这身影强烈的迷恋之情即使一千年也不会令人忘却。那是一个我所见过的最精致的女性的身影。她的脸侧向舞台，一时间我无法看到——但她的身形有如神造；其他任何词语都无法充分地形容那匀称美丽的身形——用"神造"来描述她的美丽都显得虚弱无力。

女人曼妙的身材散发着魔力——女性典雅之美的魅惑力——总是深深吸引着我，令我无法自拔，但眼前不就是优雅的化身、美神下凡，不正是我狂热追求的梦中情人吗？包厢挡住了我的视线，令我只能看到她的背影，她身材高挑，甚至可以说近乎伟岸。她体态丰腴，姿态真是秀色可餐。头部虽然仅能看到后面，但只那轮廓真可与希腊的灵魂美神塞姬媲美，那顶精致的轻纱礼帽戴在她的头上并没有遮掩她的美丽，反而使她更添几分优雅，不禁使

of Apuleius. The right arm hung over the **balustrade**[①] of the box, and thrilled every nerve of my frame with its exquisite **symmetry**[②]. Its upper portion was draperied by one of the loose open sleeves now in fashion. This extended but little below the elbow. Beneath it was worn an under one of some frail material, close-fitting, and terminated by a cuff of rich lace, which fell gracefully over the top of the hand, revealing only the delicate fingers, upon one of which **sparkled**[③] a diamond ring, which I at once saw was of extraordinary value. The admirable roundness of the wrist was well set off by a bracelet which **encircled**[④] it, and which also was **ornamented**[⑤] and clasped by a magnificent **aigrette**[⑥] of jewels — telling, in words that could not be mistaken, at once of the wealth and **fastidious**[⑦] taste of the wearer.

I gazed at this queenly apparition for at least half an hour, as if I had been suddenly converted to stone; and, during this period, I felt the full force and truth of all that has been said or sung concerning "love at first sight." My feelings were totally different from any which I had hitherto experienced, in the presence of even the most celebrated specimens of female loveliness. An unaccountable, and what I am compelled to consider a magnetic, sympathy of soul for soul, seemed to rivet, not only my vision, but my whole powers of thought and feeling, upon the admirable object before me. I saw — I felt — I knew that I was deeply, madly, irrevocably in love — and this even before seeing the face of the person beloved. So intense, indeed, was the passion that consumed me, that I really believe it would have received little if any **abatement**[⑧] had the features, yet unseen, proved of merely ordinary character, so **anomalous**[⑨] is the nature of the only true love — of the love at first sight — and so little really dependent is it upon the external conditions which only seem to create and control it.

While I was thus wrapped in admiration of this lovely vision, a sudden disturbance among the audience caused her to turn her head partially toward me, so that I beheld the entire **profile**[⑩] of the face. Its beauty even exceeded my **anticipations**[⑪] — and yet there was something about it which disappointed me without my being able to tell exactly what it was. I said "disappointed,"

① balustrade [ˌbæləs'treid] *n*. 栏杆，扶手
② symmetry ['simitri] *n*. 匀称

③ sparkle ['spɑ:kl] *v*. 闪耀，发光
④ encircle [in'sə:kl] *v*. 环绕
⑤ ornament ['ɔ:nəmənt] *v*. 装饰
⑥ aigrette ['eigret] *n*. 羽饰
⑦ fastidious [fæs'tidiəs] *a*. 挑剔的

⑧ abatement [ə'beitmənt] *n*. 减少
⑨ anomalous [ə'nɔmələs] *a*. 异常的，反常的

⑩ profile ['prəufail] *n*. 轮廓，侧脸
⑪ anticipation [æn,tisi'peiʃən] *n*. 预期

我想起著名作家阿普列乌斯说的"清风织就"。那右臂搭在包厢栏杆上，匀称的比例美得令我浑身战栗。她穿着时下流行的褶皱宽松袖口的衣服，袖子刚到肘部以下一分，里面配着那种柔软轻薄的紧身衬衣，袖口堆满的蕾丝花边优雅地衬出那纤纤玉手，指如削葱，一颗闪亮的钻石戒指闪耀其中，一看便知价值连城。微微露出的那截手腕圆润如藕，配着一只用羽状珠宝装饰的手镯，浑然天成——没错，足以显示出主人殷实的家境和不凡的品位。

我骤然石化了，盯着这高贵的背影半个多小时无法挪开视线；在这半小时里我完全感受到了一见钟情的力量，这种被传颂的异象看来是真实存在的。以前，在我面前出现过的美丽女子最惊艳的时刻也不曾令我有如此感悟。我对眼前这尤物产生了一种无以言表的情感，我不得不承认是某种磁场，是灵魂的契合，她牢牢勾住了我的眼神，更拴住了我全部的情感和思考能力。目之所至，心向往之，我意识到即便还没有见到她的真容，我就已经深沉地、疯狂地、无可救药地爱上了她。这突如其来的情感吞噬着我，即使没有见面，即使她相貌平平，我的爱也不会削减丝毫；世间唯一的真爱就是毫无章法可言——一见钟情更是如此——它并不受外界条件限制，因为被外界条件创造和控制的爱并不是真爱。

我正满心慕地欣赏着这可爱的景色，突然观众席里一阵骚动，她扭头看过来的时候，我看到了她的整个侧脸。那副美貌真是超越了我的想象——然而什么东西却有些令我失望，我也说不清楚到底是什么东西。确切地说也不是"失望"，而是爱慕之情

but this is not altogether the word. My **sentiments**[①] were at once quieted and **exalted**[②]. They partook less of transport and more of calm enthusiasm of enthusiastic **repose**[③]. This state of feeling arose, perhaps, from the Madonna-like and **matronly**[④] air of the face; and yet I at once understood that it could not have arisen entirely from this. There was something else — some mystery which I could not develope — some expression about the countenance which slightly disturbed me while it greatly heightened my interest. In fact, I was just in that condition of mind which prepares a young and susceptible man for any act of extravagance. Had the lady been alone, I should undoubtedly have entered her box and **accosted**[⑤] her at all **hazards**[⑥]; but, fortunately, she was attended by two companions — a gentleman, and a strikingly beautiful woman, to all appearance a few years younger than herself.

I revolved in my mind a thousand schemes by which I might obtain, hereafter, an introduction to the elder lady, or, for the present, at all events, a more distinct view of her beauty. I would have removed my position to one nearer her own, but the crowded state of the theatre rendered this impossible; and the **stern**[⑦] **decrees**[⑧] of Fashion had, of late, **imperatively**[⑨] prohibited the use of the opera-glass in a case such as this, even had I been so fortunate as to have one with me — but I had not — and was thus in **despair**[⑩].

At length I **bethought**[⑪] me of applying to my companion.

"Talbot," I said, "you have an opera-glass. Let me have it."

"An opera-glass! — no! — what do you suppose I would be doing with an opera-glass?" Here he turned impatiently toward the stage.

"But, Talbot," I continued, pulling him by the shoulder, "listen to me will you? Do you see the stage — box? — there! — no, the next. — did you ever behold as lovely a woman?"

"She is very beautiful, no doubt," he said.

"I wonder who she can be?"

"Why, in the name of all that is **angelic**[⑫], don't you know who she is? 'Not to know her argues yourself unknown.' She is the celebrated Madame

① sentiment ['sentimənt] *n.* 感情，情绪

② exalt [ig'zɔlt] *v.* 提升，加强

③ repose [ri'pəuz] *n.* 休息

④ matronly ['meitrənli] *a.* 稳重的

⑤ accost [ə'kɔst] *v.* 搭讪

⑥ hazard ['hæzəd] *n.* 危险，冒险

⑦ stern [stə:n] *a.* 严格的

⑧ decree [di'kri:] *n.* 法令

⑨ imperatively [im'perətivli] *ad.* 命令式地，不可避免地

⑩ despair [di'speə] *n.* 绝望

⑪ bethought [bi'θɔ:t] *v.* （bethink 的过去式）使（自己）思考或考虑

⑫ angelic [æn'dʒelik] *a.* 天使般的

稍稍冷静而升华了。我的内心依旧激情澎湃，只是稍微控制了一下而已。这份控制或许是源于她脸上圣母玛利亚般庄严的神态，而我马上意识到不可能全是因为如此。还有其他原因——某种我看不透的神秘缘由——她的面部表情令我有些不安，而这却大大燃起了我的兴趣。事实上，作为一个多情的青年，在当时那种心境下已经准备好立刻采取大胆行动。如果那位女士独自一人，我毫无疑问就会进入她的包厢冒险与她搭话；但是所幸，她有两个同 伴——一位绅士和一位和她一样光彩夺目但要年轻一些的女士。

我在头脑中构想出上千种场景，幻想着在今后该如何认识她，但现在无论如何，我也要把她的美貌看清楚。我想挪到离她更近的地方，但是剧场里太拥挤了，根本过不去；上流社会一本正经的规矩最近还严令禁止在剧院里使用小望远镜窥视其他观众，可我真希望现在身边就带着一个——但是我没有——我无计可施了。

最后我想到可以求助于我的朋友啊。

"塔尔博特，"我说，"你有小望远镜吧。借我用一下。"

"小望远镜！没有！——我带望远镜又没有用，怎么会有呢？"他不耐烦地应付我几句后又看向舞台。

"但是塔尔博特，"我并不放弃，扳着他的肩膀让他看回我这里，"听我说好吗？看到那边的舞台，不是，包厢了吗？——就是那儿！——不对，旁边那个——见过那么漂亮的女人吗？"

"的确，她很美，"他说。

"真想知道她是谁。"

"哎呀，你不知道那是谁？人人都知道那个天使，

Lalande — the beauty of the day **par excellence**①, and the talk of the whole town. Immensely wealthy too — a widow, and a great match — has just arrived from Paris."

"Do you know her?"

"Yes; I have the honor."

"Will you introduce me?"

"Assuredly, with the greatest pleasure; when shall it be?"

"To-morrow, at one, I will call upon you at B — 's."

"Very good; and now do hold your tongue, if you can."

In this latter respect I was forced to take Talbot's advice; for he remained **obstinately**② deaf to every further question or suggestion, and occupied himself exclusively for the rest of the evening with what was transacting upon the stage.

In the meantime I kept my eyes riveted on Madame Lalande, and at length had the good fortune to obtain a full front view of her face. It was exquisitely lovely — this, of course, my heart had told me before, even had not Talbot fully satisfied me upon the point — but still the **unintelligible**③ something disturbed me. I finally concluded that my senses were impressed by a certain air of gravity, sadness, or, still more properly, of **weariness**④, which took something from the youth and freshness of the countenance, only to **endow**⑤ it with a **seraphic**⑥ tenderness and majesty, and thus, of course, to my enthusiastic and romantic temperment, with an interest **tenfold**⑦.

While I thus **feasted**⑧ my eyes, I perceived, at last, to my great **trepidation**⑨, by an almost imperceptible start on the part of the lady, that she had become suddenly aware of the intensity of my gaze. Still, I was absolutely fascinated, and could not withdraw it, even for an instant. She turned aside her face, and again I saw only the **chiselled**⑩ **contour**⑪ of the back portion of the head. After some minutes, as if urged by curiosity to see if I was still looking, she gradually brought her face again around and again encountered my burning gaze. Her large dark eyes fell instantly, and a deep blush **mantled**⑫ her cheek. But what was my astonishment at perceiving that she not only did not a second time **avert**⑬ her

① par excellence 出类拔萃的，卓越的

② obstinately ['ɔbstinitli] *ad.* 顽固地

③ unintelligible [ˌʌnin'telidʒəbl] *a.* 令人费解的

④ weariness ['wiərinis] *n.* 疲劳，疲惫

⑤ endow [in'dau] *v.* 赋予

⑥ seraphic [si'ræfik] *a.* 纯洁的，美丽的

⑦ tenfold ['tenfəuld] *a.* 十倍的

⑧ feast [fi:st] *v.* 使享受

⑨ trepidation [ˌtrepidei'ʃən] *n.* 不安

⑩ chiselled ['tʃizəld] *a.* 轮廓分明的

⑪ contour ['kɔntuə] *n.* 轮廓，外形

⑫ mantle ['mæntl] *v.* 扩散，覆盖

⑬ avert [ə'və:t] *v.* 把……移开

'你不认得她，表示你自己无名。'这位是大名鼎鼎的拉兰德夫人——时下艳压群芳的美人，名震全城。她富甲一方——是位寡妇，很多人都追求她——刚从巴黎来到这儿。"

"你认识她？"

"当然，很荣幸。"

"能帮忙把我介绍给她吗？"

"当然，不胜荣幸；什么时候？"

"就明天吧，一点钟，我去 B 公寓找你。"

"很好；现在，请你别说话打扰我看戏啦。"

我再怎么向他打听，他也充耳不闻，我不得不照他说的闭嘴了。而我的这位朋友则专注地享受着接下来舞台上的剧情。

而我则专注地望着这位拉兰德夫人，最终上帝眷顾，我终于如愿看到了她的脸。如此精致美丽——当然，即使塔尔博特没有向我盛赞她的美貌，我心中也早有预感——但仍有什么东西莫名地令我不安。我终于想明白了，令我着迷的正是那一丝严肃、忧伤，更确切地说，是那份疲惫，这使她看起来并不那么妙龄清新，但这反而赋予了她天使般的温柔和庄严，这正符合我热情浪漫的性格，让我对她更加着迷十倍。

正当我享受这视觉盛宴，密切注视着这位女士的一举一动，她突然吃了一小惊，注意到了我那灼热的目光，这令我大为恐慌，然而彻底迷失在她的美丽之中，我一时无法收回自己的目光。她又背过脸去看舞台，又让我欣赏到了她那精心梳起的发髻。过了几分钟，好似忍不住好奇地想看看我是不是还在看她，她再次把脸转过来，又一次与我灼热的目光碰撞。她那双乌黑的大眼睛立刻垂下来，脸色绯红。

head, but that she actually took from her **girdle**① a double eyeglass — elevated it — adjusted it — and then regarded me through it, intently and deliberately, for the space of several minutes.

Had a **thunderbolt**② fallen at my feet I could not have been more thoroughly astounded — astounded only — not offended or disgusted in the slightest degree; although an action so bold in any other woman would have been likely to offend or disgust. But the whole thing was done with so much **quietude**③ — so much **nonchalance**④ — so much repose — with so evident an air of the highest breeding, in short — that nothing of mere **effrontery**⑤ was perceptible, and my sole sentiments were those of admiration and surprise.

I observed that, upon her first elevation of the glass, she had seemed satisfied with a momentary inspection of my person, and was withdrawing the instrument, when, as if struck by a second thought, she resumed it, and so continued to regard me with fixed attention for the space of several minutes — for five minutes, at the very least, I am sure.

This action, so remarkable in an American theatre, attracted very general observation, and gave rise to an indefinite movement, or buzz, among the audience, which for a moment filled me with confusion, but produced no visible effect upon the countenance of Madame Lalande.

Having satisfied her curiosity — if such it was — she dropped the glass, and quietly gave her attention again to the stage; her profile now being turned toward myself, as before. I continued to watch her **unremittingly**⑥, although I was fully conscious of my rudeness in so doing. Presently I saw the head slowly and slightly change its position; and soon I became convinced that the lady, while pretending to look at the stage was, in fact, attentively regarding myself. It is needless to say what effect this conduct, on the part of so fascinating a woman, had upon my excitable mind.

Having thus scrutinized me for perhaps a quarter of an hour, the fair object of my passion addressed the gentleman who attended her, and while she spoke, I saw distinctly, by the glances of both, that the conversation had reference to myself.

① girdle ['gə:dl] *n.* 腰带，
饰带

② thunderbolt ['θʌndəbəult]
n. 霹雳

③ quietude ['kwaiətju:d] *n.*
平静，宁静

④ nonchalance ['nɔnʃələns]
n. 冷静

⑤ effrontery [i'frʌntəri] *n.*
放肆，无礼

⑥ unremittingly
[ʌnri'mitiŋli] *ad.* 不间断
地

但我又惊奇地注意到，这次她并没有回过头去，而是从腰间取出一副眼镜，举起来，调整好，透过镜片大大方方、仔仔细细地观察起我来，还看了好几分钟。

好似遭遇晴天霹雳一般，我彻底震惊了——只是震惊——并没有感到被冒犯，也没有一丝鄙夷；换作其他任何一个女人这么做，我很可能会感到羞辱或者心生厌恶。但她做这一切时却如此平静——如此不动声色——如此不受惊扰——举手投足间都显露出高贵的教养，简言之——我察觉不到一丝的轻佻无礼，唯一的感觉只剩倾慕和惊喜。

我观察到她第一次抬起眼镜只看了我一眼似乎就觉得足够了，但刚要放下眼镜又把它举了起来，好像又想起什么，又仔细地打量着我足足有几分钟——我敢肯定，五分钟不止。

在美国的剧场里，私下盯着别人看是出格之举，我们的举动很快就引起了其他观众的注意，大家颇有骚动，抑或窃窃私语，当时真是令我如芒在背，但从拉兰德夫人的表情却看不出任何反应。

好奇心得到满足——如果是好奇心的话——她放下眼镜，默默地转身继续看戏；如以前以一样把侧脸留给我。而我虽然明知这样做很不礼貌，但是仍然抑制不住内心的渴望，目不转睛地看着她。当时我看到她慢慢地微微地转了一下头；很快我就确定这位女士虽然假装在看着舞台，实际上却是在关注着我。无须说，这样迷人的女士能偷偷观察我，我那情感丰富的内心真是无比愉悦。

就这样偷看了大概一刻钟后，我心相许的窈窕女子和她旁边的绅士聊起了天，在她说话间，很明显两个人都看向我，肯定是在谈论我。

Upon its conclusion, Madame Lalande again turned toward the stage, and, for a few minutes, seemed absorbed in the performance. At the **expiration**① of this period, however, I was thrown into an extremity of **agitation**② by seeing her **unfold**③, for the second time, the eye-glass which hung at her side, fully confront me as before, and, disregarding the renewed buzz of the audience, survey me, from head to foot, with the same **miraculous**④ **composure**⑤ which had previously so delighted and **confounded**⑥ my soul.

This extraordinary behavior, by throwing me into a perfect fever of excitement — into an absolute **delirium**⑦ of love — served rather to **embolden**⑧ than to **disconcert**⑨ me. In the mad intensity of my devotion, I forgot everything but the presence and the majestic loveliness of the vision which confronted my gaze. Watching my opportunity, when I thought the audience were fully engaged with the opera, I at length caught the eyes of Madame Lalande, and, upon the instant, made a slight but **unmistakable**⑩ bow.

She blushed very deeply — then averted her eyes — then slowly and cautiously looked around, apparently to see if my rash action had been noticed — then leaned over toward the gentleman who sat by her side.

I now felt a burning sense of the **impropriety**⑪ I had committed, and expected nothing less than instant **exposure**⑫; while a vision of pistols upon the morrow floated rapidly and uncomfortably through my brain. I was greatly and immediately relieved, however, when I saw the lady merely hand the gentleman a play-bill, without speaking, but the reader may form some feeble **conception**⑬ of my astonishment — of my profound amazement — my **delirious**⑭ **bewilderment**⑮ of heart and soul — when, instantly afterward, having again glanced **furtively**⑯ around, she allowed her bright eyes to set fully and steadily upon my own, and then, with a faint smile, **disclosing**⑰ a bright line of her pearly teeth, made two distinct, pointed, and unequivocal **affirmative**⑱ **inclinations**⑲ of the head.

It is useless, of course, to dwell upon my joy — upon my transport — upon my **illimitable**⑳ **ecstasy**㉑ of heart. If ever man was mad with excess of happiness,

① expiration [ˌekspi'reiʃən] n. 结束

② agitation [ˌædʒi'teiʃən] n. 烦乱，焦虑不安

③ unfold ['gəːdl] v. 打开，展开

④ miraculous [mi'rækjuləs] a. 非凡的，不可思议的

⑤ composure [kəm'pəuʒə] n. 镇静，沉着

⑥ confound [kən'faund] v. 使困惑

⑦ delirium [di'liriəm] n. 发狂

⑧ embolden [im'bəuldən] v. 鼓励，使有胆量

⑨ disconcert [ˌdiskən'səːt] v. 使焦虑，使困惑

⑩ unmistakable [ˌʌnmi'steikəbl] a. 明显的

⑪ impropriety [ˌimprə'praiəti] n. 不适当

⑫ exposure [ik'spəuʒə] n. 暴露

⑬ conception [kən'sepʃən] n. 设想

⑭ delirious [di'liriəs] a. 发狂的，极度兴奋的

⑮ bewilderment [ˌbi'wildəmənt] n. 困惑，迷惑

⑯ furtively ['fəːtivli] ad. 偷偷地

⑰ disclose [dis'kləuz] v. 使显露，使出现

⑱ affirmative [ə'fəːmətiv] a. 认可的

⑲ inclination [ˌinkli'neiʃən] n. 点头

⑳ illimitable [i'limitəbl] a. 无限的

㉑ ecstasy ['ekstəsi] n. 狂喜

交谈结束，拉兰德夫人又看向戏台，有几分钟，她似乎在专心地看歌剧。但她接下来的举动令我心潮澎湃不已。只见她不顾周围观众再次响起的窃窃私语，又一次打开别在腰间的眼镜，从头到脚正面观察着我，仍如上次那般出奇淡定，而我刚刚就已被她看得又是欢喜，又是慌乱。

这非凡的举动使我内心狂热——将我抛入爱情的痴妄——非但没有让我感到不安，反而让我更加无所顾忌。那疯狂而强烈的倾慕之情，令我忘却身在何处，眼前只有这高雅可爱的佳人。当我看到观众已经不再关注我的举动而全心投入地看戏时，我看好时机，等到拉兰德夫人的目光扫到这里，马上意味明确地向她微微颔首。

她羞得面颊绯红——移开视线——然后慢慢地小心翼翼地观察周围，很显然是在看是否有人注意到我这鲁莽的举动——随后又转向坐在身边的那位绅士。

现在我也感到刚才的行为有些冒昧，只期望不要马上被她揭发；这时脑海中居然令人不快地闪过第二天掏枪决斗的画面。但当我看到那位女士仅仅递给旁边绅士一张戏目单，并未说话，就马上松了一口气。但你对我接下来的心情也许能有些许体会——我当时无比惊愕，深为诧异——我的心和灵魂为之狂喜迷乱——因为紧接着她就再次谨慎地看了看四周，然后清澈的眼神专注地看着我，浅浅一笑，露出贻贝皓齿，十分明确地向我赞同地点了两下头。

当然，无须再描述我的欣喜——我早已迷失自我——迷失在内心无边的狂喜中。如果有人因幸福过度而癫狂，那一刻那个人就是我。我坠入爱河了，

it was myself at that moment. I loved. This was my first love — so I felt it to be. It was love supreme — indescribable. It was "love at first sight;" and at first sight, too, it had been appreciated and returned.

Yes, returned. How and why should I doubt it for an instant. What other construction could I possibly put upon such conduct, on the part of a lady so beautiful — so wealthy — evidently so accomplished — of so high breeding — of so lofty a position in society — in every regard so entirely respectable as I felt assured was Madame Lalande? Yes, she loved me — she returned the enthusiasm of my love, with an enthusiasm as blind — as uncompromising — as uncalculating — as abandoned — and as utterly **unbounded**① as my own! These delicious fancies and reflections, however, were now interrupted by the falling of the drop-curtain. The audience arose; and the usual **tumult**② immediately **supervened**③. Quitting Talbot abruptly, I made every effort to force my way into closer proximity with Madame Lalande. Having failed in this, on account of the crowd, I at length gave up the chase, and bent my steps homeward; **consoling**④ myself for my disappointment in not having been able to touch even the **hem**⑤ of her robe, by the reflection that I should be introduced by Talbot, in due form, upon the morrow.

This morrow at last came, that is to say, a day finally dawned upon a long and weary night of impatience; and then the hours until "one" were snail-paced, **dreary**⑥, and innumerable. But even Stamboul, it is said, shall have an end, and there came an end to this long delay. The clock struck. As the last echo ceased, I stepped into B — 's and inquired for Talbot.

"Out," said the footman — Talbot's own.

"Out!" I replied, staggering back half a dozen paces — "let me tell you, my fine fellow, that this thing is thoroughly impossible and **impracticable**⑦; Mr. Talbot is not out. What do you mean?"

"Nothing, sir; only Mr. Talbot is not in, that's all. He rode over to S — , immediately after breakfast, and left word that he would not be in town again for a week."

这是我第一次真正的爱——这就是我当时的感想。那是爱的极致——无以言表。"一见钟情"，一见亦被钟情。

是的，她也爱上了我。那一瞬间，我还有什么理由，怎么会有所怀疑呢。一位如此美貌，如此富有，显然如此才华卓越，如此高贵，身居上流社会，且各方面品行定当无可指摘的拉兰德夫人，不顾周围的目光，做出这样的举动，我不可能有其他理解。没错，她也爱上了我——她回应了我热烈的爱，她的热情如我一样盲目、不瞻前、不顾后、不受束、完全释放自我。然而歌剧落幕打断了我的甜美幻想和思绪。观众们都站起身，剧院立刻喧闹嘈杂。我突然起身，也不管塔尔博特，拼尽全力向拉兰德夫人的方向挤去。但人多得令我寸步难行，根本过不去，最后我放弃了追逐，只得转身回家了；连她的裙边都没碰到，真是失望极了，但我仍然安慰自己，想着明天塔尔博特就可以正式地介绍我们认识了。

煎熬过漫长疲惫的夜晚，终于等来了黎明，这个"明天"总算到来了；接着，时间像蜗牛般，不紧不慢地，一步一步地爬向"一点钟"，什么时候才能爬到啊。但是如人们所说的那样，即便是斯坦波尔大街也有尽头，漫长的等待终于结束了。钟声敲响。声音刚停，我就冲向 B 公寓找塔尔博特。

"出去了。"塔尔博特的男仆说。

"出去了！"我叫道，跟跄着后退了几步——"听我说，好兄弟，这完全不可能，这不是实情；塔尔博特先生没出门。你这么说是什么意思？"

"没别的意思，先生；就是说塔尔博特先生不在家，就这样。他骑马去了 S 市，一早吃过早饭就走了，还说得一个礼拜才回来。"

① unbounded [ʌn'baundid] v. 不受控制的

② tumult ['tju:mʌlt] n. 骚动，喧闹

③ supervene [ˌsju:pə'vi:n] v. 随后发生

④ console [kən'səul] v. 安慰

⑤ hem [hem] n. 褶边

⑥ dreary ['driəri] n. 沉闷的，枯燥的

⑦ impracticable [im'præktikəbl] a. 行不通的

I stood **petrified**① with horror and **rage**②. I endeavored to reply, but my tongue refused its office. At length I turned on my heel, **livid**ⓒ with **wrath**④, and inwardly consigning the whole tribe of the Talbots to the **innermost**⑤ regions of Erebus. It was evident that my considerate friend, il fanatico, had quite forgotten his appointment with myself — had forgotten it as soon as it was made. At no time was he a very **scrupulous**⑥ man of his word. There was no help for it; so **smothering**⑦ my **vexation**⑧ as well as I could, I strolled moodily up the street, **propounding**⑨ **futile**⑩ inquiries about Madame Lalande to every male acquaintance I met. By report she was known, I found, to all — to many by sight — but she had been in town only a few weeks, and there were very few, therefore, who claimed her personal acquaintance. These few, being still comparatively strangers, could not, or would not, take the liberty of introducing me through the formality of a morning call. While I stood thus in despair, conversing with a trio of friends upon the all absorbing subject of my heart, it so happened that the subject itself passed by.

"As I live, there she is!" cried one.

"Surprisingly beautiful!" exclaimed a second.

"An angel upon earth!" **ejaculated**⑪ a third.

I looked; and in an open carriage which approached us, passing slowly down the street, sat the **enchanting**⑫ vision of the opera, accompanied by the younger lady who had occupied a portion of her box.

"Her companion also wears remarkably well," said the one of my trio who had spoken first.

"Astonishingly," said the second; "still quite a brilliant air, but art will do wonders. Upon my word, she looks better than she did at Paris five years ago. A beautiful woman still; — don't you think so, Froissart? — Simpson, I mean."

"Still!" said I, "and why shouldn't she be? But compared with her friend she is as a rush-light to the evening star — a glow-worm to Antares."

① petrified ['petrifaid] *a.* 惊呆的

② rage [reidʒ] *n.* 愤怒，盛怒

③ livid ['livid] *a.* 乌青色的

④ wrath [ræθ] *n.* 愤怒

⑤ innermost ['inəməust] *a.* 最深处的

⑥ scrupulous ['skru:pjuləs] *n.* 小心谨慎的

⑦ smother ['smʌðə] *v.* 抑制

⑧ vexation [vek'seiʃən] *n.* 恼怒

⑨ propound [prəu'paund] *v.* 提出

⑩ futile ['fju:tail] *n.* 无用的，无效的

⑪ ejaculate [i'dʒækjuleit] *v.* 突然说出

⑫ enchanting [in'tʃɑ:ntiŋ] *a.* 令人愉悦的

　　我又惊又气地呆在那里。我努力想说点什么，但舌头根本不听使唤。最后我转身离开，气得脸色铁青，在内心深处默默地咒骂塔尔博特一家都不得安生。显然我这位体贴的朋友只爱音乐，已经彻底忘记了与我的约定——就在他答应我的那一刻就已经忘记了。他从来也不是个言而有信的人。这个塔尔博特是指望不上了；于是我强压怒火，气闷地在大街上徘徊，遇到哪个认识的先生我就上前询问是否认识拉兰德夫人，但是没用。我发现所有人都知道她——有很多人都见过她——但是，她来城里也就几个礼拜的时间，因此极少有人跟她私下里有来往。这些极少的人又与我不熟，或不能，或不愿冒昧地通过正式的午前访问把我介绍给她。正当我绝望地站在那儿和三个朋友一起谈论我魂牵梦萦的拉兰德夫人时，刚巧，她本人就从此路过了。

　　"快看，她就在那儿！"一个人喊道。

　　"真是绝色佳人！"第二个人大声说。

　　"天使下凡！"第三个突然喊道。

　　我抬眼望去；只见一辆敞篷马车正缓慢地沿着街道向我们驶来，车上就坐着剧场里我看到的佳人，那天和她一起在包厢看戏的稍年轻的女士坐在她旁边。

　　"她的女伴穿得也是光彩照人啊，"刚才第一个说话的朋友赞道。

　　"太惊人了，"第二位说；"仍然夺目，真是人靠衣装，此话不错，她比我五年前在巴黎时看起来更美。仍是个美人——你觉得呢，佛瓦萨尔？——我是说，辛普森。"

　　"的确很美！"我说，"她自然也是天生丽质。但比起她的朋友，她简直就像点点星火之于皓月——微弱萤火之于安塔利斯恒星。"

"Ha! ha! ha! — why, Simpson, you have an astonishing tact at making discoveries — original ones, I mean." And here we separated, while one of the trio began humming a gay **vaudeville**①, of which I caught only the lines —

Ninon, Ninon, Ninon a bas —

A bas Ninon De L'Enclos!

During this little scene, however, one thing had served greatly to console me, although it fed the passion by which I was consumed. As the carriage of Madame Lalande rolled by our group, I had observed that she recognized me; and more than this, she had **blessed**② me, by the most seraphic of all imaginable smiles, with no equivocal mark of the recognition.

As for an introduction, I was obliged to abandon all hope of it until such time as Talbot should think proper to return from the country. In the meantime I perseveringly frequented every **reputable**③ place of public amusement; and, at length, at the theatre, where I first saw her, I had the supreme bliss of meeting her, and of exchanging glances with her once again. This did not occur, however, until the **lapse**④ of a **fortnight**⑤. Every day, in the **interim**⑥, I had inquired for Talbot at his hotel, and every day had been thrown into a **spasm**⑦ of wrath by the everlasting "Not come home yet" of his footman.

Upon the evening in question, therefore, I was in a condition little short of madness. Madame Lalande, I had been told, was a Parisian — had lately arrived from Paris — might she not suddenly return? — return before Talbot came back — and might she not be thus lost to me forever? The thought was too terrible to bear. Since my future happiness was at issue, I resolved to act with a manly decision. In a word, upon the breaking up of the play, I traced the lady to her residence, noted the address, and the next morning sent her a full and elaborate letter, in which I poured out my whole heart.

I spoke boldly, freely — in a word, I spoke with passion. I concealed nothing — nothing even of my weakness. I **alluded**⑧ to the romantic circum-

① vaudeville ['vəudəvil] *n.*
歌舞杂耍

② bless [bles] *v.* 赐予

③ reputable ['repjutəbl] *a.*
声誉好的

④ lapse [læps] *n.*（两件事
发生的）间隔时间

⑤ fortnight ['fɔ:tnait] *n.* 两
星期

⑥ interim ['intərim] *n.* 期
间，过渡期

⑦ spasm ['spæzəm] *n.* 突
发，发作

⑧ allude [ə'lju:d] *v.* 暗指

"哈！哈！哈！——哎呀，辛普森，你善于发现的眼睛真是惊人地老练——我是说，真是眼光独到啊。"话说到此我们就各自走开了，其中一个还哼着欢快的小曲，我只听到这几句歌词——

倒在地上的是谁？妮蓉，妮蓉，妮蓉——

倒在地上的是谁？妮蓉·德·兰克罗斯！

在这次小小邂逅中，有件事情令我倍感安慰，也使我内心的激情燃得更旺了。那就是拉兰德夫人的马车从我们几个旁边驶过时，我看到她认出了我；不仅如此，她还向我打招呼了，用她那最纯洁的微笑，这毫无疑问是她认出我了。

至于正式认识拉兰德夫人，我放弃了所有的希望，只能等塔尔博特在觉得合适的时候从乡下回来再说。在等待的这段时间，我也没闲着，我执着地频繁出入各个知名剧院；终于，就在我第一次见到她的那家剧院，感谢上帝赐福，我见到了她，还像上次那样，我们四目交错。而这次剧院相见距离上次已经是两个礼拜了。在这期间，我每天都去塔尔博特的住所询问，而每天那个男仆都一字不差地用"还没回家"给我答复，气得我一阵阵火气上蹿。

重逢的那天晚上，内心的焦灼快令我发疯了。我早前听塔尔博特说过，拉兰德夫人是巴黎人——最近才从巴黎来到这里——她会不会突然返回巴黎？——在塔尔博特回来前就返回——我会不会就这样永远失去她？这样的想法折磨得我彻夜难眠。这关乎我未来的幸福，我决心像个真正的男人一样行动起来。于是就在演出散场后，我尾随夫人到了她的住所，记下地址，第二天一早我就递去了一封信，信中字字深情款款，倾吐我内心的爱慕之情。

这封信我写得大胆又直率——就是用真情写就。

stances of our first meeting — even to the glances which had passed between us. I went so far as to say that I felt assured of her love; while I offered this assurance, and my own intensity of devotion, as two excuses for my otherwise unpardonable conduct. As a third, I spoke of my fear that she might quit the city before I could have the opportunity of a formal introduction. I concluded the most wildly enthusiastic **epistle**[1] ever penned, with a frank declaration of my worldly circumstances — of my **affluence**[2] — and with an offer of my heart and of my hand.

In an agony of expectation I awaited the reply. After what seemed the lapse of a century it came.

Yes, actually came. Romantic as all this may appear, I really received a letter from Madame Lalande — the beautiful, the wealthy, the **idolized**[3] Madame Lalande. Her eyes — her magnificent eyes, had not **belied**[4] her noble heart. Like a true Frenchwoman as she was she had obeyed the frank dictates of her reason — the generous impulses of her nature — despising the **conventional**[5] **pruderies**[6] of the world. She had not **scorned**[7] my proposals. She had not sheltered herself in silence. She had not returned my letter unopened. She had even sent me, in reply, one penned by her own exquisite fingers. It ran thus:

> Monsieur Simpson vill pardonne me for not compose de butefulle tong of his contree so vell as might. It is only de late dat I am arrive, and not yet ave do opportunite for to — l'etudier.
>
> Vid dis apologie for the maniere, I vill now say dat, helas! — Monsieur Simpson ave guess but de too true. Need I say de more? Helas! am I not ready speak de too moshe?
> EUGENIE LALAND.

This noble-spirited note I kissed a million times, and committed, no

我丝毫没有隐瞒——就连我的缺点也一一详述。我还回忆了那天我们在剧院里的第一次浪漫邂逅——甚至还描写了我们之间的眼神交流。我越写越多，还说我真切地感到了她对我的爱；我确信她爱我，而我对她也爱得不能自己，这是我为自己冒昧地去信找的两个借口。除此之外，我表达了我的担心，担心她会在我们正式认识之前就离开这座城市，这是我去信的第三个借口。在这封无比热情奔放的书信末尾，我坦白了我即将继承财产的事情——表明我很富有——同时献上我的真心并向她求婚。

接下来就是焦虑地等待回信。好像过了一个世纪，信来了。

真的，的确是回信。没什么能比这更浪漫了，我真的收到了拉兰德夫人的回信——美丽富有，众人崇拜的拉兰德夫人给我回信了。她的眼睛——她瑰丽的双眸，果然展示了她高尚的内心。她如真正的法国女人般浪漫，直率地说出她的想法——慷慨冲动的天性——撇开世俗的桎梏。她并没有对我的请求嗤之以鼻。她并没有沉默躲避。她并没有把信原封退回。她亲手给我写了一封回信，拿着这封信，我似乎能感受到她那酥手划过的温柔。信中写道：

亲爱的辛普森先生请务必原谅我尚不能灵活使用贵国文字。只因我来贵国不久，仍需找机会多多学习。

很抱歉我不知该用什么方式表达，现在我只能说，唉！——辛普森先生您已经猜到我的想法。我还用多说吗？唉，我还是说得太多了吧？

尤金妮·拉兰德

我把这封高贵的回信亲吻了百万遍，无疑还在

① epistle [i'pisl] *n.* 书信
② affluence ['æfluəns] *n.* 富裕

③ idolize ['aidəlaiz] *v.* 崇拜
④ belie [bi'lai] *v.* 与……不符
⑤ conventional [kən'venʃənəl] *a.* 传统的
⑥ prudery ['pru:dəri] *n.* 拘谨
⑦ scorn [skɔːn] *v.* 鄙视，蔑视

doubt, on its account, a thousand other extravagances that have now escaped my memory. Still Talbot would not return. Alas! could he have formed even the **vaguest**① idea of the suffering his absence had occasioned his friend, would not his sympathizing nature have flown immediately to my relief? Still, however, he came not. I wrote. He replied. He was **detained**② by urgent business — but would shortly return. He begged me not to be impatient — to **moderate**③ my transports — to read **soothing**④ books — to drink nothing stronger than Hock — and to bring the **consolations**⑤ of philosophy to my aid. The fool! if he could not come himself, why, in the name of every thing rational, could he not have enclosed me a letter of presentation? I wrote him again, **entreating**⑥ him to forward one forthwith. My letter was returned by that footman, with the following **endorsement**⑦ in pencil. The *scoundrel* had joined his master in the country:

Left S — yesterday, for parts unknown — did not say where — or when be back — so thought best to return letter, knowing your handwriting, and as how you is always, more or less, in a hurry.

Yours sincerely,

STUBBS.

After this, it is needless to say, that I devoted to the **infernal**⑧ deities both master and valet: — but there was little use in anger, and no consolation at all in complaint.

But I had yet a resource left, in my constitutional **audacity**⑨. Hitherto it had served me well, and I now resolved to make it **avail**⑩ me to the end. Besides, after the correspondence which had passed between us, what act of mere informality could I commit, within bounds, that ought to be regarded as **indecorous**⑪ by Madame Lalande? Since the affair of the letter, I had been in the habit of watching her house, and thus discovered that, about twilight, it was her custom to **promenade**⑫, attended only by a negro in livery, in a public square **overlooked**⑬

① vague [veig] *a.* 含糊的

② detain [di'tein] *v.* 耽搁

③ moderate ['mɔdərət] *v.*
节制，克制

④ soothing ['su:ðiŋ] *a.* 抚
慰的，使人宽心的

⑤ consolation
[ˌkɔnsə'leiʃən] *n.* 安慰

⑥ entreat [in'tri:t] *v.* 请求

⑦ endorsement
[in'dɔ:smənt] *n.* 批注

⑧ infernal [in'fə:nəl] *a.* 阴
间的，恶魔的

⑨ audacity [ɔ:'dæsəti] *n.* 大
胆，冒昧

⑩ avail [ə'veil] *v.* 有益于

⑪ indecorous [in'dekərəs]
a. 不合礼节的，不得体
的

⑫ promenade [ˌprɔmi'nɑ:d]
v. 散步

⑬ overlook [ˌəuvə'luk] *v.*
俯瞰，眺望

这封信上倾尽了千种心思，当时的夸张之举现在已经记不清了。塔尔博特还是没回来。哎呀！他的离开让我这个做朋友的遭受多大痛苦，他一丝一毫也不知道吗？他那天生的同情心去哪儿了？为什么不能马上赶回来解除我的煎熬呢？然而他还是不回来。我写信给他。他回信说，他有急事耽搁了行程——但不久就返回。他请我不要失去耐心——好事多磨——看看书宽宽心——喝些温和的白葡萄酒，别喝烈性酒——哲学的慰藉对我也有帮助。这个笨蛋！他如果自己回不来，无论怎么笨都能想到，给我写一封引荐信不行吗？我再次写信给他提出这个请求。等到的却是男仆给我的退信，信上用铅笔背书。那该死的男仆显然去乡下见他的主人了：

　　已于昨天离开 S 市，将去几处，地址不详，归期不详。识得您的笔迹，因了解您一向有些性急，故返信为妙。

你真诚的，
斯特普斯

　　无须多说，看过之后，我真想咒这主仆二人都去阴间见鬼，但生气也没用，抱怨也无济于事。

　　但我还有一线希望，就靠我这副天生的胆量了。一直以来敢作敢为都给我帮了不少忙，现在我决心再大胆一次。加之我们之间已有书信往来，我如果做一些打破世俗但又不太过激的行为，拉兰德夫人应该不会觉得过分吧？自从收到回信，我就有意观察她的住处，发现她的窗子开向一个公共广场，每到黄昏时分她就由一位穿制服的黑奴陪同在那里散步，广场那儿有一片郁郁葱葱树影斑驳的小树林，就

by her windows. Here, amid the luxuriant and shadowing groves, in the gray gloom of a sweet midsummer evening, I observed my opportunity and accosted her.

The better to **deceive**① the servant in attendance, I did this with the assured air of an old and familiar acquaintance. With a presence of mind truly Parisian, she took the cue at once, and, to greet me, held out the most **bewitchingly**② little of hands. The valet at once fell into the rear, and now, with hearts full to overflowing, we discoursed long and **unreservedly**③ of our love.

As Madame Lalande spoke English even less fluently than she wrote it, our conversation was necessarily in French. In this sweet tongue, so adapted to passion, I gave loose to the **impetuous**④ enthusiasm of my nature, and, with all the **eloquence**⑤ I could command, **besought**⑥ her to consent to an immediate marriage.

At this impatience she smiled. She urged the old story of **decorum**⑦ — that bug-bear which **deters**⑧ so many from **bliss**⑨ until the opportunity for bliss has forever gone by. I had most imprudently made it known among my friends, she observed, that I desired her acquaintance — thus that I did not possess it — thus, again, there was no possibility of concealing the date of our first knowledge of each other. And then she adverted, with a blush, to the extreme **recency**⑩ of this date. To wed immediately would be improper — would be indecorous — would be **outre**⑪. All this she said with a charming air of **naivete**⑫ which **enraptured**⑬ while it **grieved**⑭ and convinced me. She went even so far as to accuse me, laughingly, of rashness — of **imprudence**⑮. She bade me remember that I really even knew not who she was — what were her prospects, her connections, her standing in society. She begged me, but with a sigh, to reconsider my proposal, and termed my love an **infatuation**⑯ — a will o' the wisp — a fancy or fantasy of the moment — a **baseless**⑰ and unstable creation rather of the imagination than of the heart. These things she uttered as the shadows of the sweet twilight gathered darkly and more darkly around us — and then, with a gentle pressure of her fairy-like hand, overthrew, in a

① deceive [di'si:v] v. 欺骗

② bewitchingly [bi'witʃiŋli] ad. 迷人地

③ unreservedly [ˌʌnri'zə:vdli] ad. 毫无保留地

④ impetuous [im'petjuəs] a. 冲动的，热烈的

⑤ eloquence ['eləkwəns] n. 口才

⑥ besought [bi'sɔ:t] v. （beseech 的过去式）恳求

⑦ decorum [di'kɔ:rəm] n. 礼仪，礼节

⑧ deter [di'tə:] v. 阻拦

⑨ bliss [blis] n. 福气

⑩ recency ['ri:sənsi] n. 最近

⑪ outre ['u:trei] a. 越轨的

⑫ naivete [na:'i:vtei] n. 天真烂漫

⑬ enrapture [in'ræptʃə] v. 使着迷

⑭ grieve [gri:v] v. 使苦恼

⑮ imprudence [im'pru:dəns] n. 轻率，鲁莽

⑯ infatuation [inˌfætju'eiʃən] n. 迷恋

⑰ baseless ['beislis] a. 无根据的

在那个甜蜜的仲夏傍晚，星光朦胧，我看时机已到，壮了壮胆子就走过去和她搭话了。

为了更好地骗过她的仆人，我摆出一副气定神闲的样子，用熟识已久的朋友的语气和她打了招呼。定是因为她那巴黎人特有的机智，她马上明白了我的用意，还伸出她那最迷人的纤小玉手向我问候。她的仆人马上向身后退去，现在我们终于可以毫无保留地互相倾吐那早已满溢出心房的爱慕之情了。

拉兰德夫人的英语说起来还不及写得顺畅，于是我们就用法语交流。这浪漫的语言注定就是为爱情而生的，我将我那热情冲动的性情挥洒得淋漓尽致，极尽雄辩之辞，恳求她能答应马上和我结婚。

我焦急地等待着她的回答，她却微笑着表示刚认识就谈婚论嫁有些不妥——我就担心她这么想，这老套的说辞不知耽误了多少幸福，我就怕错过了这个时机就永远与她失之交臂了。她认为我鲁莽地把想认识她这件事情搞得尽人皆知——这说明我们此前并不相识——已经不可能再向大家隐瞒我们第一次认识的日子了。一提到我们第一次相识才不过几天，她就粉面含羞。鉴于这样的情况，她认为马上结婚是不合时宜的——也不符合传统礼节——更不合体面。她说这些话时散发着一种单纯而迷人的气息，使我的内心狂喜不已；然而她说服了我，这又令我悲伤万分。她甚至笑着责怪我的轻率——做事不加考虑。她还提醒我注意，我甚至还不知道她是谁——她的财产状况、她的亲戚朋友、她的社会地位。她叹了口气，请求我重新考虑我的求婚，说我所谓的爱情只是一时的激情——一时的冲动——一时的想象或幻想——全是头脑里毫无根据不切实际的臆造而非真心。暮光渐逝，树影婆娑，夜色笼罩着我俩，她说完那些话，她用那仙子般的玉手轻轻拍了拍我，这甜

single sweet instant, all the argumentative fabric she had reared.

I replied as best I could — as only a true lover can. I spoke at length, and perseveringly of my devotion, of my passion — of her exceeding beauty, and of my own enthusiastic admiration. In conclusion, I **dwelt**, with a convincing energy, **upon**[1] the perils that **encompass**[2] the course of love — that course of true love that never did run smooth — and thus **deduced**[3] the manifest danger of rendering that course unnecessarily long.

This latter argument seemed finally to soften the **rigor**[4] of her determination. She **relented**[5]; but there was yet an obstacle, she said, which she felt assured I had not properly considered. This was a delicate point — for a woman to urge, especially so; in mentioning it, she saw that she must make a sacrifice of her feelings; still, for me, every sacrifice should be made. She alluded to the topic of age. Was I aware — was I fully aware of the **discrepancy**[6] between us? That the age of the husband, should surpass by a few years — even by fifteen or twenty — the age of the wife, was regarded by the world as **admissible**[7], and, indeed, as even proper, but she had always entertained the belief that the years of the wife should never exceed in number those of the husband. A discrepancy of this unnatural kind gave rise, too frequently, alas! to a life of unhappiness. Now she was aware that my own age did not exceed two and twenty; and I, on the contrary, perhaps, was not aware that the years of my Eugenie extended very considerably beyond that sum.

About all this there was a nobility of soul — a dignity of **candor**[8] — which delighted — which **enchanted**[9] me — which eternally riveted my chains. I could scarcely restrain the excessive transport which possessed me.

"My sweetest Eugenie," I cried, "what is all this about which you are discoursing? Your years surpass in some measure my own. But what then? The customs of the world are so many conventional follies. To those who love as ourselves, in what respect differs a year from an hour? I am twenty-two, you say, granted: indeed, you may as well call me, at once, twenty-three. Now you yourself, my dearest Eugenie, can have numbered no more than — can have numbered no more than — no more than — than — than — than — "

美的时刻推翻了她刚才那整套理论。

我像真正热恋中的男子那样向她展开了激烈的语言攻势。我一再向她倾诉我的爱恋，我的热情——盛赞她的美，吐露我对她的倾心爱慕。最后我以十分令人信服的语气告诉她求爱之路充满冒险——真爱之旅充满忐忑——为了省去不必要的弯路，我们还是放弃她那套理论，尽早结婚吧。

在我的不懈努力下她似乎终于放松了对陈规的坚守。她的态度缓和了下来；但她说还有一个问题，她认为我肯定没有认真考虑过。这是一个敏感的话题——由女士主动提出更是为难；但为了我，她认为什么牺牲都是值得的，所以还是牺牲自己的感受，把这个问题提出来了。她委婉地提出了年龄的问题。她问我是否知道——完全了解我俩之间的年龄差距。通常丈夫的年龄应该长妻子几岁——哪怕年长十五、二十岁，也能被世人所接受，甚至被视为得体，而且她一直坚信是妻子的年龄至少不能超过丈夫的年龄。哎呀！有多少夫妻就因为年龄不合适而一生不幸。如今她知道我的年龄不过二十二岁，而我或许并不知道我亲爱的尤金妮年纪比这个数字大得多。

听到这些，我欣喜若狂，死心塌地臣服于她高贵的灵魂和坦率的人格，再也抑制不住内心强烈的感情。

"我最亲爱的尤金妮，"我大声喊道，"你说的这些都算什么呢？与我相比，你是年长几岁。但那又怎样？世人行事总有许多愚蠢的条条框框。对于我们这样相爱的人，一年和一个小时有什么差别吗？你说得没错，我二十二岁；但是我马上就二十三岁了。而你，我最亲爱的尤金妮，肯定只比我大不过——肯定只比我大不过——大不过——不过——不过——不过——"

① dwell upon 细想，详述
② encompass [in'kʌmpəs] v. 包含
③ deduce [di'dju:s] v. 推断

④ rigor ['rigə] n. 苛刻
⑤ relent [ri'lent] v. 变温和

⑥ discrepancy [dis'krepənsi] n. 差别

⑦ admissible [əd'misəbl] a. 可接受的

⑧ candor ['kændə] n. 坦白，直率
⑨ enchant [in'tʃɑ:nt] v. 使陶醉，使入迷

Here I paused for an instant, in the expectation that Madame Lalande would interrupt me by supplying her true age. But a Frenchwoman is seldom direct, and has always, by way of answer to an embarrassing query, some little practical reply of her own. In the present instance, Eugenie, who for a few moments past had seemed to be searching for something in her bosom, at length let fall upon the grass a **miniature**①, which I immediately picked up and presented to her.

"Keep it!" she said, with one of her most **ravishing**② smiles. "Keep it for my sake — for the sake of her whom it too **flatteringly**③ represents. Besides, upon the back of the **trinket**④ you may discover, perhaps, the very information you seem to desire. It is now, to be sure, growing rather dark — but you can examine it at your leisure in the morning. In the meantime, you shall be my **escort**⑤ home to-night. My friends are about holding a little musical levee. I can promise you, too, some good singing. We French are not nearly so **punctilious**⑥ as you Americans, and I shall have no difficulty in **smuggling**⑦ you in, in the character of an old acquaintance."

With this, she took my arm, and I attended her home. The mansion was quite a fine one, and, I believe, furnished in good taste. Of this latter point, however, I am scarcely qualified to judge; for it was just dark as we arrived; and in American mansions of the better sort lights seldom, during the heat of summer, make their appearance at this, the most pleasant period of the day. In about an hour after my arrival, to be sure, a single shaded solar lamp was lit in the principal drawing-room; and this apartment, I could thus see, was arranged with unusual good taste and even **splendor**⑧; but two other rooms of the suite, and in which the company chiefly assembled, remained, during the whole evening, in a very agreeable shadow. This is a well-conceived custom, giving the party at least a choice of light or shade, and one which our friends over the water could not do better than immediately adopt.

The evening thus spent was unquestionably the most delicious of my life. Madame Lalande had not **overrated**⑨ the musical abilities of her friends; and the singing I here heard I had never heard excelled in any private circle out of

我在这里停顿了几下，期待着拉兰德夫人会打断我，告诉我她的真实年龄。但法国女人回答这样尴尬问题的时候向来委婉，而且总有些实用的应对之策。刚才尤金妮一直在胸前摸什么东西，摸了半天，这会儿终于摸到了，还掉在了地上，我马上帮她拾起递给她，原来是一枚袖珍肖像。

"送给你！"她说，带着那最娇羞的微笑，"为了画像中的人而珍惜它吧，这画像比我本人要美。并且它背面的信息或许能帮你解除疑惑。当然，现在天色已晚——明早你可以尽情查看。今晚你可以护送我回家。我的朋友们正要举行一个小型音乐招待会。我敢向你保证能欣赏到美妙的音乐。我们法国人不像你们美国人那么拘礼，我可以轻易把你带进去，就当你是我的老朋友。"

于是，她挽着我的手臂，我们一起回到了她家。她的宅邸十分华丽，装修也很有品位。其实我们到达时刚刚天黑，我几乎还不怎么能看得清内部的摆设；在美国很多较高雅的公馆里，盛夏时节每天的这个时候都是躲避暑热最好的一段时间，所以都像这样很少点灯。我们进屋肯定有一个小时了，客厅里才点起一盏带灯罩的白炽灯；我这才看清这间屋子里的摆设品位不凡，几近华美；但客人们大多整晚都聚在另两个套间，而那两个房间整晚都处在朦胧的阴影中。这是一个考虑周全的传统，参加聚会的人至少可以自由选择或明或暗的房间，大洋彼岸来的巴黎人也只好入乡随俗了。

这无疑是个令我回味一生的美好夜晚。拉兰德夫人对她朋友们音乐天赋的夸赞并不过分；除了在维也纳，我从没在哪个私人社交圈里听见过如此美妙的

① miniature ['miniətʃə] *n.* 袖珍画，小画饰
② ravishing ['rævɪʃɪŋ] *a.* 令人陶醉的
③ flatteringly ['flætərɪŋli] *ad.* 奉承地，讨好地
④ trinket ['trɪŋkit] *n.* 小饰品
⑤ escort ['eskɔːt] *n.* 陪同，护送者
⑥ punctilious [pʌŋk'tiliəs] *a.* 拘谨的
⑦ smuggle ['smʌgl] *v.* 偷偷携带
⑧ splendor ['splendə] *n.* 壮丽
⑨ overrate [ˌəuvə'reit] *v.* 高估

Vienna. The instrumental performers were many and of superior talents. The **vocalists**① were chiefly ladies, and no individual sang less than well. At length, upon a **peremptory**② call for "Madame Lalande," she arose at once, without affectation or demur, from the **chaise longue**③ upon which she had sat by my side, and, accompanied by one or two gentlemen and her female friend of the opera, repaired to the piano in the main drawing-room. I would have escorted her myself, but felt that, under the circumstances of my introduction to the house, I had better remain unobserved where I was. I was thus deprived of the pleasure of seeing, although not of hearing, her sing.

The impression she produced upon the company seemed electrical but the effect upon myself was something even more. I know not how adequately to describe it. It arose in part, no doubt, from the sentiment of love with which I was **imbued**④; but chiefly from my conviction of the extreme sensibility of the singer. It is beyond the reach of art to endow either air or recitative with more **impassioned**⑤ expression than was hers. Her utterance of the romance in Otello — the tone with which she gave the words "Sul mio sasso," in the Capuletti — is ringing in my memory yet. Her lower tones were absolutely miraculous. Her voice embraced three complete **octaves**⑥, extending from the **contralto**⑦ D to the D upper **soprano**⑧, and, though sufficiently powerful to have filled the San Carlos, executed, with the minutest precision, every difficulty of vocal composition — ascending and descending scales, **cadences**⑨, or fiorituri. In the final of the Somnambula, she brought about a most remarkable effect at the words:

> *Ah! non guinge uman pensiero*
> *Al contento ond 'io son piena.*

Here, in imitation of Malibran, she modified the original phrase of Bellini, so as to let her voice descend to the tenor G, when, by a rapid transition, she struck the G above the **treble**⑩ **stave**⑪, springing over an interval of two octaves.

① vocalist ['vəukəlist] *n*. 歌手

② peremptory [pə'remptəri] *a*. 强制的，专横的

③ chaise longue 贵妃椅，躺椅

④ imbue [im'bju:] *n*. 使充满

⑤ impassioned [im'pæʃənd] *a*. 充满激情的

⑥ octaves ['ɔktiv] *n*. 八度音，八度音阶

⑦ contralto [kən'træltəu] *n*. 女低音

⑧ soprano [sə'prɑ:nəu] *n*. 女高音

⑨ cadence ['keidəns] *n*. 节奏

⑩ treble ['trebl] *a*. 最高声部的

⑪ stave [steiv] *n*. 五线谱

歌喉。有好几位演奏了乐器，真是精彩绝伦。演唱的主要是女士们，每首歌曲都十分优美。最后，传来了"有请拉兰德夫人"的邀请，她并不扭捏，从我们坐的长靠椅上优雅起身，由一两位绅士护送，在剧院遇见的那位女伴陪同下走向主客室的钢琴。本来我想和她同去，但是鉴于我是以普通朋友的身份来到这里做客的，最好还是别太招摇为妙。如此一来我就无缘一睹她演唱时候的风采了，但是好在还能有她那美妙的歌声入耳。

她的歌声在客人中产生了电击般的震撼，而我受到的震撼则更为强烈。我甚至不知该如何恰当地形容当时的感受。毫无疑问，那种感受部分来源于我内心热烈的爱情，但我想，主要还是因为歌手本身的感染力打动了我。她吟唱的咏叹调和宣叙调慷慨激昂的演绎已经超越其本身的艺术感染力。她演唱《奥赛罗》片段时嗓音中洋溢的浪漫，她演唱《凯普莱特》中那句"sul mio sasso"时深情的语调，至今仍在我耳畔萦绕。她的低音简直妙不可言。她的音域宽到可以从女低音 D 到女高音 D 横跨三个八度，嗓音高亢可以穿透整个圣卡洛斯剧院，她把每个难唱的小节都拿捏得十分精准——音阶忽升偶降，节奏轻缓慢急，花音驾轻就熟。在《梦游女》的最后一章，她用优美的旋律将歌词诠释得淋漓尽致：

啊！此刻我的内心欢喜，
皆由仁慈上帝赐予。

此处她模仿玛丽波兰，对贝里尼的原曲做了改动，她先降到中音 G，然后陡然上升到高音 G，瞬间完美地跨越了两个八度。

Upon rising from the piano after these miracles of vocal execution, she resumed her seat by my side; when I expressed to her, in terms of the deepest enthusiasm, my delight at her performance. Of my surprise I said nothing, and yet was I most **unfeignedly**① surprised; for a certain feebleness, or rather a certain **tremulous**② **indecision**③ of voice in ordinary conversation, had prepared me to anticipate that, in singing, she would not **acquit**④ herself with any remarkable ability.

Our conversation was now long, **earnest**⑤, uninterrupted, and totally unreserved. She made me **relate**⑥ many of the earlier **passages**⑦ of my life, and listened with breathless attention to every word of the narrative. I concealed nothing — felt that I had a right to conceal nothing — from her confiding affection. Encouraged by her candor upon the delicate point of her age, I entered, with perfect frankness, not only into a detail of my many minor **vices**⑧, but made full confession of those moral and even of those physical **infirmities**⑨, the disclosure of which, in demanding so much higher a degree of courage, is so much surer an evidence of love. I touched upon my college **indiscretions**⑩ — upon my extravagances — upon my **carousals**⑪ — upon my debts — upon my **flirtations**⑫. I even went so far as to speak of a slightly **hectic**⑬ cough with which, at one time, I had been troubled — of a chronic **rheumatism**⑭ — of a twinge of **hereditary**⑮ **gout**⑯ — and, in conclusion, of the disagreeable and inconvenient, but hitherto carefully concealed, weakness of my eyes.

"Upon this latter point," said Madame Lalande, laughingly, "you have been surely **injudicious**⑰ in coming to confession; for, without the confession, I take it for granted that no one would have accused you of the crime. By the by," she continued, "have you any **recollection**⑱ — " and here I fancied that a blush, even through the gloom of the apartment, became distinctly visible upon her cheek — "have you any recollection, mon cher ami of this little ocular assistant, which now depends from my neck?"

As she spoke she twirled in her fingers the **identical**⑲ double eye-glass which had so overwhelmed me with confusion at the opera.

① unfeignedly [ʌn'feindli] *ad.* 由衷地

② tremulous ['temjuləs] *a.* 颤抖的

③ indecision [.indi'siʒən] *n.* 迟疑不决

④ acquit [ə'kwit] *v.* 表现

⑤ earnest ['əːnist] *a.* 真挚的

⑥ relate [ri'leit] *v.* 叙述

⑦ passage ['pæsidʒ] *n.* 旅行；（时间等的）消逝

⑧ vice [vais] *n.* 缺点

⑨ infirmity [in'fəːmti] *n.* 疾病

⑩ indiscretion [.indis'kreʃən] *a.* 轻率，言行失检

⑪ carousal [kə'rauzəl] *n.* 狂欢宴会

⑫ flirtation [fləː'teiʃən] *n.* 调情取乐

⑬ hectic ['hektik] *a.* 肺病的

⑭ rheumatism ['ruːmətizəm] *n.* 风湿病

⑮ hereditary [hi'reditəri] *a.* 遗传的

⑯ gout [gaut] *n.* 痛风

⑰ injudicious [.indʒuː'diʃəs] *a.* 不明智的

⑱ recollection [.rekə'lekʃən] *n.* 回忆

⑲ identical [ai'dentikəl] *a.* 完全相同的

展示完神奇的歌唱绝技，她从钢琴旁起身，重又回到我的身旁落座；我表达了对她唱功最真挚的赞美以及对她表演的赞叹。而我心里倍感惊讶却没有说出口的是，平时对话时她的声音有些柔弱，甚至有些微颤，底气不足，没想到唱歌时却能有如此惊人的表现力。

接下来再没人打扰了，我们进行了最真诚的毫无保留的长谈。她让我讲述了早年生活的许多经历，全神贯注倾听着我的每一句话。我对她毫无保留——我有权向她表露一切——她的依赖和深情也使我无法对她保留。既然她对如年龄这样的敏感问题都如此坦率，我坦白向她细数了许多无关大局的坏习惯，承认了所有精神上甚至身体上的缺陷，只有更加真切的爱情才能给予我莫大的勇气向她如此袒露心胸。我还谈及大学时的放荡不羁，挥霍无度，纵欲狂欢，债台高筑，以及许多风流情事。我越说越远，甚至还提到曾经有一次发烧后引起了轻微的咳嗽，提到我有类风湿病，遗传性通风令我偶感疼痛，最后终于还是说到了那我一直小心隐藏的，令我不快又给我带来不便的弱视。

"关于弱视这点，"拉兰德夫人笑着说，"你大可不必承认；因为如果你不说，我绝对看不出你眼神不好。对了，顺便提一下，"她接着说，"你是否记得——"说到此处，透过室内昏暗的光她那羞红的脸颊依稀可见——"你是否记得我这位亲爱的朋友，这个帮我看清东西的小助手呢，就是我脖子上挂着的这副眼镜？"

说着，她用手指把玩着那副她在剧场里使用的眼镜，当时就是这副眼镜让我被她看得心慌意乱。

"Full well — alas! do I remember it," I exclaimed, pressing passionately the delicate hand which offered the glasses for my inspection. They formed a complex and magnificent toy, richly **chased**① and **filigreed**②, and gleaming with jewels, which, even in the deficient light, I could not help perceiving were of high value.

"Eh bien! mon ami," she resumed with a certain empressment of manner that rather surprised me — "Eh bien! mon ami, you have earnestly besought of me a favor which you have been pleased to **denominate**③ priceless. You have demanded of me my hand upon the morrow. Should I yield to your **entreaties**④ — and, I may add, to the pleadings of my own bosom — would I not be entitled to demand of you a very — a very little boon in return?"

"Name it!" I exclaimed with an energy that had nearly drawn upon us the observation of the company, and restrained by their presence alone from throwing myself impetuously at her feet. "Name it, my beloved, my Eugenie, my own! — name it! — but, alas! it is already yielded ere named."

"You shall conquer, then, mon ami," said she, "for the sake of the Eugenie whom you love, this little weakness which you have at last confessed — this weakness more moral than physical — and which, let me assure you, is so unbecoming the nobility of your real nature — so inconsistent with the candor of your usual character — and which, if permitted further control, will assuredly involve you, sooner or later, in some very disagreeable **scrape**⑤. You shall conquer, for my sake, this affectation which leads you, as you yourself acknowledge, to the **tacit**⑥ or implied **denial**⑦ of your infirmity of vision. For, this infirmity you virtually deny, in refusing to employ the customary means for its relief. You will understand me to say, then, that I wish you to wear spectacles; — ah, hush! — you have already consented to wear them, for my sake. You shall accept the little toy which I now hold in

① chase [tʃeis] *v.* 雕镂
② filigree ['filigri:] *v.* 用金银丝细工饰品装饰

③ denominate [di'nɔmineit] *v.* 把……称作

④ entreaty [in'tri:ti] *n.* 请求，恳求

⑤ scrape [skreip] *n.* 尴尬处境
⑥ tacit ['tæsit] *a.* 默认的
⑦ denial [di'naiəl] *n.* 否认

"当然记得——哎呀！简直记忆犹新。"我叹道。她把眼镜递给我看，我赶忙热情地抓住那双拿着眼镜的玉手。这副眼镜做工复杂，设计华丽，宛若一件工艺品，镜框密密地堆着金丝，镶嵌着夺目的珠宝，即便是在昏暗的灯光下，我也能看出它绝非凡品。

"那么，好吧！我亲爱的朋友，"她继续说，她那女王般不容置疑的口吻令我吃了一惊——"好吧！我亲爱的朋友，你诚挚地向我索要一样东西，一件你称之为无价的礼物。你要我明天就把终身托付给你。如果我答应你的请求——或许也可以说是遵从我内心的愿望，那么我是不是也有权向你提出一个非常非常小的请求作为回报呢？"

"尽管提！"我大声说道，我的惊呼声让周围的客人都看向我们这边，若不是有诸多客人在场，我真想当场就不管不顾地跪在她脚下。"有什么请求尽管说，我亲爱的，我的尤金妮，我的最爱！——你要什么！尽管说吧！你要什么我都答应。"

"那么，我的朋友，我说了，"她说，"为了你深爱的尤金妮，请克服你的弱点吧。你最后坦白弱视这一缺点已经不仅是身体上的问题了，它已经变成你的心理问题了——这么和你说吧，这非常不符合你高贵的本性，与你一贯坦率的性格也相差甚远——若不防微杜渐，迟早会给你带来不良后果。就算为了我，你就克服这份误导你的虚荣吧，你自己也承认了，你一直在有意无意地回避你弱视的事实。你完全否认自己视力的缺陷，拒绝采用常规的方法调节视力，这已经是一种心理疾病。所以我现在说希望你能佩戴眼镜，你能理解吗？——啊，嘘！——你说过了，为了我，你已经答应戴眼镜了。那么就请你接受我手里的这副眼镜吧，它虽然对视力大有助益，但作为首饰它并不

my hand, and which, though admirable as an aid to vision, is really of no very immense value as a **gem**①. You perceive that, by a **trifling**② **modification**③ thus — or thus — it can be adapted to the eyes in the form of spectacles, or worn in the waistcoat pocket as an eye-glass. It is in the former mode, however, and habitually, that you have already consented to wear it for my sake."

This request — must I confess it? — confused me in no little degree. But the condition with which it was coupled rendered hesitation, of course, a matter altogether out of the question.

"It is done!" I cried, with all the enthusiasm that I could **muster**④ at the moment. "It is done — it is most cheerfully agreed. I sacrifice every feeling for your sake. To-night I wear this dear eye-glass, as an eye-glass, and upon my heart; but with the earliest dawn of that morning which gives me the pleasure of calling you wife, I will place it upon my — upon my nose, — and there wear it ever afterward, in the less romantic, and less fashionable, but certainly in the more **serviceable**⑤, form which you desire."

Our conversation now turned upon the details of our arrangements for the morrow. Talbot, I learned from my **betrothed**⑥, had just arrived in town. I was to see him at once, and procure a carriage. The **soiree**⑦ would scarcely break up before two; and by this hour the vehicle was to be at the door, when, in the confusion occasioned by the departure of the company, Madame L. could easily enter it unobserved. We were then to call at the house of a **clergyman**⑧ who would be in waiting; there be married, drop Talbot, and proceed on a short tour to the East, leaving the fashionable world at home to make whatever comments upon the matter it thought best.

Having planned all this, I immediately took leave, and went in search of Talbot, but, on the way, I could not **refrain**⑨ from stepping into a hotel, for the purpose of inspecting the miniature; and this I did by the powerful aid of the glasses. The countenance was a surpassingly beautiful one! Those

① gem [dʒem] *n.* 宝石，珍
宝

② trifling ['traifliŋ] *a.* 微不
足道的

③ modification
[ˌmɔdifi'keiʃən] *n.* 修改，
修正

④ muster ['mʌstə] *v.* 鼓起，
激起

⑤ serviceable ['sə:visəbl] *a.*
有用的，耐用的

⑥ betrothed [bi'trəuðd] *n.*
未婚妻

⑦ soiree ['swɑ:rei] *n.*〈法〉
晚会，社交聚会

⑧ clergyman ['klə:dʒimən]
n. 牧师，教士

⑨ refrain [ˌri:'frein] *v.* 忍
住，克制

值什么大价钱。你看，这么轻轻一掰就开，一折就合，它能变成双片眼镜轻松戴在眼睛上，也可以变成单片眼镜装在上衣口袋里。然而我希望你能习惯用前一种方法把它戴在眼睛上。哎呀，为了我，你已经答应这么做了不是吗。"

这一要求——让我说实话？——真的令我困惑不已。她在当时的情形下提出这个请求，当然容不得我有半点犹豫。

"我答应！"我用尽全身的激情大喊道，"没问题——我欣然接受。虽然我对眼镜没什么好感，但为了你我可以克服一切。今晚，我把这亲爱的眼镜变成单片眼镜装在口袋里感受我的心跳；明天一大早，当我荣幸地娶你为妻，我就第一时间把它放在　　　　我的——我的鼻梁上——从此以后不再取下，如你所愿，虽然这种佩戴方式让我显得不那么浪漫时尚，但一定更加方便耐用。"

接下来我们就开始谈明天的详细安排。我从未来妻子口中得知，塔尔博特刚刚回城。我现在需要马上去见他，还要准备一辆马车。晚会两点前不会结束；到时塔尔博特事先准备好的马车就等在门口，趁着宾客们纷纷离开时的混乱，拉兰德夫人可以不被察觉地溜进马车。然后我们找一所教堂，会有牧师在那儿等我们；婚礼秘密举行，我们把塔尔博特送回家，然后往东做一场短途旅行，让上流社交圈的人们尽情猜测评论去吧。

事不宜迟，我马上离开晚会去找塔尔博特，但是在路上我忍不住走进一家旅店好仔细查看那枚小像；有了那副眼镜，我看得清清楚楚。那容貌足以闭月羞花！炯炯有神的大眼睛！玲珑挺拔的希腊鼻！

large **luminous**① eyes! — that proud Grecian nose! — those dark luxuriant curls! — "Ah!" said I, exultingly to myself, "this is indeed the speaking image of my beloved!" I turned the reverse, and discovered the words — "Eugenie Lalande — aged twenty-seven years and seven months."

I found Talbot at home, and proceeded at once to **acquaint**② him with my good fortune. He professed excessive astonishment, of course, but congratulated me most **cordially**③, and **proffered**④ every assistance in his power. In a word, we carried out our arrangement to the letter, and, at two in the morning, just ten minutes after the ceremony, I found myself in a close carriage with Madame Lalande — with Mrs. Simpson, I should say — and driving at a great rate out of town, in a direction Northeast by North, half-North.

It had been determined for us by Talbot, that, as we were to be up all night, we should make our first stop at C —, a village about twenty miles from the city, and there get an early breakfast and some repose, before proceeding upon our route. At four **precisely**⑤, therefore, the carriage drew up at the door of the principal inn. I handed my **adored**⑥ wife out, and ordered breakfast forthwith. In the meantime we were shown into a small **parlor**⑦, and sat down.

It was now nearly if not altogether daylight; and, as I gazed, enraptured, at the angel by my side, the singular idea came, all at once, into my head, that this was really the very first moment since my acquaintance with the celebrated loveliness of Madame Lalande, that I had enjoyed a near inspection of that loveliness by daylight at all.

"And now, mon ami," said she, taking my hand, and so interrupting this train of reflection, "and now, mon cher ami, since we are **indissolubly**⑧ one — since I have yielded to your passionate entreaties, and performed my portion of our agreement — I presume you have not forgotten that you also have a little favor to bestow — a little promise which it is your intention to keep. Ah! let me see! Let me remember! Yes; full easily do I call to mind the precise words of the dear promise you made to Eugenie last night. Listen! You spoke thus: 'It is

① luminous ['lju:minəs] *a.*
明亮的

② acquaint [ə'kweint] *v.* 使
知道

③ cordially ['kɔːdjəli] *ad.*
诚挚地

④ proffer ['prɔfə] *v.* 提供

⑤ precisely [pri'saisli] *ad.*
精确地

⑥ adore [ə'dɔ:] *v.* 爱慕

⑦ parlor ['pɑːlə] *n.* 客厅

⑧ indissolubly
[,indi'sɔljubli] *ad.* 不能
分离地

浓密乌黑的长卷发！——"啊！"我得意地自言自语，"我最亲爱的，你真如传说中那般美丽啊！"翻过来看到小像背面写着——"尤金妮·拉兰德，时年二十七岁零七个月。"

塔尔博特在家，找到他后我马上向他讲述了我的艳遇。他表现出极度的惊讶，但是仍然送上了诚挚的祝福，还表示他会鼎力相助。闲言少叙，计划顺利进行，凌晨两点，舞会刚结束十分钟，我就和拉兰德夫人——不，应该说是辛普森夫人——乘着一辆舒适的马车朝着东北偏北的方向一路狂奔驶出城外。

塔尔博特帮我们计划好了，今夜注定无眠，我们首先将马车驶到距离市中心大约二十英里的 C 庄园，稍事休息，吃点早餐，以便继续赶路。因此按照计划，马车跑到四点整就来到一家大客栈门口。我一边把爱妻扶下马车，一边命人准备早餐。我们被引到一个小会客厅坐了下来。

天色虽未大亮，东方却已见白；我抑制不住内心狂喜，凝视着旁边的天使，兀然间心中闪过一个奇怪的想法：自从我认识这位漂亮可爱又知名的拉兰德夫人以来，这是我第一次也是唯一一次在白天这么近距离地观察这位美人。

"看够了吧，我的朋友，"她拉着我的手说，打断了我的思绪，"别看了，我亲爱的朋友，既然现在你我已经结为连理——既然我已经接受了你热烈的追求，完成了我的诺言——我想你应该没有忘记曾经答应过我的那件小事吧——那个你决心践行的小小诺言。啊！让我想想！我记起来了！对；你昨晚对亲爱的尤金妮许下的承诺我一字没忘，字字在耳畔回响。听！你说：'没问题——我欣然接受。虽然我

done! — it is most cheerfully agreed! I sacrifice every feeling for your sake. To-night I wear this dear eye-glass as an eye-glass, and upon my heart; but with the earliest dawn of that morning which gives me the privilege of calling you wife, I will place it upon my — upon my nose, — and there wear it ever afterward, in the less romantic, and less fashionable, but certainly in the more serviceable, form which you desire.' These were the exact words, my beloved husband, were they not?"

"They were," I said; "you have an excellent memory; and assuredly, my beautiful Eugenie, there is no disposition on my part to **evade**① the performance of the **trivial**② promise they imply. See! Behold! they are becoming — rather — are they not?" And here, having arranged the glasses in the ordinary form of spectacles, I applied them **gingerly**③ in their proper position; while Madame Simpson, adjusting her cap, and folding her arms, sat bolt **upright**④ in her chair, in a somewhat stiff and **prim**⑤, and indeed, in a somewhat **undignified**⑥ position.

"Goodness gracious me!" I exclaimed, almost at the very instant that the rim of the spectacles had settled upon my nose — "My goodness gracious me! — why, what can be the matter with these glasses?" and taking them quickly off, I wiped them carefully with a silk handkerchief, and adjusted them again.

But if, in the first instance, there had occurred something which occasioned me surprise, in the second, this surprise became elevated into astonishment; and this astonishment was profound — was extreme — indeed I may say it was horrific. What, in the name of everything hideous, did this mean? Could I believe my eyes? — could I? — that was the question. Was that — was that — was that **rouge**⑦? And were those — and were those — were those wrinkles, upon the **visage**⑧ of Eugenie Lalande? And oh! Jupiter, and every one of the gods and goddesses, little and big! what — what — what — what had become of her teeth? I dashed the spectacles violently to the ground, and, leaping to my feet, stood erect in the middle of the floor, confronting Mrs. Simpson, with my

对眼镜没什么好感，但为了你我可以克服一切。今晚，我把这亲爱的眼镜变成单片眼镜装在口袋里感受我的心跳；明天早晨，当我荣幸地娶你为妻，我就第一时间把它放在我的——我的鼻梁上，——从此以后不再取下，如你所愿，虽然这种佩戴方式让我显得不那么浪漫时尚，但一定更加方便耐用。'这是你的原话，我亲爱的夫君，还记得吗？"

"当然没忘，"我说，"你的记忆力可真好；确实，我美丽的尤金妮，我绝对无意逃避兑现昨晚所说的那个小小的诺言。看！注意看！它挺好看的——真的——不是吗？"说着我就把镜框掰开形成可以佩戴的眼镜，小心翼翼地把它放在鼻梁上；这时，辛普森夫人整理了一下帽子，双臂抱在胸前，僵直地坐在椅子上，十分拘谨又一本正经的样子看起来真的有失尊严。

"我的上帝老天啊！"眼镜刚刚碰到我的鼻梁，我就忍不住惊呼道——"天哪，我的仁慈的上帝啊！——怎么回事，这副眼镜有什么毛病吧？"我一把摘下眼镜，用真丝手帕认真地擦了又擦，重新戴了回去。

可是，若说第一次戴上眼镜看到的画面令我吃惊，那么第二次就升级为惊愕了；惊愕到了极点——实际上可以说我受到了惊吓。这奇丑无比的画面到底是怎么回事？我还能相信我的眼睛吗？——能相信吗？——心里只剩这个问题。那是——那是——那是胭脂吗？还有啊，那些——那些——那些爬在尤金妮·拉兰德脸上的是皱纹吗？啊！哦！爱神啊，大大小小的天神啊，女神啊！她的——她的——她的——她的牙去哪儿了？我把眼镜使劲摔在地上，一跃而

① evade [i'veid] *v.* 逃避，回避
② trivial ['triviəl] *a.* 琐碎的，无关紧要的
③ gingerly [dʒindʒəli] *ad.* 小心翼翼地
④ upright ['ʌprait] *ad.* 笔直地
⑤ prim [prim] *a.* 端端正正的
⑥ undignified [ʌn'dignifaid] *a.* 不像样子的，不庄重的
⑦ rouge [ru:ʒ] *n.* 胭脂
⑧ visage ['vizidʒ] *n.* 面貌，容貌

arms set a-kimbo, and **grinning**[1] and **foaming**[2], but, at the same time, utterly speechless with terror and with rage.

Now I have already said that Madame Eugenie Lalande — that is to say, Simpson — spoke the English language but very little better than she wrote it, and for this reason she very properly never attempted to speak it upon ordinary occasions. But rage will carry a lady to any extreme; and in the present cose it carried Mrs. Simpson to the very extraordinary extreme of attempting to hold a conversation in a tongue that she did not altogether understand.

"Vell, Monsieur," said she, after surveying me, in great apparent astonishment, for some moments — "Vell, Monsieur? — and vat den? — vat de matter now? Is it de dance of de Saint itusse dat you ave? If not like me, vat for vy buy de pig in the poke?"

"You **wretch**[3]!" said I, catching my breath — "you — you — you **villainous**[4] old **hag**[5]!"

"Ag? — ole? — me not so ver ole, after all! Me not one single day more dan de eighty-doo."

"Eighty-two!" I ejaculated, staggering to the wall — "eighty-two hundred thousand **baboons**[6]! The miniature said twenty-seven years and seven months!"

"To be sure! — dat is so! — ver true! but den de portraite has been take for dese fifty-five year. Ven I go marry my segonde usbande, Monsieur Lalande, at dat time I had de portraite take for my daughter by my first usbande, Monsieur Moissart!"

"Moissart!" said I.

"Yes, Moissart," said she, **mimicking**[7] my pronunciation, which, to speak the truth, was none of the best, — "and vat den? Vat you know about de Moissart?"

"Nothing, you old fright! — I know nothing about him at all; only I had an ancestor of that name, once upon a time."

"Dat name! and vat you ave for say to dat name? 'Tis ver goot name; and so

① grin [grin] *v.* 咧嘴
② foam [fəum] *v.* 大怒

起，直直地立在当庭，恐惧和愤怒令我完全说不出话，只能对着辛普森夫人掐着腰，牙齿咬得咯吱响。

我曾说过尤金妮·拉兰德夫人——现在是辛普森夫人了——英语说得写得都不太熟练，也正因如此，她在一般场合为了礼貌得体从不尝试说英语。但是愤怒的女人真是无所不能；看到我这一连串行为，辛普森夫人被激怒，开始试图用这门她并不完全理解的语言对我发难。

"哎呀，先生，"显然十分吃惊地打量了我许久后，她说——"哎呀，先生？——怎么了？——你到底怎么了？这么快就不喜欢我了吗？如果你不喜欢我，为什么还这么急着要娶我呢？"

③ wretch [retʃ] *n.* 坏蛋
④ villainous ['vilənəs] *a.* 恶毒的
⑤ hag [hæg] *n.* 丑老太婆

"你个老妖精！"我错愕得喘不过气——"你——你——你这个该下地狱的老巫婆！"

"老？——妖精？——我也并不是太老！我还不过八十二岁而已。"

"八十二！"我失声惊叫，踉跄着靠在了墙上——"你看起来有八百二十万岁都不止！可你的小像上却写着二十七岁零七个月！"

⑥ baboon [bə'bu:n] *n.* 丑陋的人

"没错！——就是！——一点儿没错！但那张小像是五十五年前画的。当时我和第二任丈夫拉兰德先生结婚，画这张像是为了送给我和第一任丈夫莫瓦萨尔先生所生的女儿！"

"莫瓦萨尔！"我说。

⑦ mimic ['mimik] *v.* 模仿

"没错，莫瓦萨尔，"她模仿我的发音说，但讲实话，学得并不像——"又怎么了？你又知道些什么莫瓦萨尔的事？"

"我什么也不知道，你这个可怕的老东西！——我不认识他，只不过以前我祖上有人姓那个姓。"

"那个姓！你对'那个姓'又有什么意见吗？它

is Voissart — dat is ver goot name too. My daughter, Mademoiselle Moissart, she marry von Monsieur Voissart, — and de name is bot ver respectaable name."

"Moissart?" I exclaimed, "and Voissart! Why, what is it you mean?"

"Vat I mean? — I mean Moissart and Voissart; and for de matter of dat, I mean Croissart and Froisart, too, if I only tink proper to mean it. My daughter's daughter, Mademoiselle Voissart, she marry von Monsieur Croissart, and den again, my daughter's grande daughter, Mademoiselle Croissart, she marry von Monsieur Froissart; and I suppose you say dat dat is not von ver respectaable name."

"Froissart!" said I, beginning to **faint**[①], "why, surely you don't say Moissart, and Voissart, and Croissart, and Froissart?"

"Yes," she replied, leaning fully back in her chair, and stretching out her lower limbs at great length; "yes, Moissart, and Voissart, and Croissart, and Froissart. But Monsieur Froissart, he vas von ver big vat you call fool — he vas von ver great big donce like yourself — for he lef la belle France for come to dis stupide Amerique — and ven he get here he went and ave von ver stupide, von ver, ver stupide sonn, so I hear, dough I not yet av ad de plaisir to meet vid him — neither me nor my companion, de Madame Stephanie Lalande. He is name de Napoleon Bonaparte Froissart, and I suppose you say dat dat, too, is not von ver respectable name."

Either the length or the nature of this speech, had the effect of working up Mrs. Simpson into a very extraordinary passion indeed; and as she made an end of it, with great labor, she lumped up from her chair like somebody **bewitched**[②], dropping upon the floor an entire universe of **bustle**[③] as she lumped. Once upon her feet, she **gnashed**[④] her gums, **brandished**[⑤] her arms, rolled up her sleeves, shook her fist in my face, and concluded the performance by tearing the cap from her head, and with it an immense **wig**[⑥] of the most valuable and beautiful black hair, the whole of which she dashed upon the

和沃瓦萨尔都是显赫的姓氏。我的女儿莫瓦萨尔小姐嫁给了沃瓦萨尔先生——他的姓氏也是倍受尊敬的。

"莫瓦萨尔？"我惊呼，"还有沃瓦萨尔！天，你到底要说什么？"

"说什么？——我是说莫瓦萨尔和沃瓦萨尔，都曾辉煌；还有科瓦萨尔和佛瓦萨尔，也算显贵的姓氏。我女儿的女儿，沃瓦萨尔小姐嫁给了科瓦萨尔先生，后来，我女儿的外孙女科瓦萨尔小姐又和佛瓦萨尔先生结了婚；我想你可能觉得除了佛瓦萨尔这个姓氏之外还都是很体面的吧。"

"佛瓦萨尔！"说着我都快晕过去了，"天哪，我不会听错了吧，你刚才不是说莫瓦萨尔、沃瓦萨尔、科瓦萨尔和佛瓦萨尔吧？"

"正是，"她答道，把腿向前伸得很长，使身体完全靠向椅背；"正是，莫瓦萨尔、沃瓦萨尔、科瓦萨尔和佛瓦萨尔这几个姓氏。但是佛瓦萨尔先生，他是一个你可以称为败类的傻瓜——他真是愚蠢透顶，就像你一样——因为他离开富饶的法国来到这荒蛮的美利坚——到了这里后仍然犯傻，我听说，还生了一个一样愚蠢透顶的儿子，但是我还没能有幸和他见面——我和我的同伴斯蒂芬妮·拉兰德夫人都与他素未谋面。他的名字叫拿破仑·波拿巴·佛瓦萨尔，我想你一定觉得这个名字也不怎么体面吧。"

繁长复杂的意思加之颇费精力的表达令辛普森夫人越说越生气，终于控制不住情绪，就在讲完话的那一瞬间，她像着了魔一般从椅子上一下子跳起来，将里三层外三层的衣裙都脱掉扔在地上。站稳了脚跟，她就咬着牙龈，挥舞着手臂，撸起衣袖，挥舞着拳头在我面前示威，最后还气急败坏地叫喊着把帽子从头上扯下，带着那昂贵而秀美的浓密黑色假发，猛地摔

① faint ['feint] *v.* 昏倒

② bewitched [bi'witʃt] *a.* 着魔的

③ bustle ['bʌsl] *n.* (旧时好用的) 裙撑

④ gnash [næʃ] *v.* 用牙咬

⑤ brandish ['brændiʃ] *v.* 挥舞

⑥ wig [wig] *n.* 假发

ground with a yell, and there **trampled**① and danced a **fandango**② upon it, in an absolute ecstasy and agony of rage.

Meantime I sank **aghast**③ into the chair which she had **vacated**④. "Moissart and Voissart!" I repeated, thoughtfully, as she cut one of her pigeon-wings, and "Croissart and Froissart!" as she completed another — "Moissart and Voissart and Croissart and Napoleon Bonaparte Froissart! — why, you **ineffable**⑤ old **serpent**⑥, that's me — that's me — d'ye hear? that's me" — here I screamed at the top of my voice — "that's me-e-e! I am Napoleon Bonaparte Froissart! and if I havn't married my great, great, grandmother, I wish I may be everlastingly confounded!"

Madame Eugenie Lalande, quasi Simpson — formerly Moissart — was, in sober fact, my great, great, grandmother. In her youth she had been beautiful, and even at eighty-two, **retained**⑦ the majestic height, the **sculptural**⑧ **contour**⑨ of head, the fine eyes and the Grecian nose of her girlhood. By the aid of these, of pearl-powder, of rouge, of false hair, false teeth, and false tournure, as well as of the most skilful **modistes**⑩ of Paris, she **contrived**⑪ to hold a respectable footing among the beauties en peu passees of the French metropolis. In this respect, indeed, she might have been regarded as little less than the equal of the celebrated Ninon De L'Enclos.

She was immensely wealthy, and being left, for the second time, a widow without children, she bethought herself of my existence in America, and for the purpose of making me her heir, paid a visit to the United States, in company with a distant and exceedingly lovely relative of her second husband's — a Madame Stephanie Lalande.

At the opera, my great, great, grandmother's attention was arrested by my notice; and, upon surveying me through her eye-glass, she was struck with a certain family **resemblance**⑫ to herself. Thus interested, and knowing that the heir she sought was actually in the city, she made inquiries of her

① trample ['træmpl] v. 践踏

② fandango [fæn'dæŋɡəu] n. 方丹戈舞

③ aghast [ə'ɡɑ:st] a. 吓呆的，惊骇的

④ vacate [və'keit] v. 腾出，空出

⑤ ineffable [in'efəbl] a. 不可言喻的

⑥ serpent ['sə:pənt] n. 狡猾的人

⑦ retain [ri'tein] v. 保持，保留

⑧ sculptural ['skʌlptrərəl] a. 雕刻般的

⑨ contour ['kɔntuə] n. 轮廓

⑩ modiste [məu'di:st] n. 时尚女装裁缝

⑪ contrive [kən'traiv] v. 设计，设法做到

⑫ resemblance [ri'zembləns] n. 相似

到地上一通乱踩，那步伐好似在跳西班牙凡丹戈舞。

我被吓呆了，一下子瘫坐到她刚刚坐过的椅子里。"莫瓦萨尔和沃瓦萨尔！"我若有所思地重复着，而她则在一边跳脚，好像在跳鸽翼式[1]，"还有科瓦萨尔和佛瓦萨尔！"说话间她又跳完了一段。"莫瓦萨尔、沃瓦萨尔、科瓦萨尔，还有那个拿破仑·波拿巴·佛瓦萨尔！啊！你这个可恶的老蛇蝎，是我——是我——听到没？你说的那个人就是我，"——我声嘶力竭地大叫着——"那个人是我！我就是拿破仑·波拿巴·佛瓦萨尔！我居然娶了我的曾曾外祖母，我真该受到无尽的诅咒！"

我现在恍然大悟，原来尤金妮·拉兰德夫人，准辛普森夫人——原莫瓦萨尔夫人——就是我的曾曾外祖母。年轻时她是个美人，即便到了八十二岁，仍然保持着少女时的高挑身段，面部轮廓依然分明，眼睛仍然炯炯有神，那挺拔的希腊鼻也没有一点塌陷。在此基础上，外加珍珠粉、胭脂、假发、假牙、腰垫，以及巴黎女装裁缝精湛的手艺的帮助，她在法国大都市的成熟美女圈仍然占有一席之地，颇受尊敬。从这点来看，她与声名显赫的妮蓉·德·兰克罗斯真是不分伯仲了。

她家财万贯，但第二任丈夫撒手人寰时却没能给她留下子嗣，她想起了美国还有一个她的后人，也就是我，此次她由第二任丈夫的一位品貌超群的远房亲戚斯蒂芬妮·拉兰德夫人陪同来到美利坚，目的就是为了让我成为她的继承人。

那天在剧院，由于我对她的过分关注，我的曾曾外祖母也注意到了我；通过眼镜观察，她发现我的相貌和她有几分相似。这引起了她的兴趣，加上知道她

1　一种跳起后并合双腿的花式舞步。

party respecting me. The gentleman who attended her knew my person, and told her who I was. The information thus obtained induced her to renew her scrutiny; and this scrutiny it was which so emboldened me that I **behaved**① in the absurd manner already detailed. She returned my bow, however, under the impression that, by some odd accident, I had discovered her identity. When, deceived by my weakness of vision, and the arts of the toilet, in respect to the age and charms of the strange lady, I demanded so enthusiastically of Talbot who she was, he concluded that I meant the younger beauty, as a matter of course, and so informed me, with perfect truth, that she was "the celebrated widow, Madame Lalande."

In the street, next morning, my great, great, grandmother encountered Talbot, an old Parisian acquaintance; and the conversation, very naturally turned upon myself. My deficiencies of vision were then explained; for these were **notorious**②, although I was entirely **ignorant**③ of their notoriety, and my good old relative discovered, much to her **chagrin**④, that she had been deceived in supposing me aware of her identity, and that I had been merely making a fool of myself in making open love, in a theatre, to an old woman unknown. By way of punishing me for this imprudence, she **concocted**⑤ with Talbot a plot. He purposely kept out of my way to avoid giving me the introduction. My street inquiries about "the lovely widow, Madame Lalande," were supposed to refer to the younger lady, of course, and thus the conversation with the three gentlemen whom I encountered shortly after leaving Talbot's hotel will be easily explained, as also their allusion to Ninon De L'Enclos. I had no opportunity of seeing Madame Lalande closely during daylight; and, at her musical soiree, my silly weakness in refusing the aid of glasses effectually prevented me from making a discovery of her age. When "Madame Lalande" was called upon to sing, the younger lady was intended; and it was she who arose to obey the call; my great, great, grandmother,

要找的继承人刚巧也在这座城市，她便向同行者询问了我的事情。陪同她的那位绅士刚好认识我，便把我的姓名告诉了她。得知这些后她又重新对我进行观察，这一看居然就令我误会从而引出了刚才讲述的那些荒诞的行为。当时我向她点头，她以为我已经通过某种巧合知道了她的身份，所以才以点头回敬。我的弱视让我看不清她，而她的化妆之术又掩盖了她的年龄而展示出陌生女人的美丽，这时，我急切地向塔尔博特询问她的身份，他还以为我指的是那位年轻的美人，因此就跟我说那位是"很有名的寡妇，拉兰德夫人"，而那位美丽女士的确是。

其实，第二天早上，我的曾曾外祖母在街上遇到了巴黎的旧相识塔尔博特；一番寒暄后他们自然地提到了我。塔尔博特向她解释说误会是我的弱视造成的；我还完全不知道原来我的视力问题已经人尽皆知了，而我那位善良的亲戚懊恼地发现，原来我并不知道她的身份，而我向她点头是在剧院里公开调戏一位素不相识的老太太，真是太丢人了。为了惩罚我的轻佻行为，她与塔尔博特合谋制订了一个计划。塔尔博特故意外出就是为了不给我做引荐。我在街上到处打听的"美丽的寡妇拉兰德夫人"当然也被人误以为是那位年轻的女士，因此离开塔尔博特住处后不久在大街上和那三位友人的谈话中的疑惑就迎刃而解了，他们用妮蓉·德·兰克罗斯影射的人正是我的这位曾曾外祖母。我在白天没有机会近距离地观察拉兰德夫人；而在那晚的音乐会上，如果我克服了我那愚蠢的心理障碍戴上眼镜，那么也就能发现她的真实年龄了。被叫去唱歌的"拉兰德夫人"其实是那位年轻的女士；也是这位年轻的拉兰德夫人应邀起身歌唱；为了继续骗局，我的曾曾外祖母也陪

① behave [bi'heiv] *v.* 表现

② notorious [nəu'tɔ:riəs] *a.* 臭名昭著的
③ ignorant ['ignərənt] *a.* 无知的，愚昧的
④ chagrin ['ʃægrin] *n.* 懊恼，气愤
⑤ concoct [kən'kɔkt] *v.* 捏造，编造

to further the **deception**①, arising at the same moment and accompanying her to the piano in the main drawing-room. Had I decided upon escorting her thither, it had been her design to suggest the propriety of my remaining where I was; but my own **prudential**② views rendered this unnecessary. The songs which I so much admired, and which so confirmed my impression of the youth of my **mistress**③, were executed by Madame Stephanie Lalande. The eyeglass was presented by way of adding a **reproof**④ to the **hoax**⑤ — a sting to the epigram of the deception. Its presentation afforded an opportunity for the lecture upon affectation with which I was so especially **edified**⑥. It is almost **superfluous**⑦ to add that the glasses of the instrument, as worn by the old lady, had been exchanged by her for a pair better adapted to my years. They suited me, in fact, to a T.

The clergyman, who merely pretended to tie the fatal knot, was a boon companion of Talbot's, and no priest. He was an excellent "whip," however; and having **doffed**⑧ his **cassock**⑨ to put on a great-coat, he drove the hack which conveyed the "happy couple" out of town. Talbot took a seat at his side. The two scoundrels were thus "in at the death," and through a half-open window of the back parlor of the inn, amused themselves in grinning at the **denouement**⑩ of the drama. I believe I shall be forced to call them both out.

Nevertheless, I am not the husband of my great, great, grandmother; and this is a reflection which affords me infinite relief, — but I am the husband of Madame Lalande — of Madame Stephanie Lalande — with whom my good old relative, besides making me her sole heir when she dies — if she ever does — has been at the trouble of concocting me a match. In conclusion: I am done forever with billets doux and am never to be met without SPECTACLES.

① deception [di'sepʃən] n. 欺骗

② prudential [pru:'denʃəl] a. 谨慎的

③ mistress ['mistris] n. 情妇

④ reproof [ri'pru:f] n. 谴责

⑤ hoax [həuks] n. 骗局

⑥ edify ['edifai] v. 启发，教诲

⑦ superfluous [sju'pə:fluəs] a. 多余的，不必要的

⑧ doff [dɔf] v. 脱（衣、帽等）

⑨ cassock ['kæsək] n. 教士服

⑩ denouement [deinu:'mɔŋ] n.（戏剧、小说等的）结局

同她走到了主会客厅的钢琴旁。她已经设计好了，如果我执意陪她同去，她就会劝我说这不符合礼节；而我自己当时谨慎小心，也没跟她一同走进主会客厅。让我赞叹不已的演唱事实上是出自斯蒂芬妮·拉兰德夫人之口，我当时还笃定地认为那饱满甜润的声音是发自我年轻的爱人。至于为什么送我眼镜，那是为给这个骗局增加一种惩罚的色彩——也是这个骗局谱写的讽刺诗的关键词。我的曾曾外祖母借着赠眼镜的机会长篇大论地数落我的虚荣，实实在在地给我上了一课。不用多说您也能知道，我的曾曾外祖母佩戴的那副眼镜已经被改装过，刚好适合我这个年龄的人戴。太适合我了，简直是量身定做的。

那位"牧师"其实并不是什么牧师，而是塔尔博特的一位好友。然而他却使得一手"好鞭子"，假装为我们证过婚，他便脱下牧师长袍，换上马夫的大衣，正是他驾着马车将这对"幸福的新人"带出城外。塔尔博特和他在车上并肩而坐，这两个坏蛋因此目睹了我所受的"致命一击"，他们通过旅店后客厅半掩的窗户看到了这出闹剧的结局，笑得直不起腰来。等有机会我一定得教训他们一顿。

不过值得欣慰的是，我并没有同我曾曾外祖母结婚；每想到此事我都庆幸不已——但是我还是娶了拉兰德夫人——斯蒂芬妮·拉兰德夫人——这都是我这位善良的老亲戚一手撮合的，同时她还指定我为她遗产的唯一继承人，当然要等到她去世那天——那可真是遥遥无期。最后总结一句话：我从此再也不写情书，再也不摘下眼镜了。

The Murders in the Rue Morgue

*What song the **Syrens**① sang, or what name Achilles assumed when he hid himself among women, although puzzling questions, are not beyond all **conjecture**②.*

— Sir Thomas Browne.

The mental features discoursed of as the analytical, are, in themselves, but little susceptible of analysis. We appreciate them only in their effects. We know of them, among other things, that they are always to their possessor, when inordinately possessed, a source of the liveliest enjoyment. As the strong man exults in his physical ability, delighting in such exercises as call his muscles into action, so glories the analyst in that moral activity which ***disentangles***③. He derives pleasure from even the most trivial occupations bringing his talent into play. He is fond of **enigmas**④, of **conundrums**⑤, of **hieroglyphics**⑥; exhibiting in his solutions of each a degree of ***acumen***⑦ which appears to the ordinary apprehension **preternatural**⑧. His results, brought about by the very soul and essence of method, have, in truth, the whole air of intuition.

The faculty of re-solution is possibly much **invigorated**⑨ by mathematical study, and especially by that highest branch of it which, unjustly, and merely on account of its **retrograde**⑩ operations, has been called, as if par excellence,

魔阁街凶杀案

① syren ['saiərən] *n.* 塞壬
（希腊神话中的女妖）

② conjecture [kən'dʒektʃə]
n. 推测，猜想

③ disentangle [ˌdisin'tæŋgl]
v. 解决，使摆脱

④ enigma [i'nigmə] *n.* 难解
之谜

⑤ conundrum [kə'nʌndrəm]
n. 难题

⑥ hieroglyphic
[ˌhaiərəu'glifik] *n.* 象形
文字，难懂的文字

⑦ acumen [ə'kju:men] *n.*
聪明，敏锐

⑧ preternatural
[ˌpri:tə'nætʃərəl] *a.* 超自
然的，异常的

⑨ invigorate [in'vigəreit] *v.*
鼓舞，激励

⑩ retrograde ['retrəugreid]
a. 退化的，向后的

海上的妖女吟唱什么歌曲，阿基里斯混迹
女人堆里又冒的什么名，虽似无法揣度，却非
无迹可寻。

——托马斯·布朗尼爵士

我们称之为分析能力的心理特质，其本身却难
以分析，我们只能通过其产生的结果加以理解。我
们也听说若是谁拥有强大的分析能力，那么他也就拥
有了一种乐趣之源。正如体魄强健者因体能而欢跃，
尤喜锻炼身体的体力活动，擅长分析者也为其智力
而骄傲，乐于释难解惑的脑力活动。即便一些琐事
微不足道，只要值得分析，他都会乐此不疲。他偏
爱猜谜解惑、探赜索隐、析文解字，在解决问题的
过程中展示出的敏锐程度超乎常人所能理解。他解
开谜题靠的是条理分析的精髓和灵魂，而在别人看
来实在是有种全凭直觉的意味。

学习数学也许可以大大激活释疑的才能，尤其
是学习数学那门最高深的分支——这一分支仅仅因
为其逆推运算的方法就被称作是分析学，这名字看

analysis. Yet to calculate is not in itself to analyse. A chess-player, for example, does the one without effort at the other. It follows that the game of chess, in its effects upon mental character, is greatly misunderstood. I am not now writing a **treatise**①, but simply **prefacing**② a somewhat peculiar narrative by observations very much at random; I will, therefore, take occasion to assert that the higher powers of the reflective intellect are more decidedly and more usefully tasked by the **unostentatious**③ game of **draughts**④ than by all the elaborate **frivolity**⑤ of chess. In this latter, where the pieces have different and *bizarre*⑥ motions, with various and variable values, what is only complex is mistaken (a not unusual error) for what is profound. The *attention* is here called powerfully into play. If it flag for an instant, an oversight is committed resulting in injury or defeat. The possible moves being not only **manifold**⑦ but **involute**⑧, the chances of such oversights are multiplied; and in nine cases out of ten it is the more concentrative rather than the more acute player who conquers. In draughts, on the contrary, where the moves are *unique* and have but little variation, the probabilities of **inadvertence**⑨ are diminished, and the mere attention being left comparatively unemployed, what advantages are obtained by either party are obtained by superior *acumen*. To be less abstract — Let us suppose a game of draughts where the pieces are reduced to four kings, and where, of course, no oversight is to be expected. It is obvious that here the victory can be decided (the players being at all equal) only by some *recherché* movement, the result of some strong **exertion**⑩ of the intellect. Deprived of ordinary resources, the analyst throws himself into the spirit of his opponent, identifies himself therewith, and not unfrequently sees thus, at a glance, the sole methods (sometime indeed absurdly simple ones) by which he may **seduce**⑪ into error or hurry into **miscalculation**⑫.

Whist⑬ has long been noted for its influence upon what is termed the calculating power; and men of the highest order of intellect have been known to take an apparently unaccountable delight in it, while **eschewing**⑭ chess as frivolous. Beyond doubt there is nothing of a similar nature so greatly tasking the faculty of analysis. The best chess-player in Christendom *may* be little more

似极为高深，实际上计算本身并不是分析。比如下象棋的人就只需计算，不用分析。这样看来，象棋对下棋者心理因素的影响就被极大地误解了。我并不是要写一篇论文，而只是想在讲述一件离奇事件之前开篇闲叙几点我自己的看法；因此我也借此机会宣布，低调的国际跳棋比繁复又肤浅的国际象棋更需要果断有效地应用较强的思考能力。国际象棋中各子走法不同，行棋古怪，棋子的价值多样亦多变，因其复杂而被人误以为深奥（人们普遍的误解）。下象棋需要精力高度集中。稍有懈怠就会疏忽，轻者损兵折将，重者全盘皆输。象棋走法多种多样且布局错综复杂，出错的概率因此倍增；胜者十之有九是赢在专注而非聪明。相反，在跳棋中，走法单一且缺乏变数，因此精力分散的可能性大大减少，相对而言无需太强的专注力，往往更聪明的一方会取得对局的优势。更具体地说，让我们假设有一局跳棋只剩四个棋，双方并不存在疏漏。显然（如果双方势均力敌）胜负已定，赢家注定是走法精湛的一方，或者说善用智力的一方。若不采取寻常对策，善分析者会设身处地揣摩对手心思，往往看一眼就能找到诱对手入陷阱或者令对手忙中算错的方法（有时那几招真是会简单到荒唐）。

惠斯特牌向来以其对计算能力的高要求著称；众所周知，智力超群者显然都莫名地更加偏爱惠斯特，对毫无思维挑战的象棋则是避而远之。毫无疑问，类似的游戏中，再没有什么比惠斯特更能挑战选手的分析能力。在基督教国家，最好的国际象棋选手也不过仅仅是最好的棋手；而精通惠斯特牌则

① treatise ['tri:tiz] n. 论文
② preface ['prefis] v. 作为……的开端
③ unostentatious [ˌʌn,ɔsten'teiʃəs] a. 不虚饰的，不夸耀的
④ draughts [drɑ:fts] n. 国际跳棋
⑤ frivolity [fri'vɔliti] n. 轻浮，轻率
⑥ bizarre [bi'zɑ:] a. 古怪的
⑦ manifold ['mænifəuld] a. 多种多样的
⑧ involute ['invəlju:t] a. 错综复杂的
⑨ inadvertence [ˌinəd'və:təns] n. 不注意

⑩ exertion [ig'zə:ʃən] n. 发挥，运用
⑪ seduce [si'dju:s] v. 使误入歧途
⑫ miscalculation ['mis,kælkju'leiʃən] n. 错误判断
⑬ whist [hwist] n. 惠斯特（类似桥牌的一种四人玩的纸牌游戏）
⑭ eschew [is'tʃu:] v. 避开，回避

than the best player of chess; but **proficiency**① in whist implies capacity for success in all those more important undertakings where mind struggles with mind. When I say proficiency, I mean that perfection in the game which includes a comprehension of *all* the sources whence **legitimate**② advantage may be derived. These are not only manifold but **multiform**③, and lie frequently among **recesses**④ of thought altogether **inaccessible**⑤ to the ordinary understanding. To observe attentively is to remember distinctly; and, so far, the concentrative chess-player will do very well at whist; while the rules of Hoyle (themselves based upon the mere mechanism of the game) are sufficiently and generally comprehensible. Thus to have a **retentive**⑥ memory, and to proceed by "the book," are points commonly regarded as the sum total of good playing. But it is in matters beyond the limits of mere rule that the skill of the analyst is evinced. He makes, in silence, a host of observations and **inferences**⑦. So, perhaps, do his companions; and the difference in the extent of the information obtained, lies not so much in the validity of the inference as in the quality of the observation. The necessary knowledge is that of *what* to observe. Our player confines himself not at all; nor, because the game is the object, does he reject **deductions**⑧ from things external to the game. He examines the countenance of his partner, comparing it carefully with that of each of his opponents. He considers the mode of assorting the cards in each hand; often counting **trump**⑨ by trump, and honor by honor, through the glances bestowed by their holders upon each. He notes every variation of face as the play progresses, gathering **a fund of**⑩ thought from the differences in the expression of certainty, of surprise, of triumph, or of chagrin. From the manner of gathering up a trick he judges whether the person taking it can make another in the suit. He recognises what is played through **feint**⑪, by the air with which it is thrown upon the table. A casual or inadvertent word; the accidental dropping or turning of a card, with the accompanying anxiety or carelessness in regard to its **concealment**⑫; the counting of the tricks, with the order of their arrangement; embarrassment, hesitation, eagerness or trepidation — all afford, to his apparently **intuitive**⑬ **perception**⑭, indications

① proficiency [prəuˈfiʃənsi]
n. 精通，熟练

② legitimate [liˈdʒitimət] a.
合理的

③ multiform [ˈmʌltifɔːm] a.
多样的，多种形式的

④ recess [riˈses] n.（思想、
灵魂的）深处

⑤ inaccessible
[ˌinækˈsesəbl] a. 难达到
的

⑥ retentive [riˈtentiv] a. 记
忆力强的

⑦ inference [ˈinfərəns] n.
推论，推断

⑧ deduction [diˈdʌkʃən] n.
推论

⑨ trump [trʌmp] n.（牌戏
中的）王牌，将牌

⑩ a fund of 大量的，丰富
的

⑪ feint [feint] n. 佯攻

⑫ concealment
[kənˈsiːlmənt] n. 隐藏，
隐蔽

⑬ intuitive [inˈtjuːitiv] a. 直
觉的

⑭ perception [pəˈsepʃən] n.
理解，看法

意味着你在任何更重要的智力相斗的场合都具有获胜的能力。我所说的精通，指的是通晓所有获取正当优势渠道的精湛牌技。这些渠道繁多且形式多样，通常潜伏于思维深处，非常人所能企及。凝神观察定会清晰记忆；因此，专注的棋手，只要他通晓足够的纸牌规则（霍伊尔牌谱，以实战技巧为基础的规则），在一定程度上讲，也可以是玩惠斯特牌的好手。这样看来，精于牌技便可以总结为拥有一副好记性并按"规则"行事。但超越规则的情况下，善分析者的技巧才得以展示。他默默地做足观察和推断。或许对手也如此；因此，所获信息的差异与其说是在于推断得正确与否，倒不如说更在于观察的质量。所以，知道该观察什么是必不可少的技巧。我们的选手丝毫不限制自己；也不会因为专注于牌局本身就拒绝用外部事件作推断。他会研究对手的表情，将其与另两位对手仔细比对。他考虑每人手中配牌的状况，经常通过他人得到牌时的眼神就能一张一张地算计出王牌和大牌的所在。他观察出牌过程中其他人表情的变化，从肯定、惊讶、得意、懊丧等表情的差异中搜罗推测的依据。从对手拿到赢墩时的表现他可以判断对手是否能用同样的花色再赢一墩。他可以从对手把牌放在桌子上的姿态看出那是不是在佯攻。不经意的只字片语，失手掉牌或翻牌，以及伴随的为了掩饰而产生的焦虑或不屑，以什么样的顺序查点牌张以及摆法，任何窘迫、迟

of the true state of affairs. The first two or three rounds having been played, he is in full possession of the contents of each hand, and thenceforward puts down his cards with as absolute a precision of purpose as if the rest of the party had turned outward the faces of their own.

The analytical power should not be confounded with ample ingenuity; for while the analyst is necessarily ingenious, the ingenious man is often remarkably incapable of analysis. The constructive or combining power, by which ingenuity is usually **manifested**①, and to which the **phrenologists**② (I believe **erroneously**③) have assigned a separate organ, supposing it a primitive faculty, has been so frequently seen in those whose intellect bordered otherwise upon **idiocy**④, as to have attracted general observation among writers on morals. Between ingenuity and the analytic ability there exists a difference far greater, indeed, than that between the fancy and the imagination, but of a character very strictly **analogous**⑤. It will be found, in fact, that the ingenious are always fanciful, and the *truly* imaginative never otherwise than analytic.

The narrative which follows will appear to the reader somewhat in the light of a commentary upon the propositions just advanced.

Residing⑥ in Paris during the spring and part of the summer of 18 — , I there became acquainted with a Monsieur C. Auguste Dupin. This young gentleman was of an excellent — indeed of an **illustrious**⑦ family, but, by a variety of **untoward**⑧ events, had been reduced to such poverty that the energy of his character **succumbed**⑨ beneath it, and he ceased to **bestir**⑩ himself in the world, or to care for the **retrieval**⑪ of his fortunes. By **courtesy**⑫ of his creditors, there still remained in his possession a small **remnant**⑬ of his **patrimony**⑭; and, upon the income arising from this, he managed, by means of a rigorous economy, to procure the necessaries of life, without troubling himself about its **superfluities**⑮. Books, indeed, were his sole luxuries, and in Paris these are easily obtained.

Our first meeting was at an **obscure**⑯ library in the Rue Montmartre, where the accident of our both being in search of the same very rare and very remarkable volume, brought us into closer communion. We saw each other

疑、急切、焦虑——都躲不过他貌似直觉的洞察力，并向他展现牌局的真实状况。开局两三回合，他便对各家配牌了如指掌，以后他出的每张牌都精准无误，好似对手们的牌都摆明了放在桌上一般。

分析能力不应与足智多谋混淆；因为善分析者必然足智多谋，而足智多谋者往往出人意料地不善分析。颅相学者（错误地）将足智多谋者所展示的推理或归纳能力归因为某独立器官，并认为这些能力是原始能力，其实这些能力常见于在其他方面智力几近白痴的人身上，因此这些能力引起了伦理方面作家的普遍关注。善谋者与善分析者之间实则存在着一种比幻想和想象之间大得多的差异，但二者之间有一极其相似的特征。事实上你将发现，善谋者往往爱幻想，而真正富于想象力的人向来不缺少分析能力。

下面要向各位讲述的事件多少可以被看成是以上命题的详释。

18××年整个春天和初夏我都住在巴黎，在这期间，我结识了一位 C. 奥古斯特·杜宾先生。这位年轻的绅士出身于一个高贵的——实际上十分显赫的家族，但是因多种变故，他当时穷困潦倒以致意志消沉，颓废不振，更无心重振家业。多亏债主手下留情，给他留下些许祖产；仅凭那份薄产的收入，加之精打细算，他才得以维持基本生活，除此之外也别无他求。实际上，书对于他来讲就是唯一的奢侈品了，好在巴黎到处都能找到书。

与他相遇是在蒙马特街一家冷清的图书馆里，当时我们都在寻找同一本珍奇的书册，从此我们一见如故。后来我们经常见面。他以法国人那种一谈

① manifest ['mænifest] *v.* 显现，显露

② phrenologist [fri'nɔ:ədʒist] *n.* 颅相学者

③ erroneously [i'rəuniəsli] *ad.* 错误地

④ idiocy ['idiəsi] *n.* 愚蠢的行为

⑤ analogous [ə'næləgəs] *a.* 类似的

⑥ reside [ri'zaid] *v.* 居住

⑦ illustrious [i'lʌstriəs] *a.* 显赫的

⑧ untoward [ʌntə'wɔ:d] *a.* 不幸的

⑨ succumb [sə'kʌm] *v.* 屈服，屈从

⑩ bestir [bi'stə:] *v.* 激励

⑪ retrieval [ri'tri:vəl] *n.* 恢复

⑫ courtesy ['kɔ:tisi] *n.* 好意

⑬ remnant ['remnənt] *n.* 剩余

⑭ patrimony ['pætriməni] *n.* 遗产

⑮ superfluity [,sju:pə'fluiti] *n.* 多余，过剩

⑯ obscure [əb'skjuə] *a.* 昏暗的

again and again. I was deeply interested in the little family history which he detailed to me with all that candor which a Frenchman **indulges**① whenever mere self is his theme. I was astonished, too, at the vast extent of his reading; and, above all, I felt my soul **enkindled**② within me by the wild **fervor**③, and the vivid freshness of his imagination. Seeking in Paris the objects I then sought, I felt that the society of such a man would be to me a treasure beyond price; and this feeling I frankly **confided**④ to him. It was at length arranged that we should live together during my stay in the city; and as my worldly circumstances were somewhat less embarrassed than his own, I was permitted to be at the expense of renting, and furnishing in a style which suited the rather fantastic gloom of our common temper, a time-eaten and **grotesque**⑤ mansion, long deserted through superstitions into which we did not inquire, and **tottering**⑥ to its fall in a retired and desolate portion of the Faubourg St. Germain.

Had the routine of our life at this place been known to the world, we should have been regarded as madmen — although, perhaps, as madmen of a harmless nature. Our **seclusion**⑦ was perfect. We admitted no visitors. Indeed the locality of our retirement had been carefully kept a secret from my own former **associates**⑧; and it had been many years since Dupin had ceased to know or be known in Paris. We existed within ourselves alone.

It was a freak of fancy in my friend (for what else shall I call it?) to be **enamored**⑨ of the Night for her own sake; and into this *bizarrerie*, as into all his others, I quietly fell; giving myself up to his wild **whims**⑩ with a perfect *abandon*. The **sable**⑪ divinity would not herself dwell with us always; but we could **counterfeit**⑫ her presence. At the first dawn of the morning we closed all the **messy**⑬ shutters of our old building; lighting a couple of **tapers**⑭ which, strongly perfumed, threw out only the **ghastliest**⑮ and feeblest of rays. By the aid of these we then busied our souls in dreams — reading, writing, or conversing, until warned by the clock of the advent of the true Darkness. Then we **sallied forth**⑯ into the streets arm in arm, continuing the topics of the day,

① indulge [in'dʌldʒ] v. 沉
溺，满足

② enkindle [in'kindl] v. 燃
起（激情等）

③ fervor ['fə:və] n. 热情

④ confide [kən'faid] v. 吐
露

⑤ grotesque [grəu'tesk] a.
怪异的

⑥ totter ['tɔtə] v. 蹒跚，踉
跄

⑦ seclusion [si:'klu:ʒən] n.
隐蔽之处

⑧ associate [ə'səuʃieit] n.
同事，伙伴

⑨ enamor [i'næmə] v. 使倾
心，使迷恋

⑩ whim [hwim] n. 奇想

⑪ sable ['seibl] a. 阴森可
怕的

⑫ counterfeit ['kauntəfit] v.
假装

⑬ messy ['mesi] a. 凌乱
的，肮脏的

⑭ taper ['teipə] n. 细长的
蜡烛

⑮ ghastly ['gɑ:stli] a. 可怕
的

⑯ sally forth 出发，动身

及自己就滔滔不绝的坦率向我细数他的家史，我听
得津津有味。同时我也惊讶于他涉猎之广，最重要
的是我感到他热情奔放、生动鲜活的想象在我的灵
魂深处燃起了熊熊烈火。当时我在巴黎寻找着自己
的目标，我感到有这样一位朋友做伴对我来说是无
价之宝；我也向他坦白了我的感受。最后我们商定
在我逗留巴黎期间我们将住在一起；我当时的境遇
多少不像他那般窘迫，他同意由我出钱租下了圣杰
曼郊区一处偏远荒凉的角落里一幢年久失修、样式
古怪的房子，传说这房子因什么迷信的原因而许久
无人居住，摇摇欲坠，我俩并未深究那些迷信，只
是把房子按照我们共有的那种喜欢幻想又忧郁的性
情装饰了一番。

　　若世人了解我俩在这里居住的日常，定会把我
们看成疯子——不过或许是不会伤人的那种疯子。我
们完全避世隐居，闭门谢客。实际上就连我们隐居
的地址我都小心翼翼地对我以前的朋友保密；而杜宾
也和友人断绝来往多年，在巴黎也已鲜有人知。我
俩就这样避世蛰居着。

　　我的朋友有一个怪诞的癖好（除了怪诞我还能称
为什么呢？），他仅仅因为黑夜的缘故而迷恋黑夜；
而我也不知不觉地染上了他这个怪癖，就像染上他的
其他怪癖一样；我完全放任自己心甘情愿地服从他的
奇思狂想。夜神不可能总是伴随我们，可我们能够伪
造黑夜。每当东方露出第一抹曙光，我们就把那幢老
屋脏兮兮的百叶窗统统关上，再点上两支散发出浓烈
香气、放射出幽幽微光的小蜡烛。借着那点微光，我
们各自沉浸于自己的梦幻——阅读、书写，或是交谈，
直到时钟报告真正的黑夜降临。这时我俩便手挽手出

or roaming far and wide until a late hour, seeking, amid the wild lights and shadows of the populous city, that **infinity**① of mental excitement which quiet observation can afford.

At such times I could not help remarking and admiring (although from his rich ideality I had been prepared to expect it) a peculiar analytic ability in Dupin. He seemed, too, to take an eager delight in its exercise — if not exactly in its display — and did not hesitate to confess the pleasure thus derived. He boasted to me, with a low chuckling laugh, that most men, in respect to himself, wore windows in their bosoms, and was **wont**② to follow up such assertions by direct and very startling proofs of his intimate knowledge of my own. His manner at these moments was **frigid**③ and **abstract**④; his eyes were vacant in expression; while his voice, usually a rich **tenor**⑤, rose into a treble which would have sounded **petulantly**⑥ but for the **deliberateness**⑦ and entire distinctness of the **enunciation**⑧. Observing him in these moods, I often dwelt **meditatively**⑨ upon the old philosophy of the Bi-Part Soul, and amused myself with the fancy of a double Dupin — the creative and the resolvent.

Let it not be supposed, from what I have just said, that I am detailing any mystery, or penning any romance. What I have described in the Frenchman, was merely the result of an excited, or perhaps of a **diseased**⑩ intelligence. But of the character of his remarks at the periods in question an example will best convey the idea.

We were strolling one night down a long dirty street in the vicinity of the Palais Royal. Being both, apparently, occupied with thought, neither of us had spoken a syllable for fifteen minutes at least. All at once Dupin broke forth with these words:

"He is a very little fellow, that's true, and would do better for the *Théâtre des Variétés*."

"There can be no doubt of that," I replied **unwittingly**⑪, and not at first observing (so much had I been absorbed in reflection) the extraordinary manner

① infinity [in'finəti] *n.* 无穷，无限

② wont [wəunt] *a.* 习惯于，习以为常的

③ frigd ['fridʒid] *a.* 冷淡的

④ abstract ['æbstrækt] *a.* 难以理解的

⑤ tenor ['tenə] *n.* 男高音

⑥ petulantly ['petjuləntli] *ad.* 脾气坏地

⑦ deliberateness [di'libəreitənis] *n.* 深思熟虑

⑧ enunciation [i,nʌnsi'eiʃən] *n.* 阐明，表明

⑨ meditatively ['medi,tətivli] *ad.* 沉思地，冥想地

⑩ diseased [di'zi:zd] *a.* 患病的

⑪ unwittingly [,ʌn'witiŋli] *ad.* 不知不觉地

门上街，继续着白天讨论的话题，或是尽兴漫步到深更半夜，在那座繁华都市的万家灯火与阴影之中，寻求唯有冷眼静观方能领略到的无限心灵悸动。

每当此时，我不禁注意到并赞叹（虽然从他丰富的想象力中我早能预料）杜宾非同寻常的分析能力。他似乎也渴望施展这种能力带来的乐趣——若说不是炫耀的话——也毫不犹疑地向我承认他的确以此为乐。他常得意地笑着向我自夸说，在他看来，人们大多在胸前都开着一扇窗，他还习惯在这番言论后用对我的深入了解作为直接又惊人的证据加以证明。这种时候他总是表现得冷漠而高深，双眼空灵，那平时洪亮的男高音更高到颤抖，若非他言辞审慎并思路清晰，那声音听着就像在发怒。观察到他的性情如此，我经常会神往于那有关双重灵魂的古老哲学，还打趣地幻想有两个杜宾——富于想象的杜宾和辨析一切的杜宾。

请不要以为我刚才在讲天方夜谭或是在杜撰浪漫传奇。我所描述的这位法国人的上述种种表现，不过是由他那敏感，或者说病态的才智所催生的。至于他在这些时候都发些什么样的高论，下面这个例子最能说明问题。

一天晚上，我俩正沿着皇家宫殿附近的一条又长又脏的街道散步，有至少十五分钟我们谁也没发一言，显然各自在思考问题。杜宾突然张口就说："他是个小矮个，的确，更适合去杂耍剧院。"

"那是毫无疑问的。"我不假思索地回答，一开始并未察觉到（当时我深陷于自己所思索的问题中）杜宾这话竟然以奇妙的方式洞悉了我的思维。随后我回过神来，不由得大吃一惊。

"杜宾，"我严肃地说，"这真令我难以理解。直说吧，我被你惊到了，都不敢相信自己的感觉了。你

in which the speaker had **chimed in with**① my meditations. In an instant afterward I recollected myself, and my astonishment was profound.

"Dupin," said I, **gravely**②, "this is beyond my comprehension. I do not hesitate to say that I am amazed, and can scarcely credit my senses. How was it possible you should know I was thinking of — ?" Here I paused, to ascertain beyond a doubt whether he really knew of whom I thought.

— "of Chantilly," said he, "why do you pause? You were remarking to yourself that his **diminutive**③ figure unfitted him for tragedy."

This was precisely what had formed the subject of my reflections. Chantilly was a *quondam*④ **cobbler**⑤ of the Rue St. Denis, who, becoming stage-mad, had attempted the *rôle* of Xerxes, in Crébillon's tragedy so called, and been notoriously Pasquinaded for his pains.

"Tell me, for Heaven's sake," I exclaimed, "the method — if method there is — by which you have been enabled to **fathom**⑥ my soul in this matter." In fact I was even more startled than I would have been willing to express.

"It was the fruiterer," replied my friend, "who brought you to the conclusion that the mender of soles was not of sufficient height for Xerxes *et id genus omne.*"

"The fruiterer! — you astonish me — I know no fruiterer whomsoever."

"The man who ran up against you as we entered the street — it may have been fifteen minutes ago."

I now remembered that, in fact, a fruiterer, carrying upon his head a large basket of apples, had nearly thrown me down, by accident, as we passed from the Rue C — into the **thoroughfare**⑦ where we stood; but what this had to do with Chantilly I could not possibly understand.

There was not a particle of *charlatanerie* about Dupin. "I will explain," he said, "and that you may comprehend all clearly, we will first retrace the course of your meditations, from the moment in which I spoke to you until that of the *rencontre*⑧ with the fruiterer in question. The larger links of the chain run thus — Chantilly, Orion, Dr. Nichols, Epicurus, **Stereotomy**⑨, the street stones, the fruiterer."

① chime in with 与……一致

② gravely ['greivli] ad. 严肃地

③ diminutive [di'minjutiv] a. 矮小的

④ quondam ['kwɔndæm] a. 原来的，以前的

⑤ cobbler ['kɔblə] n. 补鞋匠

⑥ fathom ['fæðəm] v. 看穿

⑦ thoroughfare ['θʌrəfeə] n. 大街，大道

⑧ rencontre [ren'kɔntə] n. 邂逅

⑨ stereotomy [steri'ɔtəmi] n. 立体切割技术

怎么可能知道我正在想——？”我故意停顿了一下，想百分百地确认他是否真的知道我想到的那人是谁。

“正在想尚蒂利，”他说，“你怎么说到一半就停了？你在想他那矮小的身材不适合演悲剧。”

这正是我在脑海中形成的想法。尚蒂利原来是圣丹尼斯街的一个修鞋匠，后来疯狂地迷恋舞台，曾尝试表演克雷比隆的悲剧《泽克西斯王》中泽克西斯一角，结果却遭冷嘲热讽，声名扫地。

“看在上帝的分上，请告诉我，”我惊呼道，“你到底用什么方法——若真的有这样的方法——推测出我内心所想的。”我是极力不表现出来，仍掩饰不住内心的惊奇。

“是那个卖水果的小贩，”我的朋友答道，“是他让你得出结论，认为那个修鞋匠饰演泽克西斯这类的角色不够高。”

“水果小贩！——你真令我吃惊——我并不认识什么卖水果的啊。”

“就是我们走上这条街时向你迎头走来的那个人——可能十五分钟前吧。”

现在我想起来了，的确有个水果小贩，头上顶着一大篮苹果，就在我们从 C 街转到这条大街时，一不小心差点把我撞倒。但是这又和尚蒂利有什么关联呢，我真是不能理解。

杜宾一丝一毫也没有弄虚作假。“听我解释，”他说，“你就完全清楚了。从我刚才开口和你说话到与那个卖水果的小贩相撞，让我们首先追溯一下你思绪的走向。大致环节是这样的——尚蒂利、猎户座、尼科尔斯博士、伊壁鸠鲁、切石法、街上的铺路石、水果小贩。”

There are few persons who have not, at some period of their lives, amused themselves in retracing the steps by which particular conclusions of their own minds have been attained. The occupation is often full of interest and he who attempts it for the first time is astonished by the apparently illimitable distance and incoherence between the starting-point and the goal. What, then, must have been my amazement when I heard the Frenchman speak what he had just spoken, and when I could not help acknowledging that he had spoken the truth. He continued:

"We had been talking of horses, if I remember aright, just before leaving the Rue C — . This was the last subject we discussed. As we crossed into this street, a fruiterer, with a large basket upon his head, brushing quickly past us, **thrust**① you upon a pile of paving stones collected at a spot where the causeway is undergoing repair. You stepped upon one of the loose fragments, slipped, slightly **strained**② your ankle, appeared **vexed**③ or sulky, **muttered**④ a few words, turned to look at the pile, and then proceeded in silence. I was not particularly attentive to what you did; but observation has become with me, of late, a species of necessity.

"You kept your eyes upon the ground — glancing, with a petulant expression, at the holes and **ruts**⑤ in the pavement, (so that I saw you were still thinking of the stones,) until we reached the little alley called Lamartine, which has been paved, by way of experiment, with the overlapping and riveted blocks. Here your countenance brightened up, and, perceiving your lips move, I could not doubt that you murmured the word 'stereotomy,' a term very affectedly applied to this species of pavement. I knew that you could not say to yourself 'stereotomy' without being brought to think of atomies, and thus of the theories of Epicurus; and since, when we discussed this subject not very long ago, I mentioned to you how singularly, yet with how little notice, the vague guesses of that noble Greek had met with confirmation in the late **nebular**⑥ **cosmogony**⑦, I felt that you could not avoid casting your eyes upward to the great *nebula* in Orion, and I certainly expected that you would do so. You did

　　几乎每个人都会在生命中的某时自娱自乐地逐步回顾自己的思路是如何得到某些结论的。回顾的过程充满乐趣，但初次尝试的人都会惊讶于起点与目标之间相隔十万八千里，完全风马牛不相及。因此当我听到身旁的这位法国人将我的思路原原本本地说了出来，我当然惊讶至极。

　　他接着说道："如果我没记错，就在我们走出 C 街前一刻，我们正在谈论马，那是我们沉默之前谈论的最后一个话题。当我们拐入这条街时，一个水果小贩头顶大果篮从我们俩身旁匆匆擦过，将你撞到了一堆因修路而堆起来的修路石上。你踩到一个松动的石块，脚下一滑，有点崴到脚踝，你看起来有点恼火，或者生气了，嘟哝着说了些什么，回头又看了看那堆石头，然后我们再接着走的时候你就默不作声了。我也不是特意观察你的举动；但是最近，观察已经深入我的骨髓，成为我的日常必然了。

　　"你两眼盯着地面——面带怒容地看着路上的坑洼和车辙，（所以我看出你还在想着那些石头，）然后我们走到了一条叫作拉玛丁的小巷，这条巷子的路面是试用将砌石交搭铆接的方法铺的。看到这，你面露喜色，我还看到你的嘴唇微微动了一下，我毫不怀疑你念叨的是'切石法'，这个词描述那种路面实在大词小用。我知道你一说到'切石法'肯定就会联想到'原子'这个同根词，进而想到伊壁鸠鲁，因为我们不久前刚讨论过这个话题，我向你提到那位杰出的希腊人那些模糊的猜测是多么奇妙又多么不为人知，他的那些猜测在后来的星云宇宙进化说中得到了证实。我感觉你难免会抬头看那一大团猎户座星云，我当然也预料到你会这样做。你果然抬头看了；

① thrust [θrʌst] v. 猛推
② strain [strein] v. 扭伤
③ vexed [vekst] a. 恼火的
④ mutter ['mʌtə] v. 咕哝，喃喃自语

⑤ rut [rʌt] n. 车辙

⑥ nebular ['nebjulə] a. 星云的，星云状的
⑦ cosmogony [kɔz'mɔgəni] n. 天体演化学

look up; and I was now assured that I had correctly followed your steps. But in that bitter **tirade**① upon Chantilly, which appeared in yesterday's '*Musée*,' the satirist, making some disgraceful allusions to the cobbler's change of name upon assuming the **buskin**②, quoted a Latin line about which we have often conversed. I mean the line

Perdidit antiquum litera sonum.

"I had told you that this was in reference to Orion, formerly written Urion; and, from certain **pungencies**③ connected with this explanation, I was aware that you could not have forgotten it. It was clear, therefore, that you would not fail to combine the two ideas of Orion and Chantilly. That you did combine them I saw by the character of the smile which passed over your lips. You thought of the poor cobbler's **immolation**④. So far, you had been stooping in your **gait**⑤; but now I saw you draw yourself up to your full height. I was then sure that you reflected upon the diminutive figure of Chantilly. At this point I interrupted your meditations to remark that as, in fact, he was a very little fellow — that Chantilly — he would do better at the *Théâtre des Variétés*."

Not long after this, we were looking over an evening edition of the "Gazette des Tribunaux," when the following paragraphs **arrested**⑥ our attention.

"EXTRAORDINARY MURDERS. — This morning, about three o'clock, the inhabitants of the Quartier St. Roch were aroused from sleep by a succession of terrific **shrieks**⑦, issuing, apparently, from the fourth story of a house in the Rue Morgue, known to be in the sole occupancy of one Madame L'Espanaye, and her daughter Mademoiselle Camille L'Espanaye. After some delay, occasioned by a **fruitless**⑧ attempt to procure admission in the usual manner, the gateway was broken in with a **crowbar**⑨, and eight or ten of the neighbors entered accompanied by two **gendarmes**⑩. By this time the cries had ceased; but, as the party rushed up the first flight of stairs, two or more rough voices in angry **contention**⑪ were distinguished and seemed to proceed from the upper

现在我可以肯定我和你的思路相吻合。但在昨天的《博物馆》报纸上有一篇针对尚蒂利的语气辛辣的长篇讽刺文章，那位讽刺作家毫不留情地挖苦修鞋匠穿上唱戏的中筒靴就改了名字，还引用了我们常谈起的一句拉丁文，就是那句：

第一个字母已经失去原来发音。

"我告诉过你这句诗指的就是猎户座，原来拼作'Urion'现在拼作'Orion'；我当时的解释也带有辛辣的语气，我想你不可能忘记此事。因此就清楚了，你肯定会把猎户座和尚蒂利联系到一起。通过掠过你嘴角的微笑我证实了你的确是这样联想的。你想到那可怜的修鞋匠成了牺牲品。到此为止你一直在弯腰走路，但是现在我看到你挺直了腰板。那么我就能确定你是想到了尚蒂利的矮小身材。于是我就在这时打断了你的思绪，说他的确是个非常矮的家伙——那个尚蒂利——他更适合在杂耍剧院干活。"

这件事后不久，有一天我们在看《法院公报》的晚间版，下面一则信息引起了我们的注意。

"离奇凶案——今晨约三点，圣洛奇街的居民被接连惨叫声惊醒，叫声明显是从魔阁街一幢房子的四楼发出，该楼只住着勒斯潘纳耶夫人和她的女儿卡米尔·勒斯潘纳耶小姐。邻居们尝试用常规方式进入未果，稍后门被用铁撬棍撬开，八到十位邻居由两位警察陪同进入房子。此时尖叫声已经停止；但当人们冲上一楼楼梯时，明显听到至少有两个声音在激烈地粗声争吵，声音似乎是从楼上传出。当

① tirade [tai'reid] *n.* 激烈的长篇演说

② buskin ['bʌskin] *n.*（古希腊或罗马悲剧演员穿的）厚底高靴

③ pungency ['pʌndʒənsi] *n.* 辛辣，尖刻

④ immolation [,iməu'leiʃən] *n.* 牺牲，牺牲品

⑤ gait [geit] *n.* 步伐

⑥ arrest [ə'rest] *v.* 吸引

⑦ shriek [ʃri:k] *n.* 尖叫

⑧ fruitless ['fru:tlis] *a.* 徒劳的

⑨ crowbar ['krəu,ba:] *n.* 撬棍

⑩ gendarme ['ʒɔnda:m] *n.*〈法〉警察

⑪ contention [kən'tenʃən] *n.* 争论，冲突

part of the house. As the second landing was reached, these sounds, also, had ceased and everything remained perfectly quiet. The party spread themselves and hurried from room to room. Upon arriving at a large back chamber in the fourth story, (the door of which, being found locked, with the key inside, was forced open,) a spectacle presented itself which struck every one present not less with horror than with astonishment.

"The apartment was in the wildest disorder — the furniture broken and thrown about in all directions. There was only one **bedstead**①; and from this the bed had been removed, and thrown into the middle of the floor. On a chair lay a **razor**②, **besmeared**③ with blood. On the hearth were two or three long and thick **tresses**④ of grey human hair, also **dabbled**⑤ in blood, and seeming to have been pulled out by the roots. Upon the floor were found four Napoleons, an ear-ring of **topaz**⑥, three large silver spoons, three smaller of *métal d'Alger*, and two bags, containing nearly four thousand **francs**⑦ in gold. The drawers of a *bureau*, which stood in one corner were open, and had been, apparently, **rifled**⑧, although many articles still remained in them. A small iron safe was discovered under the *bed* (not under the bedstead). It was open, with the key still in the door. It had no contents beyond a few old letters, and other papers of little consequence.

"Of Madame L'Espanaye no traces were here seen; but an unusual quantity of **soot**⑨ being observed in the fire-place, a search was made in the chimney, and (horrible to relate!) the corpse of the daughter, head downward, was dragged therefrom; it having been thus forced up the narrow **aperture**⑩ for a considerable distance. The body was quite warm. Upon examining it, many **excoriations**⑪ were perceived, no doubt occasioned by the violence with which it had been thrust up and **disengaged**⑫. Upon the face were many severe scratches, and, upon the throat, dark **bruises**⑬, and deep **indentations**⑭ of finger nails, as if the deceased had been **throttled**⑮ to death.

"After a thorough investigation of every portion of the house, without farther discovery, the party made its way into a small paved yard in the rear of the building, where lay the corpse of the old lady, with her throat so entirely cut

大家到达二楼，争吵声消失了，一切恢复平静。人们分头搜索每个房间。当到达四楼的一个大卧室时（门从内部反锁，钥匙在屋内，人们破门而入），室内景象令在场的每一位都又惊又惧。

"屋里乱七八糟——家具被砸碎了，扔得四处都是。床垫被扔到屋子中央的地上，空剩一个床架。有一把椅子上放着一把沾满血迹的剃刀。在壁炉旁的地面上有两三绺灰白的、又长又粗的头发，也都浸满了鲜血，看样子像是连头皮一起扯下。地上散落着四枚金币、一只黄宝石耳环、三把大银勺、三把小铜勺，另外还有两个小袋子，里面装着将近四千枚金法郎。角落里有一张书桌，抽屉开着，虽然里面物品仍在，但显然被匆匆翻过。在床垫下（不是床架下）人们发现一个打开的金属保险箱，钥匙还插在门上。箱里只有几封旧信和几张无关紧要的文件。

"屋内并没有发现勒斯潘纳耶夫人；但是人们看到壁炉里异常大量的烟灰，就搜看了一下烟囱，（说来恐怖！）女儿的尸体被头朝下脚朝上从狭窄的烟道塞进去一大截。尸体被发现时尚有余温。细查后发现身体有许多擦伤，无疑是在暴力地塞入和拉出烟道过程中产生的。面部有许多抓伤，喉部有深色瘀青和深陷的指甲印，死者似乎是被掐死的。

"彻底搜查了房子的每个部分都没有进一步发现，一行人来到楼后一块石块铺地的小院，在那里发现了老夫人的尸体，喉咙被彻底割断，在人们试图抬起尸体时，头从身体脱落下来。身体和头都已

① bedstead ['bedsted] *n.* 床架

② razor ['reizə] *n.* 剃刀

③ besmear [bi'smiə] *v.* 弄脏，涂抹

④ tress [tres] *n.* 一绺头发，一束头发

⑤ dabble ['dæbl] *v.* 溅湿

⑥ topaz ['təupæz] *n.* 黄玉

⑦ franc [fræŋk] *n.* 法郎

⑧ rifle ['raifl] *v.* 迅速翻找（尤指偷窃）

⑨ soot [su:t] *n.* 烟灰

⑩ aperture ['æpə,tjuə] *n.* 缝隙

⑪ excoriation [ek,skɔ:ri'eiʃən] *n.* 剥皮

⑫ disengage [,disin'geidʒ] *v.* 分开，分离

⑬ bruise [bru:z] *n.* 青肿，瘀伤

⑭ indentation [,inden'teiʃən] *n.* 压痕

⑮ throttle ['θrɔtl] *v.* 掐死

that, upon an attempt to raise her, the head fell off. The body, as well as the head, was fearfully **mutilated**① — the former so much so as scarcely to retain any **semblance**② of humanity.

"To this horrible mystery there is not as yet, we believe, the slightest clew."

The next day's paper had these additional particulars.

"*The Tragedy in the Rue Morgue*. Many individuals have been examined in relation to this most extraordinary and frightful affair." [The word 'affaire' has not yet, in France, that levity of import which it conveys with us,] "but nothing whatever has **transpired**③ to throw light upon it. We give below all the material **testimony**④ **elicited**⑤.

"*Pauline Dubourg*, laundress, **deposes**⑥ that she has known both the deceased for three years, having washed for them during that period. The old lady and her daughter seemed on good terms — very **affectionate**⑦ towards each other. They were excellent pay. Could not speak in regard to their mode or means of living. Believed that Madame L. told fortunes for a living. Was reputed to have money put by. Never met any persons in the house when she called for the clothes or took them home. Was sure that they had no servant in employ. There appeared to be no furniture in any part of the building except in the fourth story.

"*Pierre Moreau*, tobacconist, deposes that he has been in the habit of selling small quantities of tobacco and **snuff**⑧ to Madame L'Espanaye for nearly four years. Was born in the neighborhood, and has always resided there. The deceased and her daughter had occupied the house in which the corpses were found, for more than six years. It was formerly occupied by a jeweller, who under-let the upper rooms to various persons. The house was the property of Madame L. She became dissatisfied with the abuse of the **premises**⑨ by her tenant, and moved into them herself, refusing to let any portion. The old lady was childish. Witness had seen the daughter some five or six times during the six years. The two lived an exceedingly retired life — were reputed to have money. Had heard it said among the neighbors that Madame L. told fortunes — did not believe it. Had never seen any person enter the door except the old lady and her daughter, a

经血肉模糊——尤其身体已经看不出人形了。

"本报认为，这桩恐怖谜案尚无丝毫线索。"

第二天报纸增载了如下详情。

"魔阁街悲剧。多人因此离奇恐怖事件被传讯。"（"事件"这词在法国尚未有我们赋予的轻薄之意。）"但证词并未能使案情明朗。现本报将所有重要证词摘引如下。

"波林·杜堡，洗衣女工，宣誓称她与受害人母女相识三年，一直为她们洗衣。老夫人与女儿关系良好——相亲相爱。说不出她们的生活方式和收入来源，但是她们给的报酬颇丰。相信老夫人给人算命谋生。据说有存款。取衣服和送衣服的时候都没见房子里有别人。确认没有雇佣人。除了四楼好像其他楼层都没有什么家具。

"皮埃尔·莫罗，烟草商，宣誓称他平时向老夫人零售烟草和鼻烟将近四年了。出生在当地，从小住在这里。死者母女在案发房屋居住长达六年多。之前那里租住着一位珠宝商，曾把上层房间分租给三教九流。这房子是勒斯潘纳耶老夫人的财产。因不满租客肆意破坏而收回房屋，自己居住，不再租出任何房间。老夫人很孩子气。在这六年里只看到她女儿五六次。母女俩过着极度与世隔离的生活——据说有存款。邻居们都传说老夫人给人算命——本人不信。除了老夫人和她女儿，没见过别人进她家，只有搬运工来过一两次，一位大夫来过八到十次。

① mutilate ['mju:tileit] *v.*
严重损毁

② semblance ['sembləns] *n.*
外貌

③ transpire [træn'spaiə] *v.*
发生

④ testimony ['testiməni] *n.*
证词，口供

⑤ elicit [i'lisit] *v.* 引出，得出

⑥ depose [di'pəuz] *v.* 作证

⑦ affectionate [ə'fekʃənət]
a. 充满爱的，深情的

⑧ snuff [snʌf] *n.* 鼻烟

⑨ premise ['premis] *n.* 房屋

porter once or twice, and a physician some eight or ten times.

"Many other persons, neighbors, gave evidence to the same effect. No one was spoken of as frequenting the house. It was not known whether there were any living connexions of Madame L. and her daughter. The shutters of the front windows were seldom opened. Those in the rear were always closed, with the exception of the large back room, fourth story. The house was a good house — not very old.

"*Isidore Muset, gendarme,* deposes that he was called to the house about three o'clock in the morning, and found some twenty or thirty persons at the gateway, endeavoring to gain admittance. Forced it open, at length, with a **bayonet**① — not with a crowbar. Had but little difficulty in getting it open, on account of its being a double or folding gate, and bolted neither at bottom not top. The shrieks were continued until the gate was forced — and then suddenly ceased. They seemed to be screams of some person (or persons) in great agony — were loud and drawn out, not short and quick. Witness led the way up stairs. Upon reaching the first landing, heard two voices in loud and angry contention — the one a **gruff**② voice, the other much **shriller**③ — a very strange voice. Could distinguish some words of the former, which was that of a Frenchman. Was positive that it was not a woman's voice. Could distinguish the words '*sacré*' and '*diable.*' The shrill voice was that of a foreigner. Could not be sure whether it was the voice of a man or of a woman. Could not make out what was said, but believed the language to be Spanish. The state of the room and of the bodies was described by this witness as we described them yesterday.

"*Henri Duval*, a neighbor, and by trade a silver-smith, deposes that he was one of the party who first entered the house. **Corroborates**④ the testimony of Muset in general. As soon as they forced an entrance, they reclosed the door, to keep out the crowd, which collected very fast, notwithstanding the lateness of the hour. The shrill voice, this witness thinks, was that of an Italian. Was certain it was not French. Could not be sure that it was a man's voice. It might have been a woman's. Was not acquainted with the Italian language. Could not

"其他邻居作为证人提供的证词大致相同。都说没见到有人经常出入那座房子。不知道勒斯潘纳耶老夫人和女儿是否有健在的亲朋好友。房子前面窗户的百叶窗很少打开。后面的百叶窗除了四楼那个大卧室的，其他从来都是关着的，这房子状况不错——不太旧。

"伊西多尔·穆塞，警察，宣誓称约凌晨三点他被召到那座房子，到时发现在门口有二三十人试图进入未果。最后用一把刺刀①——不是撬棍——将门撬开。因为那是一个双扇门或叫对折门，上下没有插插销，所以很容易就撬开了。撬门时还能听见尖叫声——撬开门后就戛然而止了。听起来像是某人（也可能是几个人）极度痛苦的喊叫——叫声很尖拖得很长，不是又短又急。证人带着大家上楼。在到达第一层楼梯平台时听到两个愤怒的声音在高声大吵——一个声音粗哑②，另一个很尖厉③——听起来很奇怪。粗哑的声音讲的是法语，从中能分辨出一些词。确定不是女人的声音。能清楚听到'该死'和'见鬼'。尖厉的声音说的是外语。分辨不清男女。也听不清说的内容，但相信是西班牙语。证人所述房间和尸体的状态与本报昨日刊登内容相同。

"亨利·杜瓦尔，邻居，银匠，宣誓称他是最先进屋的几个人之一。大体证实④了穆塞的证词。他们一闯进房子就重新关闭大门，以免有围观者进入，因为尽管已经夜深，好事者还是迅速聚拢过来围观。证人认为那个尖利的声音在讲意大利语。确定不是法语。不确定那是男人的声音。可能是女人的。证人并不会说意大利语。无法分辨说的是什么，但是从语调断定说话人是意大利人。证人认识勒斯潘纳耶夫人

① bayonet ['beiənit] *n*. 刺刀

② gruff [grʌf] *a*. 粗哑的
③ shrill [ʃril] *a*. 尖锐的，刺耳的

④ corroborate [kə'rɔbə,reit] *v*. 证实，确证

distinguish the words, but was convinced by the **intonation**① that the speaker was an Italian. Knew Madame L. and her daughter. Had **conversed**② with both frequently. Was sure that the shrill voice was not that of either of the deceased.

" — *Odenheimer, restaurateur.* This witness volunteered his testimony. Not speaking French, was examined through an interpreter. Is a native of Amsterdam. Was passing the house at the time of the shrieks. They lasted for several minutes — probably ten. They were long and loud — very awful and distressing. Was one of those who entered the building. Corroborated the previous evidence in every respect but one. Was sure that the shrill voice was that of a man — of a Frenchman. Could not distinguish the words uttered. They were loud and quick — unequal — spoken apparently in fear as well as in anger. The voice was **harsh**③ — not so much shrill as harsh. Could not call it a shrill voice. The gruff voice said repeatedly '*sacré*,' '*diable*,' and once '*mon Dieu*.'

"*Jules Mignaud*, banker, of the firm of Mignaud et Fils, Rue Deloraine. Is the elder Mignaud. Madame L'Espanaye had some property. Had opened an account with his banking house in the spring of the year — (eight years previously). Made frequent deposits in small sums. Had checked for nothing until the third day before her death, when she took out in person the sum of 4000 francs. This sum was paid in gold, and a clerk went home with the money.

"*Adolphe Le Bon*, clerk to Mignaud et Fils, deposes that on the day in question, about noon, he accompanied Madame L'Espanaye to her residence with the 4000 francs, put up in two bags. Upon the door being opened, Mademoiselle L. appeared and took from his hands one of the bags, while the old lady relieved him of the other. He then bowed and **departed**④. Did not see any person in the street at the time. It is a bye-street — very lonely.

"*William Bird*, tailor deposes that he was one of the party who entered the house. Is an Englishman. Has lived in Paris two years. Was one of the first to ascend the stairs. Heard the voices in contention. The gruff voice was that of a Frenchman. Could make out several words, but cannot now remember all. Heard distinctly '*sacré*' and '*mon Dieu*.' There was a sound at the moment as

① intonation [ˌɪntəʊ'neɪʃən]
n. 语调，声调

② converse [kən'vɜːs] v. 交谈

③ harsh [hɑːʃ] a. 刺耳的

④ depart [dɪ'pɑːt] v. 离开

及其女儿。经常与她二人交谈。确定尖厉的声音不是出自两位受害人。

"奥登海默，餐馆老板。该证人自愿提供证词。不会讲法语，通过翻译员接受问讯。阿姆斯特丹人。传出尖叫声时他刚好经过那房子。尖叫声持续了几分钟——可能有十分钟。叫声很响且拖得很长——十分可怕又凄惨。证人也进入了房子。证实前述证词均无误，但有一点除外。可以确定尖厉的声音来自一位法国男子。说出的词分辨不清。声音很大又急促——忽高忽低——显然说话时又惧怕又愤怒。那嗓音很刺耳——与其说尖厉不如说刺耳。不能说是尖厉的声音。另一个粗哑的声音重复地说着'该死''见鬼'，还有一声'我的天啊'。

"朱尔斯·米哥尼亚，银行家，在德罗兰街开有一家父子银行。证人为老米哥尼亚。宣誓称勒斯潘纳耶夫人有些财产。一年春天（八年前）在他家银行开了一个账户。经常存入小额存款。八年间从未取款，直到死者被害三天前亲自取出四千法郎。全是金币，由一位职员送到她家。

"阿道夫·勒邦，米哥尼亚银行职员，宣誓称案发当天大约中午，他陪同勒斯潘纳耶夫人将四千金法郎送到她住所，共分装两袋。开门后勒斯潘纳耶小姐过来从他手中接过一个袋子，夫人拿过另一袋。他鞠了一躬就告辞离开了。当时并没有在街上看到其他人。那是一条背街——很冷清。

"威廉·伯德，裁缝，宣誓称他是进入房子的人之一。英国人。在巴黎居住两年。最先上楼梯的人之一。听到争吵声。粗哑的声音讲的是法语。能分辨出几个词，但现在记不全了。清晰地听到'该死'和'我的天啊'。当时好像有几个人打斗的声音——一种刮

if of several persons struggling — a scraping and **scuffling**① sound. The shrill voice was very loud — louder than the gruff one. Is sure that it was not the voice of an Englishman. Appeared to be that of a German. Might have been a woman's voice. Does not understand German.

"Four of the above-named witnesses, being recalled, deposed that the door of the chamber in which was found the body of Mademoiselle L. was locked on the inside when the party reached it. Every thing was perfectly silent — no **groans**② or noises of any kind. Upon forcing the door no person was seen. The windows, both of the back and front room, were down and firmly fastened from within. A door between the two rooms was closed, but not locked. The door leading from the front room into the passage was locked, with the key on the inside. A small room in the front of the house, on the fourth story, at the head of the passage was open, the door being **ajar**③. This room was crowded with old beds, boxes, and so forth. These were carefully removed and searched. There was not an inch of any portion of the house which was not carefully searched. Sweeps were sent up and down the chimneys. The house was a four story one, with **garrets**④ (*mansardes.*) A trap-door on the roof was nailed down very securely — did not appear to have been opened for years. The time **elapsing**⑤ between the hearing of the voices in contention and the breaking open of the room door, was variously stated by the witnesses. Some made it as short as three minutes — some as long as five. The door was opened with difficulty.

"*Alfonzo Garcio*, undertaker, deposes that he resides in the Rue Morgue. Is a native of Spain. Was one of the party who entered the house. Did not proceed up stairs. Is nervous, and was **apprehensive**⑥ of the consequences of agitation. Heard the voices in contention. The gruff voice was that of a Frenchman. Could not distinguish what was said. The shrill voice was that of an Englishman — is sure of this. Does not understand the English language, but judges by the intonation.

"*Alberto Montani*, **confectioner**⑦, deposes that he was among the first to ascend the stairs. Heard the voices in question. The gruff voice was that of a Frenchman. Distinguished several words. The speaker appeared to be

① scuffle ['skʌfl] *v.* 扭打

② groan [grəun] *n.* 呻吟

③ ajar [ə'dʒɑ:] *a.* 半开的

④ garret ['gærət] *n.* 阁楼
⑤ elapse [i'læps] *v.* (时间)
流逝

⑥ apprehensive
[ˌæpri'hensiv] *a.* 忧虑的，
不安的

⑦ confectioner
[kən'fekʃənə] *n.* 糖果商

擦扭打的声音。尖厉的声音很响——比那个粗哑的声音更响。确定那尖声说的不是英语。说的似乎是德语。可能是女人的声音。不懂德语。

"上述四位证人经再次传讯，宣誓称当众人到达发现勒斯潘纳耶小姐尸体的大卧室时，门是从里面锁住的。屋里一片死寂——没有呻吟声或任何吵闹声。破门而入后没见到任何人。大卧室前后屋的窗户都从里面关闭并锁紧。两屋之间的门关着，但是没锁。前屋通向走廊的门从里面锁着，钥匙在屋内。四楼走廊尽头临街的一间小屋房门半开着。那里面堆满了破床旧箱子之类的杂物。把这些都小心搬开并搜查了一遍。整幢房子没有一处不被仔细搜查过。烟囱上下也派人清扫。房子一共四层，带有阁楼（斜顶小屋）。屋顶有个活板门也被牢牢钉紧——貌似多年来也未曾打开。从听到争吵声到破门而入过了多久，证人们说法不一。有的说只有三分钟——有的长到五分钟。开房门很费工夫。

"阿方索·卡西奥，殡仪员，宣誓称他住在魔阁街。西班牙人。进入案发楼房的人之一。并未上楼。当时很紧张，担心被吓出病。听到争吵声。粗哑的声音是男人在说法语。分辨不清说的什么。尖利的声音在说英语——这点很肯定。不懂英语，但从语调判定是英语。

"阿尔伯托·蒙塔尼，糖果店老板，宣誓称他在最先上楼的人之中。听到了案发时的两个声音。粗哑的声音是一个男人在讲法语。能分辨其中几个词语。说话人似乎在规劝什么人。听不出尖厉的声音在说什么，那声音急促且音调高低起伏。认为是俄语。

expostulating[①]. Could not make out the words of the shrill voice. Spoke quick and **unevenly**[②]. Thinks it the voice of a Russian. Corroborates the general testimony. Is an Italian. Never conversed with a native of Russia.

"Several witnesses, recalled, here testified that the chimneys of all the rooms on the fourth story were too narrow to admit the passage of a human being. By 'sweeps' were meant **cylindrical**[③] sweeping brushes, such as are employed by those who clean chimneys. These brushes were passed up and down every flue in the house. There is no back passage by which any one could have descended while the party proceeded up stairs. The body of Mademoiselle L'Espanaye was so firmly **wedged**[④] in the chimney that it could not be got down until four or five of the party united their strength.

"*Paul Dumas*, physician, deposes that he was called to view the bodies about day-break. They were both then lying on the **sacking**[⑤] of the bedstead in the chamber where Mademoiselle L. was found. The corpse of the young lady was much bruised and excoriated. The fact that it had been thrust up the chimney would sufficiently account for these appearances. The throat was greatly **chafed**[⑥]. There were several deep scratches just below the chin, together with a series of livid spots which were evidently the impression of fingers. The face was fearfully **discolored**[⑦], and the eye-balls **protruded**[⑧]. The tongue had been partially bitten through. A large bruise was discovered upon the pit of the stomach, produced, apparently, by the pressure of a knee. In the opinion of M. Dumas, Mademoiselle L'Espanaye had been throttled to death by some person or persons unknown. The corpse of the mother was horribly mutilated. All the bones of the right leg and arm were more or less shattered. The left *tibia*[⑨] much **splintered**[⑩], as well as all the **ribs**[⑪] of the left side. Whole body dreadfully bruised and discolored. It was not possible to say how the injuries had been **inflicted**[⑫]. A heavy club of wood, or a broad bar of iron — a chair — any large, heavy, and **obtuse**[⑬] weapon would have produced such results, if wielded by the hands of a very powerful man. No woman could have inflicted the blows with any weapon. The head of the deceased, when seen by witness, was entirely

① expostulate [ik'spɔstjuleit]
　　v. 规劝，争论

② unevenly [ʌn'ivənli] *ad.*
　　不均匀地

③ cylindrical [si'lindrikəl]
　　a. 圆柱形的

④ wedge [wedʒ] *v.* 将……
　　塞入

⑤ sacking ['sækiŋ] *n.* 粗麻
　　布

⑥ chafe [tʃeif] *v.* 擦伤

⑦ discolor [dis'kʌlə] *v.* 使
　　变色

⑧ protrude [prəu'tru:d] *v.* 突
　　出

⑨ tibia ['tibiə] *n.* 胫骨

⑩ splinter ['splintə] *v.* 分
　　裂，裂成碎片

⑪ rib [rib] *n.* 肋骨

⑫ inflict [in'flikt] *v.* 造成

⑬ obtuse [əb'tju:s] *a.* 不锋
　　利的

大体证实其他人证词无误。证人是意大利人。未曾与俄国人交谈。

"几名证人再次被传讯，证实四楼所有房间内的烟囱都十分狭窄，不足以让人体通过。所说的'清扫'烟囱是指用扫烟囱用的柱形扫帚进行清扫，并没有进入烟囱。用这种扫帚清扫了房子里的每个烟道。房子没有后门通道，因此当众人冲上楼时，不可能有人从后面下楼。勒斯潘纳耶小姐的尸体在烟囱里楔得太紧，四五个人一起用力才把它拖出来。

"保罗·仲马，医生，宣誓称案发当天清晨被请去验尸。当时两位被害者都被放在发现小姐那个大卧室的床架的粗麻布垫上。年轻女人的尸体遍身瘀青和擦伤。尸体曾被塞入烟囱，这足以解释这些擦伤和瘀青产生的原因。喉部被严重擦伤。紧挨颌下有几处深划痕，并有一串显然是指印的乌黑斑点。死者面部严重变色，眼球突出。舌头被部分咬穿。腹部一大块瘀青，显然是由膝盖压迫造成。仲马先生的意见为：勒斯潘纳耶小姐是被一人或多人掐住喉咙窒息而亡。那位老夫人的尸体支离破碎。右侧手臂和腿部的骨骼有多处不同程度碎裂。左侧胫骨及左侧全部肋骨均被严重粉碎。整个尸体严重变色并呈现出可怕的瘀青。无法判断这些伤是如何造成的。强壮男子双手挥动硬木棍、粗铁棍、椅子或任何体积大又沉重的钝器方能造成如此伤害。女人使用任何凶器都不可能造成这种重伤。证人查看时，被害者头部完全与身体分离，头骨碎裂严重。

separated from the body, and was also greatly shattered. The throat had evidently been cut with some very sharp instrument — probably with a razor.

"*Alexandre Etienne*, surgeon, was called with M. Dumas to view the bodies. Corroborated the testimony, and the opinions of M. Dumas.

"Nothing farther of importance was elicited, although several other persons were examined. A murder so mysterious, and so **perplexing**① in all its particulars, was never before committed in Paris — if indeed a murder has been committed at all. The police are entirely at fault — an unusual occurrence in affairs of this nature. There is not, however, the shadow of a clew apparent."

The evening edition of the paper stated that the greatest excitement still continued in the Quartier St. Roch — that the premises in question had been carefully re-searched, and fresh examinations of witnesses **instituted**②, but all to no purpose. A **postscript**③, however, mentioned that Adolphe Le Bon had been arrested and **imprisoned**④ — although nothing appeared to **criminate**⑤ him, beyond the facts already detailed.

Dupin seemed singularly interested in the progress of this affair — at least so I judged from his manner, for he made no comments. It was only after the announcement that Le Bon had been imprisoned, that he asked me my opinion respecting the murders.

I could merely agree with all Paris in considering them an insoluble mystery. I saw no means by which it would be possible to trace the murderer.

"We must not judge of the means," said Dupin, "by this shell of an examination. The Parisian police, so much **extolled**⑥ for *acumen*, are **cunning**⑦, but no more. There is no method in their proceedings, beyond the method of the moment. They make a vast parade of measures; but, not unfrequently, these are so ill adapted to the objects proposed, as to put us in mind of Monsieur Jourdain's calling for his *robe-de-chambre — pour mieux entendre la musique*. The results attained by them are not unfrequently surprising, but, for the most part, are brought about by simple diligence and activity. When these qualities are **unavailing**⑧, their schemes fail. Vidocq, for example, was a good guesser and a **persevering**⑨

喉部显然是被某种利器割断——可能是一把剃刀。

"亚历山大·艾蒂安，外科医生，同仲马先生一起被召来验尸。证实了上述证词与仲马先生见解一致。

"虽然还传讯了其他几位证人，并没有进一步的重要发现。这桩案情如此复杂神秘又扑朔迷离的凶案在巴黎可谓前所未有——如果巴黎真的发生过凶案的话。面对性质如此不同寻常的案件，巴黎警方表示要全权负责。然而却查不到任何明显的线索。"

该报晚间版称，圣洛奇声势浩大的调查行动仍在继续——凶案发生的房子被再次仔细勘察，证人再次接受警方传讯，但均徒劳无获。然而报道后的补充消息提及阿道夫·勒邦已被捕入狱——虽然根据已载情节，并没有任何证据证明他有罪。

杜宾似乎对此事的发展格外关注——他并未发表任何评论，但至少我从他的神情可以作此判断。就在报纸公布勒邦被捕的消息后，他问我对这桩凶案的看法。

我只能跟所有巴黎人一样认为这是一桩无解谜案。我看不出有任何可以追踪凶手的方法。

"我们千万不能凭借口供的表象，"杜宾说，"来判断查找凶手的方法。让巴黎警察备受赞誉的敏锐，其实不过是机灵，仅此而已。他们在办案过程中使用的方法仅局限于当时当刻。他们大肆炫耀办案手法的精妙；但往往在涉及具体案件时，这些手法均不得其所，这就使我们想到茹尔丹先生想要睡衣——以便更好地听音乐[1]。巴黎警方的办案业绩是惊人的，但是这大多归因于他们勤劳肯干。当这一优良作风不管用时，他们的策略就会以失败告终。例如，维多克[2]是个推测高手，也极富毅

1　出自莫里哀《贵人迷》第一幕第二场。

2　弗朗索瓦·欧仁·维多克，曾为拿破仑组建过国家警察总队，后建立私人侦探所。

---

① perplexing [pə'pleksiŋ] *a.* 复杂的，令人费解的

② institute ['institjut] *v.* 开始（调查）

③ postscript ['pəustskript] *n.* 附言

④ imprison [im'prizən] *v.* 监禁，关押

⑤ criminate ['krimineit] *v.* 定罪

⑥ extol [ik'stəul] *v.* 赞美

⑦ cunning ['kʌniŋ] *a.* 狡猾的

⑧ unavailing [ˌʌnə'veiliŋ] *a.* 无效的

⑨ persevering [ˌpə:si'viəriŋ] *a.* 坚忍的，坚持不懈的

man. But, without educated thought, he **erred**① continually by the very intensity of his investigations. He **impaired**② his vision by holding the object too close. He might see, perhaps, one or two points with unusual clearness, but in so doing he, necessarily, lost sight of the matter as a whole. Thus there is such a thing as being too profound. Truth is not always in a well. In fact, as regards the more important knowledge, I do believe that she is invariably **superficial**③. The depth lies in the valleys where we seek her, and not upon the mountain-tops where she is found. The modes and sources of this kind of error are well **typified**④ in the **contemplation**⑤ of the **heavenly bodies**⑥. To look at a star by glances — to view it in a side-long way, by turning toward it the exterior portions of the *retina*⑦ (more susceptible of feeble impressions of light than the interior), is to behold the star distinctly — is to have the best appreciation of its lustre — a lustre which grows dim just in proportion as we turn our vision *fully* upon it. A greater number of rays actually fall upon the eye in the latter case, but, in the former, there is the more refined capacity for comprehension. By undue profundity we perplex and **enfeeble**⑧ thought; and it is possible to make even Venus herself vanish from the **firmament**⑨ by a scrutiny too sustained, too concentrated, or too direct.

"As for these murders, let us enter into some examinations for ourselves, before we make up an opinion respecting them. An inquiry will afford us amusement," [I thought this an odd term, so applied, but said nothing] "and, besides, Le Bon once rendered me a service for which I am not ungrateful. We will go and see the premises with our own eyes. I know G — , the Prefect of Police, and shall have no difficulty in obtaining the necessary permission."

The permission was obtained, and we proceeded at once to the Rue Morgue. This is one of those miserable thoroughfares which **intervene**⑩ between the Rue Richelieu and the Rue St. Roch. It was late in the afternoon when we reached it; as this quarter is at a great distance from that in which we resided. The house was readily found; for there were still many persons gazing up at the closed shutters, with an **objectless**⑪ curiosity, from the opposite side of the way. It was an ordinary Parisian house, with a gateway, on one side of which was a glazed

① err [ə:] v. 犯错
② impair [im'peə] v. 损害，
损伤

③ superficial [,sju:pə'fiʃəl]
a. 肤浅的

④ typify ['tipifai] v. 作
为……的典型
⑤ contemplation
[kɒntem'pleiʃən] n. 注视
⑥ heavenly body 天体
⑦ retina ['retinə] n. 视网膜

⑧ enfeeble [in'fi:bl] v. 使衰
弱，使无力
⑨ firmament ['fə:məmənt]
n. 天空

⑩ intervene [,intə'vi:n] v.
介于中间

⑪ objectless ['ɒbdʒiktlis] a.
无目的的

力。但是他的头脑没经过训练，就会因调查过度而频繁出错。距离被调查的对象太近也会限制他的视野。或许他能把一两点看得尤为清晰，但正因如此，他必然会看不清全局。这样，他就调查得过于深入了。其实真相并不总是存在于井底。实际上，我认为越是重要的真知就越会显而易见。我们到深谷中去搜寻真相，殊不知在山顶才能发现它的踪迹。这一错误背后的思维模式和成因很典型地表现在观星这件事上。当我们瞥见一颗星，也就是用斜向视线观察，将视网膜的外层（比视网膜内层更能灵敏地感受到光留下的微弱影像）转向这颗星，就能把它看得清清楚楚——这样最能够欣赏它的璀璨——当我们把视线灌注在它身上时，这璀璨却会变暗。正视这颗星时，会有更多的星光投射到眼睛上，但是，斜向视线却对星光有着更敏锐的感知力。所以说，过分深究会搅乱并弱化我们的思维能力；过于细致、持久、专注、直接地凝望，金星也会在苍穹下黯然失色。

"至于这起凶案，在我们对它形成观点前先让我们自己来调查一番，权且把它当作消遣吧。"（我觉得消遣这词用在这里很怪，但我也没说什么）"而且勒邦曾帮过我，我不能不感恩，他含冤入狱我不能袖手旁观。我们要亲眼看看那幢房子。我认识警察局长 G，拿到相关的许可令应该不难。"

就这样，我们拿到许可令后，径直向魔阁街走去。它是位于黎塞留街和洛奇街之间的一条脏乱的街道。因为这个街区距离我们的住所较远，我们到那儿时已经接近傍晚。那幢房子很好找；因为仍然有人从街对面带着毫无目的的好奇心盯着那紧闭的百叶窗看。那是一幢普通的巴黎式房子，有一个大门，大门的一侧有一个装玻璃窗的小房，窗户上装有一个滑动的小格窗，说明那是一间门房。进入房子前我们沿着街道往

watch-box, with a sliding panel in the window, indicating a *loge de concierge*. Before going in we walked up the street, turned down an alley, and then, again turning, passed in the rear of the building — Dupin, meanwhile examining the whole neighborhood, as well as the house, with a **minuteness**[1] of attention for which I could see no possible object.

Retracing our steps, we came again to the front of the dwelling, rang, and, having shown our **credentials**[2], were admitted by the agents in charge. We went up stairs — into the chamber where the body of Mademoiselle L'Espanaye had been found, and where both the deceased still lay. The disorders of the room had, as usual, been suffered to exist. I saw nothing beyond what had been stated in the "Gazette des Tribunaux." Dupin scrutinized every thing — not excepting the bodies of the victims. We then went into the other rooms, and into the yard; a *gendarme* accompanying us throughout. The examination occupied us until dark, when we took our departure. On our way home my companion stepped in for a moment at the office of one of the daily papers.

I have said that the whims of my friend were manifold, and that *Je les ménageais*: — for this phrase there is no English equivalent. It was his humor, now, to decline all conversation on the subject of the murder, until about noon the next day. He then asked me, suddenly, if I had observed any thing *peculiar* at the scene of the *atrocity*.

There was something in his manner of emphasizing the word "peculiar," which caused me to shudder, without knowing why.

"No, nothing *peculiar*," I said; "nothing more, at least, than we both saw stated in the paper."

"The 'Gazette,'" he replied, "has not entered, I fear, into the unusual horror of the thing. But dismiss the idle opinions of this print. It appears to me that this mystery is considered insoluble, for the very reason which should cause it to be regarded as easy of solution — I mean for the *outré* character of its features. The police are confounded by the seeming absence of **motive**[3] — not for the

前走下，拐入一个小巷，然后再一拐就到了房子的后面——杜宾一面查看那房子，一面细致专注地审视周边的状况，可我却看不出他这番查看有什么目的。

我们又按原路返回到正门前，按响门铃，出示了许可令，警方负责守卫的人员就给我们放行了。我们上了楼——进入发现勒斯潘纳耶小姐的那个大卧室，两位死者的尸体仍停放在那里。按照案发现场一贯的处理方式，房间的杂乱状态仍保持原样。除了《法院公报》描述的细节外，我并没有其他发现。杜宾仔细检查了每样东西——两名被害人的尸体也不例外。然后我们进入另外的房间，又进到那个小院；一位警察全程跟随着我们。检查完已近天黑，我们就离开了。回家途中，我的那位朋友在一家每日出刊的报馆停留了片刻。

我曾说过，我的这位朋友奇思怪想层出不穷，然而 Je les ménageais（他这些点子我不得不谨慎对待）——这句话在英文里我找不到对应的说法。现在他对这桩凶案的话题避而不谈，这就是他的一贯的古怪脾气，直到第二天中午，他突然问我在案发现场是否观察到任何异常。

他在强调"异常"这两个字的口气使我莫名地一惊，但又说不上为什么。

"没有，没什么异常，"我说，"至少除了我俩在报纸上都看到的信息之外我没发现什么别的。"

"恐怕那份《公报》，"他答道，"并没有领略到这桩案件的异常恐怖性。但我们还是暂且不提报纸上的那些无用累述吧。在我看来，这桩谜案被认为无法破解的原因，反而可以解释我为什么认为它容易破解——我是说案件本身具有超出常规性质的特点。看似没有作案动机使得警方困惑不已——不是困惑于为何行凶——而是困惑于作案手段为何如此凶残。看似

① minuteness [mai'nju:tnis] *n.* 微小，精密

② credential [kri'denʃəl] *n.* 证书，凭证

③ motive ['məutiv] *n.* 动机

murder itself — but for the atrocity of the murder. They are puzzled, too, by the seeming impossibility of **reconciling**① the voices heard in contention, with the facts that no one was discovered up stairs but the **assassinated**② Mademoiselle L'Espanaye, and that there were no means of **egress**③ without the notice of the party ascending. The wild disorder of the room; the corpse thrust, with the head downward, up the chimney; the frightful **mutilation**④ of the body of the old lady; these considerations, with those just mentioned, and others which I need not mention, have sufficed to **paralyze**⑤ the powers, by putting completely **at fault**⑥ the boasted *acumen*, of the government agents. They have fallen into the gross but common error of confounding the unusual with the abstruse. But it is by these **deviations**⑦ from the plane of the ordinary, that reason feels its way, if at all, in its search for the true. In investigations such as we are now pursuing, it should not be so much asked 'what has occurred,' as 'what has occurred that has never occurred before.' In fact, the facility with which I shall arrive, or have arrived, at the solution of this mystery, is in the direct ratio of its apparent insolubility in the eyes of the police."

I stared at the speaker in **mute**⑧ astonishment.

"I am now awaiting," continued he, looking toward the door of our apartment — "I am now awaiting a person who, although perhaps not the **perpetrator**⑨ of these **butcheries**⑩, must have been in some measure **implicated**⑪ in their perpetration. Of the worst portion of the crimes committed, it is probable that he is innocent. I hope that I am right in this supposition; for upon it I build my expectation of reading the entire riddle. I look for the man here — in this room — every moment. It is true that he may not arrive; but the probability is that he will. Should he come, it will be necessary to detain him. Here are **pistols**⑫; and we both know how to use them when occasion demands their use."

I took the pistols, scarcely knowing what I did, or believing what I heard, while Dupin went on, very much as if in a soliloquy. I have already spoken of

① reconcile ['rekənsail] v. 使一致，使协调

② assassinate [ə'sæsineit] v. 暗杀

③ egress ['i:gres] n. 外出，出口

④ mutilation [.mju:ti'leiʃən] n. 毁损，切断

⑤ paralyze ['pærəlaiz] v. 使无力

⑥ at fault 出毛病，靠不住

⑦ deviation [.di:vi'eiʃən] n. 偏差，偏离

⑧ mute [mju:t] a. 无声的，缄默的

⑨ perpetrator ['pə:pitreitə] n. 行凶者

⑩ butchery ['butʃəri] n. 残杀

⑪ implicate ['implikeit] v. 使卷入

⑫ pistol ['pistl] n. 手枪

无法调和的事实也使他们不解：证人都听到了争吵声，然而除了被害的勒斯潘纳耶小姐楼上并没有发现其他人，而且没有任何出口能让凶手在不被冲上楼的人们发现的情况下离开。房间被翻腾得乱七八糟，尸体被倒楔进烟囱，老夫人的尸体遭到残酷蹂躏——考虑到这些以及之前提到的几点事实，加之一些无需我提及的情况，足以使政府的警力完全瘫痪，令他们对外夸耀的敏锐全无用武之地。他们已经陷入一个重大又常见的谬误之中：混淆了不同寻常与深不可测这两个概念。但正是通过这些偏离寻常的事实，理性才能在探明真相过程中找到自己的方向，若理性真的有方向的话。就好比我们现在正进行的调查，不应该问'发生了什么'，更该问'发生了什么以前没发生过的事情。'事实上我应该，或者说已经，破解了这谜案。警方眼中此案越是无法侦破，在我看来就越有办法轻而易举地破解。"

我盯着杜宾，惊得哑口无言。

"我此刻正在等，"他一边接着说，一边望向我们住所的房门——"我此刻在等一个人，他或许不是本案的凶手，但也一定与凶案的发生有所牵连。他可能并未参与凶案最残忍的那部分。我希望我的推测没错，因为我解开整个谜案的关键就是这个推测。我料到那个人会来这儿——这个房间——随时都会。也很有可能他不会来，但是他来的可能性更大。如果他来了，我们得把他稳住。手枪在这儿；若有必要，你我都知道如何使用。"

我拿着枪，几乎不知道自己在干什么，也不相信自己听到了什么，此时杜宾还在继续说着，更像是在自言自语。我曾提过他在这种时候这种抽离现实的神情。他的话是讲给我听的；他的声音虽不太高，

his abstract manner at such times. His discourse was addressed to myself; but his voice, although by no means loud, had that intonation which is commonly employed in speaking to some one at a great distance. His eyes, vacant in expression, regarded only the wall.

"That the voices heard in contention," he said, "by the party upon the stairs, were not the voices of the women themselves, was fully proved by the evidence. This relieves us of all doubt upon the question whether the old lady could have first destroyed the daughter and afterward have committed suicide. I speak of this point chiefly for the sake of method; for the strength of Madame L'Espanaye would have been utterly unequal to the task of thrusting her daughter's corpse up the chimney as it was found; and the nature of the wounds upon her own person entirely **preclude**① the idea of self-destruction. Murder, then, has been committed by some third party; and the voices of this third party were those heard in contention. Let me now advert — not to the whole testimony respecting these voices — but to what was *peculiar* in that testimony. Did you observe any thing peculiar about it?"

I remarked that, while all the witnesses agreed in supposing the gruff voice to be that of a Frenchman, there was much disagreement in regard to the shrill, or, as one individual termed it, the harsh voice.

"That was the evidence itself," said Dupin, "but it was not the peculiarity of the evidence. You have observed nothing distinctive. Yet there *was* something to be observed. The witnesses, as you remark, agreed about the gruff voice; they were here **unanimous**②. But in regard to the shrill voice, the peculiarity is — not that they disagreed — but that, while an Italian, an Englishman, a Spaniard, a Hollander, and a Frenchman attempted to describe it, each one spoke of it as that *of a foreigner*. Each is sure that it was not the voice of one of his own countrymen. Each **likens**③ it — not to the voice of an individual of any nation with whose language he is conversant — but the **converse**④. The Frenchman supposes it the voice of a Spaniard, and 'might have distinguished some words *had he been acquainted with the Spanish.*' The Dutchman maintains

却带着那种说给远处的人听的语调。他的眼睛茫然地望向墙壁。

"种种证据都已证明，人们上楼时听到的争吵声，"他说，"不是被害人母女的。这使我们排除了老夫人谋杀女儿而后自杀的怀疑。我说起这点，主要是为了严谨起见；勒斯潘纳耶夫人的力量完全不足以将她女儿的尸体塞到壁炉里呈现人们发现的状态，从她自己的伤势来看也可以完全排除自杀的可能。因此，谋杀是由第三者所为；这第三者的声音就包含在人们听到的争吵声中。我们现在需要关注的不是与这些争吵声相关的整体证词，而是指出证词中的异常之处。你有没有看出有什么异常？"

我指出所有证人都听出那个粗哑的声音说的是法语，而关于那个尖厉的声音——其中一位证人说是刺耳的声音——证人们却各执一词。

"这本身就是证据，"杜宾说，"但这并不是证据的异常之处。你并没有注意到什么特别的事情，而这其中并非没有非常之处。如你所说，证人们对粗哑的声音证词一致，可以说是众口一词。但说到那个尖厉的声音，异常之处并不在于他们说法不一，而是在于当一个意大利人、一个英国人、一个西班牙人、一个荷兰人和一个法国人尝试描述这个声音的时候，每个人都说那声音是一个外国人的。每个人都确定那不是自己国家的语言。每个证人都认为那声音不像自己熟悉的那个国家的语言，反倒更像其他国家的语言。那个法国人认为那是西班牙语，还说'若是他能听懂西班牙语或许能分辨出几个字来'。那个荷兰人执意称那是法国人的声音；但是我们却发现报上说他'不会讲法语，通过翻译员接受问讯'。那个英国人认为那声音讲的是德语，却'不懂德语'。那个西

① preclude [pri'klu:d] v. 排除

② unanimous [ju:'nænɪməs] a. 意见一致的

③ liken ['laɪkən] v. 把……比作

④ converse [kən'vɜ:s] a. 相反的

it to have been that of a Frenchman; but we find it stated that '*not understanding French this witness was examined through an interpreter.*' The Englishman thinks it the voice of a German, and '*does not understand German.*' The Spaniard 'is sure' that it was that of an Englishman, but 'judges by the intonation' altogether, '*as he has no knowledge of the English.*' The Italian believes it the voice of a Russian, but '*has never conversed with a native of Russia.*' A second Frenchman differs, moreover, with the first, and is positive that the voice was that of an Italian; but, *not being cognizant of that tongue*, is, like the Spaniard, 'convinced by the intonation.' Now, how strangely unusual must that voice have really been, about which such testimony as this *could* have been elicited! — in whose *tones*, even, **denizens**① of the five great divisions of Europe could recognise nothing familiar! You will say that it might have been the voice of an **Asiatic**② — of an African. Neither Asiatics nor Africans abound in Paris; but, without denying the inference, I will now merely call your attention to three points. The voice is termed by one witness 'harsh rather than shrill.' It is represented by two others to have been 'quick and *unequal*.' No words — no sounds resembling words — were by any witness mentioned as **distinguishable**③.

"I know not," continued Dupin, "what impression I may have made, so far, upon your own understanding; but I do not hesitate to say that legitimate deductions even from this portion of the testimony — the portion respecting the gruff and shrill voices — are in themselves sufficient to **engender**④ a suspicion which should give direction to all farther progress in the investigation of the mystery. I said 'legitimate deductions;' but my meaning is not thus fully expressed. I designed to imply that the deductions are the *sole* proper ones, and that the suspicion arises *inevitably* from them as the single result. What the suspicion is, however, I will not say just yet. I merely wish you to bear in mind that, with myself, it was sufficiently **forcible**⑤ to give a definite form — a certain tendency — to my inquiries in the chamber.

"Let us now transport ourselves, in fancy, to this chamber. What shall we first seek here? The means of egress employed by the murderers. It is not too

班牙人'肯定'那是英语，但总的来说是'从语调判定'，因为他'不懂英语'。那个意大利人相信那声音是在说俄语，但是'未曾与俄国人交谈'。另外，第二个法国人与第一个法国人说法不同，他确认那声音是意大利语；但是并不懂那种语言，与那位西班牙人一样，是'从语调断定'。瞧瞧，那声音可真是奇特到不同寻常，居然能引出如此言人人殊的证词！——甚至欧洲五大区域的移民都不熟悉那语调！你会说那声音也许是亚洲人的——或者非洲人的。在巴黎的亚洲人或非洲人数量都不多；但我并不否认这一推断，现在我只让你注意三点。有一位证人称那声音'与其说尖厉不如说刺耳'。还有两位证人将它描述成'急促而忽高忽低'。没有哪位证人提到可分辨其中的词句——没有类似词句的声音。

"我不知道，"杜宾接着说，"至此我刚才所说对你的理解有什么影响；但我可以毫不迟疑地说，仅从这部分证词——有关粗哑和尖厉的声音这部分——作出的合理推断就足以让我们产生一种怀疑，而这个怀疑就为谜案调查的所有后续发展指明了方向。我说的'合理推断'并没有完全表达我的意思。我想表达的意思是，这种推断是唯一适当的推断，因该推断引出的怀疑是唯一必然的结果。然而这个怀疑是什么，我尚不能透露。我只希望你记得，对我来说，这种怀疑有力到足以使我在那个大卧室里的调查形成一个确定形式——或说是某种意向。

"现在想象我们回到那个大卧室。在那里我们首先应该寻找什么？凶手遁逃的途径。无须多说，我们俩都不相信有超自然事件存在。勒斯潘纳耶母女也不是被幽灵所杀。犯案的凶手是肉体凡胎，逃走方式也有迹可循。那他是如何逃走的呢？幸运的

① denizen ['denizən] *n.* 外籍居民

② Asiatic [ˌeiʃi'ætik] *n.* 亚洲人

③ distinguishable [dis'tiŋgwiʃəbl] *a.* 可辨识的

④ engender [in'dʒendə] *v.* 产生，造成

⑤ forcible ['fɔ:səbl] *a.* 有说服力的

much to say that neither of us believe in preternatural events. Madame and Mademoiselle L'Espanaye were not destroyed by spirits. The doers of the deed were material, and escaped materially. Then how? Fortunately, there is but one mode of reasoning upon the point, and that mode *must* lead us to a definite decision. — Let us examine, each by each, the possible means of egress. It is clear that the assassins were in the room where Mademoiselle L'Espanaye was found, or at least in the room **adjoining**①, when the party ascended the stairs. It is then only from these two apartments that we have to seek issues. The police have **laid bare**② the floors, the ceilings, and the **masonry**③ of the walls, in every direction. No *secret* issues could have escaped their **vigilance**④. But, not trusting to *their* eyes, I examined with my own. There were, then, no secret issues. Both doors leading from the rooms into the passage were securely locked, with the keys inside. Let us turn to the chimneys. These, although of ordinary width for some eight or ten feet above the hearths, will not admit, throughout their extent, the body of a large cat. The impossibility of egress, by means already stated, being thus absolute, we are reduced to the windows. Through those of the front room no one could have escaped without notice from the crowd in the street. The murderers *must* have passed, then, through those of the back room. Now, brought to this conclusion in so unequivocal a manner as we are, it is not our part, as reasoners, to reject it on account of apparent impossibilities. It is only left for us to prove that these apparent 'impossibilities' are, in reality, not such.

"There are two windows in the chamber. One of them is **unobstructed**⑤ by furniture, and is wholly visible. The lower portion of the other is hidden from view by the head of the **unwieldy**⑥ bedstead which is thrust close up against it. The former was found securely fastened from within. It resisted the utmost force of those who endeavored to raise it. A large gimlet-hole had been pierced in its frame to the left, and a very stout nail was found fitted therein, nearly to the head. Upon examining the other window, a similar nail was seen similarly fitted in it; and a vigorous attempt to raise this **sash**⑦, failed also. The police were now entirely satisfied that egress had not been in these directions.

是，关于这个问题只有一种推理方式，而这一方式必定将我们引入一个明确的结论。让我们逐一排查凶手可能的逃走路径。有一点很清楚，当人们冲上楼梯时，凶手就在勒斯潘纳耶小姐被发现的那个房间，或在隔壁房间。那么我们只需从这两个房间寻找线索。警方已经彻底搜查了地板、天花板，以及房间的每面墙壁。没有任何秘密出口可以逃过警方的检查。但我信不过他们，自己检查了一遍。的确没有秘密通道。房间通往过道的两扇门都牢牢锁着，钥匙都在房间里。我们再看烟囱。虽然壁炉往上八到十英尺，烟囱都是正常粗细，但里面的通道连体型较大的猫都无法通过。可以肯定地说，上述途径都不可能逃脱，那我们就只好看看窗户了。没人能从前面的窗户逃走而不引起街上人群的注意。那么凶手一定是从后面房间的某个窗户逃出去的。现在，我们用十分明确的分析方法得出了这一结论，那么作为推理者，我们就不能因其表象上的不可能性而否定它。我们只需证明表象上的'不可能'实际上并非不可能。

"这个大卧室有两扇窗。其中一扇没有被家具遮挡，完全暴露在外。另一扇窗的下半部分被紧紧顶住它的笨重床架遮挡住了。没被挡住的那扇窗从里面牢牢闩紧。任凭谁用多大力气也无法把它抬起。窗框左侧钻有一个大孔，一根结实的长钉刚好深深钉入孔内，只露出钉头。另一扇窗户经查也有一颗同样的钉子以同样的方式钉住窗框，用力也同样无法提起。警方也就完全相信出口并不是这两扇窗。因此，拔下钉子开窗查看便显得多此一举。

"我自己的查看要比警察多少更仔细些，为何更仔细，我刚刚已经解释——因为我知道，正是在此

---

① adjoining [ə'dʒɔiniŋ] *a.* 隔壁的

② lay bare 暴露
③ masonry ['meisənri] *n.* 砖石
④ vigilance ['vidʒiləns] *n.* 警戒

⑤ unobstructed [ʌnəb'strʌktid] *a.* 没有障碍的
⑥ unwieldy [ʌn'wi:ldi] *a.* 笨重的

⑦ sash [sæʃ] *n.*（门、窗上装玻璃的）框格

And, *therefore*, it was thought a matter of **supererogation**① to **withdraw**② the nails and open the windows.

"My own examination was somewhat more particular, and was so for the reason I have just given — because here it was, I knew, that all apparent impossibilities *must* be proved to be not such in reality.

"I proceeded to think thus — *a posteriori*. The murderers did escape from one of these windows. This being so, they could not have **refastened**③ the sashes from the inside, as they were found fastened; — the consideration which put a stop, through its obviousness, to the scrutiny of the police in this quarter. Yet the sashes *were* fastened. They *must*, then, have the power of fastening themselves. There was no escape from this conclusion. I stepped to the unobstructed **casement**④, withdrew the nail with some difficulty and attempted to raise the sash. It resisted all my efforts, as I had anticipated. A concealed spring must, I now know, exist; and this **corroboration**⑤ of my idea convinced me that my premises at least, were correct, however mysterious still appeared the circumstances attending the nails. A careful search soon brought to light the hidden spring. I pressed it, and, satisfied with the discovery, **forbore**⑥ to **upraise**⑦ the sash.

"I now replaced the nail and regarded it attentively. A person passing out through this window might have reclosed it, and the spring would have caught — but the nail could not have been replaced. The conclusion was plain, and again narrowed in the field of my investigations. The assassins *must* have escaped through the other window. Supposing, then, the springs upon each sash to be the same, as was probable, there *must* be found a difference between the nails, or at least between the modes of their fixture. Getting upon the sacking of the bedstead, I looked over the **head-board**⑧ minutely at the second casement. Passing my hand down behind the board, I readily discovered and pressed the spring, which was, as I had supposed, identical in character with its neighbor. I now looked at the nail. It was as stout as the other, and apparently fitted in the same manner — driven in nearly up to the head.

① supererogation
['sju:pə,reərə'geiʃən] *n.*
分外工作

② withdraw [wið'drɔ:] *v.* 拿
出，取出

③ refasten [ri:'fɑ:sən] *v.* 再
次固定

④ casement ['keismənt] *n.*
窗扉

⑤ corroboration
[kə,rɔbə'reiʃən] *n.* 确证，
证实

⑥ forbore [fɔ:'bɔ:] *v.*
（ forbear 的过去式）克
制

⑦ upraise [ʌp'reiz] *v.* 举起，
抬起

⑧ head-board 床头板

处，所有表象上的不可能必然被证明实际上并非不可能。

"我就沿着这条思路走——后验。凶犯肯定是从其中一扇窗户逃出去的。如果是这样，他们不可能从里面重新闩紧窗框，就如我们发现时那样——考虑到这一点，警方停止了向这方面调查，因为事实显而易见。然而窗户既然是闩紧的，那它必然能够自动上闩。这个结论无懈可击。我走到那个没被遮挡的窗前，费些力气拔出钉子，试图抬起窗框。如我所料，我使尽全身力气也抬不起。现在我知道了，一定有一个隐藏的弹簧；我的想法得到了证实，这样一来无论钉子的情况显得多么神秘，至少我能确信我的前提是正确的。仔细搜查后我很快就发现了那个隐藏的弹簧。我按了按弹簧，这一发现已经令我很满足了，于是我忍住并没有抬起窗框。

"我把钉子插回孔中，仔细研究。一个人完全可以从这扇窗户出去在外面把窗户关闭，弹簧会自动把窗户卡住——但是钉子却没办法插回原位。这样一来结论就清晰了，再次缩小了我的调查范围。凶犯一定是通过另一扇窗户逃跑的。假设两扇窗框上的弹簧装置相同，那么两边的钉子肯定不同，至少在固定方式上有差别。站在床架的粗麻布上，我仔细地查看了床头后面的那扇窗。我把手伸到床头板后面，轻易地就发现了弹簧装置，按了一下，正如我所料，和旁边的弹簧作用一样。我再看看钉子。看起来和旁边那扇窗的钉子一样结实地钉在那里——孔外只露出钉头。

"你会说这让我大惑不解；可如果你这么想，那你就误解归纳的本质了。用打猎时的一句话说，就是我从未曾'失去嗅迹'。猎物的味道片刻也未丢失。

"You will say that I was puzzled; but, if you think so, you must have misunderstood the nature of the inductions. To use a sporting phrase, I had not been once '**at fault**①.' The scent had never for an instant been lost. There was no flaw in any link of the chain. I had traced the secret to its ultimate result, — and that result was *the nail*. It had, I say, in every respect, the appearance of its fellow in the other window; but this fact was an absolute **nullity**② (conclusive as it might seem to be) when compared with the consideration that here, at this point, terminated the clew. 'There *must* be something wrong,' I said, 'about the nail.' I touched it; and the head, with about a quarter of an inch of the shank, came off in my fingers. The rest of the shank was in the gimlet-hole where it had been broken off. The fracture was an old one (for its edges were **incrusted**③ with rust), and had apparently been accomplished by the blow of a hammer, which had partially **imbedded**④, in the top of the bottom sash, the head portion of the nail. I now carefully replaced this head portion in the **indentation**⑤ whence I had taken it, and the resemblance to a perfect nail was complete — the **fissure**⑥ was invisible. Pressing the spring, I gently raised the sash for a few inches; the head went up with it, remaining firm in its bed. I closed the window, and the semblance of the whole nail was again perfect.

"The riddle, so far, was now **unriddled**⑦. The assassin had escaped through the window which looked upon the bed. Dropping of its own accord upon his exit (or perhaps purposely closed), it had become fastened by the spring; and it was the **retention**⑧ of this spring which had been mistaken by the police for that of the nail, — farther inquiry being thus considered unnecessary.

"The next question is that of the mode of descent. Upon this point I had been satisfied in my walk with you around the building. About five feet and a half from the casement in question there runs a **lightning-rod**⑨. From this rod it would have been impossible for any one to reach the window itself, to say nothing of entering it. I observed, however, that the shutters of the fourth story were of the peculiar kind called by Parisian carpenters *ferrades* — a kind rarely employed at the present day, but frequently seen upon very old mansions

① at fault 失误；失去臭迹

② nullity ['nʌləti] n. 无效

③ incrust ['in'krʌst] v. 生外皮

④ imbed [im'bed] v. 嵌入

⑤ indentation [.inden'teiʃən] n. 缺口

⑥ fissure ['fiʃə] n. 裂缝

⑦ unriddle [ʌn'ridl] v. 解决

⑧ retention [ri'tenʃən] n. 保留

⑨ lighting-rod 避雷针

我的推理链条每个环节都毫无瑕疵。我已经追踪到了谜团的终点——终点就是那颗钉子。表面上看起来它和旁边窗户上的钉子各方面都相同，这是事实；但相比之下，考虑到这就是线索的终点，那么这一事实无论多么具有决定性，都变得毫无意义了。'那颗钉子肯定有问题。'我说着晃了晃钉子头，钉头就带着四分之一英尺长的钉身掉下来了，剩下的部分仍旧嵌在钉子孔里。断口很旧（因为断口表面已经生锈），显然是用锤子钉的时候把钉子敲断了，但钉头连着部分钉身还是被从顶上敲进了下窗框里。我小心地把那小截钉子放回到凹孔，钉头复位，看上去又是一颗完整的钉子——完全看不见断口。我按压弹簧，轻轻地把窗向上提起几英寸；钉头随着窗框一起上升，还牢牢地嵌在凹孔里。我把窗户放下来，那颗钉子看起来又完好无损了。

"至此，谜底揭开。凶手就是从床头后面的窗户逃脱的。凶手离开后，窗户自动关闭（或许是凶手故意关闭的），弹簧装置把它闩紧；窗户抬不起来是因为弹簧装置，而警方却误认为是钉子的作用——如此一来，他们就认为没有必要进一步探究了。

"下一个问题是凶手如何下楼。关于这点，我在和你绕着那幢房子外面走的时候就已经有了满意的答案。距离刚才说的窗户大约五英尺半的地方竖着一根避雷针。任何人都不可能从这根避雷针直接够到那扇窗户，更不可能借此进入窗户。但我观察到四楼的百叶窗很特殊，是巴黎木匠所称的铁格火印窗——时下很少有人装这种样式的窗户，但在里昂和波尔多地区的老宅子里还很常见。这种窗样式像普通的门（单扇门，不是折叠门），但与普通的门不同的地方是这种百叶窗下半部分装有格子，或铸有

at Lyons and Bordeaux. They are in the form of an ordinary door, (a single, not a folding door) except that the lower half is **latticed**[①] or worked in open **trellis**[②] — thus affording an excellent hold for the hands. In the present instance these shutters are fully three feet and a half broad. When we saw them from the rear of the house, they were both about half open — that is to say, they stood off at right angles from the wall. It is probable that the police, as well as myself, examined the back of the **tenement**[③]; but, if so, in looking at these *ferrades* in the line of their breadth (as they must have done), they did not perceive this great breadth itself, or, at all events, failed to take it into due consideration. In fact, having once satisfied themselves that no egress could have been made in this quarter, they would naturally bestow here a very **cursory**[④] examination. It was clear to me, however, that the shutter belonging to the window at the head of the bed, would, if swung fully back to the wall, reach to within two feet of the lightning-rod. It was also evident that, by exertion of a very unusual degree of activity and courage, an entrance into the window, from the rod, might have been thus effected. — By reaching to the distance of two feet and a half (we now suppose the shutter open to its whole extent) a robber might have taken a firm grasp upon the trellis-work. Letting go, then, his hold upon the rod, placing his feet securely against the wall, and springing boldly from it, he might have swung the shutter so as to close it, and, if we imagine the window open at the time, might even have swung himself into the room.

"I wish you to bear especially in mind that I have spoken of a *very* unusual degree of activity as **requisite**[⑤] to success in so **hazardous**[⑥] and so difficult a **feat**[⑦]. It is my design to show you, first, that the thing might possibly have been accomplished: — but, secondly and *chiefly*, I wish to impress upon your understanding the *very extraordinary* — the almost præternatural character of that **agility**[⑧] which could have accomplished it.

"You will say, no doubt, using the language of the law, that 'to make out my case,' I should rather undervalue, than insist upon a full estimation of the activity required in this matter. This may be the practice in law, but it is not the usage of

花式格架——这就提供了完美的抓手。这幢房子的百叶窗足有三英尺半宽。我们从房子后面看的时候，窗是半开着的——也就是说，窗和墙成直角。也许同我一样，警方也检查过房屋的后面；但即便如此，他们从平行方向看到那铁格火印窗时（他们肯定看到了），并没有察觉到它的宽度，抑或怎么也没将宽度列入应当考虑的因素中去。事实上，警方已经先入为主地认为凶犯不可能从这边逃走，他们对这里的查看自然就会十分草率。然而对我来说再清晰不过，百叶窗紧挨着床头的上滑窗，如果完全被推开，那么距避雷针仅两英尺。还有一点很明显，凭借异常敏捷的身手和超乎寻常的勇气，就可以利用避雷针进入窗口——（现在我们假设百叶窗完全打开）跨越两英尺半的距离，盗贼就可以稳稳抓住百叶窗的格架。然后手松开避雷针，用脚猛地蹬一下墙，他就有可能将百叶窗摆回关闭的位置，若我们想象当时的滑窗是开着的，他甚至可以顺势跳进屋子里。

"我希望你特别牢记，我刚才说要完成这一冒险又困难的动作，超常的矫捷是必要因素。我这么说是要向你表明两点：首先，翻窗入室是可以实现的——但是，第二，也是我的主要目的，是希望你能深刻领悟完成这个动作需要怎样超乎寻常——近乎超自然的敏捷度。

"无疑，你会说，法律用语称，'为了证明我的案例'，在这件事情上，我应该低估凶犯的能力，而不该一直过分地强调他所需要的敏捷力。这可能是法律上的惯例，但不是推理的惯例。我的终极目标是找出真相。我现在的目的是向你同时呈现几个事实：我刚才提到的异常敏捷的身手；特别尖厉（或刺耳）且忽高忽低的声音；那声音说的是哪国语言，证

① lattice ['lætis] *v.* 使成格子状
② trellis ['trelis] *n.* 格子结构
③ tenement ['tenimənt] *n.* 房屋
④ cursory ['kə:səri] *a.* 粗略的，草率的
⑤ requisite ['rekwizit] *a.* 必不可少的
⑥ hazardous ['hæzədəs] *a.* 危险的
⑦ feat [fi:t] *n.* 壮举，技艺表演
⑧ agility [ə'dʒiləti] *n.* 敏捷，灵活

reason. My ultimate object is only the truth. My immediate purpose is to lead you to place in juxtaposition, that *very unusual* activity of which I have just spoken with that *very peculiar* shrill (or harsh) and *unequal* voice, about whose nationality no two persons could be found to agree, and in whose **utterance**[1] no **syllabification**[2] could be detected."

At these words a vague and half-formed conception of the meaning of Dupin **flitted**[3] over my mind. I seemed to be upon the **verge**[4] of comprehension without power to comprehend — men, at times, find themselves upon the brink of remembrance without being able, in the end, to remember. My friend went on with his discourse.

"You will see," he said, "that I have shifted the question from the mode of egress to that of **ingress**[5]. It was my design to convey the idea that both were effected in the same manner, at the same point. Let us now revert to the interior of the room. Let us survey the appearances here. The drawers of the bureau, it is said, had been rifled, although many articles of **apparel**[6] still remained within them. The conclusion here is absurd. It is a mere guess — a very silly one — and no more. How are we to know that the articles found in the drawers were not all these drawers had originally contained? Madame L'Espanaye and her daughter lived an exceedingly retired life — saw no company — seldom went out — had little use for numerous changes of **habiliment**[7]. Those found were at least of as good quality as any likely to be possessed by these ladies. If a thief had taken any, why did he not take the best — why did he not take all? In a word, why did he abandon four thousand francs in gold to encumber himself with a **bundle**[8] of **linen**[9]? The gold *was* abandoned. Nearly the whole sum mentioned by Monsieur Mignaud, the banker, was discovered, in bags, upon the floor. I wish you, therefore, to discard from your thoughts the **blundering**[10] idea of *motive*, engendered in the brains of the police by that portion of the evidence which speaks of money delivered at the door of the house. Coincidences ten times as remarkable as this (the delivery of the money, and murder committed within three days upon the party receiving it), happen to all of us every hour of our lives, without attracting

人们的证言莫衷一是；从那声音中没人听到清晰可辨的音节。"

听了杜宾最后这番话，我的脑海中掠过一个模糊但几近成型的概念。我似乎就要理解了，但是却不得要领——人有的时候觉得自己马上就记起某件事了，却终究没能想起。我的朋友继续他的推理。

"你注意到了吧，"他说，"我已经把问题从逃跑的方法转为入室的方法。我想传达的观点是，出入是在同一个地点以同样的方式完成的。现在我们再回到室内。看看案发现场。据说，桌子的抽屉被翻查过，而许多衣服留在里面。这就得出一个荒诞的结论。这仅是猜测——十分愚蠢的猜测——仅此而已。我们怎么知道抽屉里发现的衣服不是抽屉里本来装的全部东西呢？勒斯潘纳耶母女极度深居简出——不会客——少外出——不用频繁换衣服。抽屉里发现的衣服至少可以说是这母女俩拥有的最好的服装了。如果盗贼入室想拿走衣服，为什么不拿最好的——为什么不都拿走？话说回来，他为什么放弃四千法郎的黄金去费劲地偷一堆衣服呢？然而事实是金币却被弃置不顾。那位银行家米哥尼亚先生提及的几乎所有金币都还装在袋子里，放在地板上。因此我希望你抛开动机这个误导的想法，不要像警方那样仅仅根据提及把钱送到家的这部分证词就将劫财作为杀人动机。十倍于此（送钱到家，收到钱后三天内遇害）的巧合随时都会悄然发生在我们每个人的生活里。通常，巧合就是那类受过教育却不知晓概率理论的人们思维中的障碍——得益于概率理论，人类调查中最辉煌的目标才能获得最清晰的例证。就目前这个事例而言，如果金币丢了，那么三天前

---

① utterance ['ʌtərəns] *n.* 表达，话语
② syllabification [si,læbifi'keiʃən] *n.* 音节划分
③ flit [flit] *v.* 掠过
④ verge [və:dʒ] *n.* 边缘

⑤ ingress ['ingres] *n.* 入口

⑥ apparel [ə'pærəl] *n.* 服装

⑦ habiliment [hə'bilimənt] *n.* 服装

⑧ bundle ['bʌndl] *n.* 捆
⑨ linen ['linin] *n.* 日用织品
⑩ blundering ['blʌndəriŋ] *a.* 愚蠢的

even momentary notice. Coincidences, in general, are great stumbling-blocks in the way of that class of thinkers who have been educated to know nothing of the theory of probabilities — that theory to which the most glorious objects of human research are indebted for the most glorious of illustration. In the present instance, had the gold been gone, the fact of its delivery three days before would have formed something more than a coincidence. It would have been corroborative of this idea of motive. But, under the real circumstances of the case, if we are to suppose gold the motive of this **outrage**①, we must also imagine the perpetrator so **vacillating**② an idiot as to have abandoned his gold and his motive together.

"Keeping now steadily in mind the points to which I have drawn your attention — that peculiar voice, that unusual agility, and that startling absence of motive in a murder so singularly **atrocious**③ as this — let us glance at the butchery itself. Here is a woman **strangled**④ to death by manual strength, and thrust up a chimney, head downward. Ordinary assassins employ no such modes of murder as this. Least of all, do they thus **dispose**⑤ of the murdered. In the manner of thrusting the corpse up the chimney, you will admit that there was something *excessively outré* — something altogether **irreconcilable**⑥ with our common notions of human action, even when we suppose the actors the most **depraved**⑦ of men. Think, too, how great must have been that strength which could have thrust the body *up* such an aperture so forcibly that the united vigor of several persons was found barely sufficient to drag it *down*!

"Turn, now, to other indications of the employment of a vigor most marvellous. On the hearth were thick tresses — very thick tresses — of grey human hair. These had been torn out by the roots. You are aware of the great force necessary in tearing thus from the head even twenty or thirty hairs together. You saw the locks in question as well as myself. Their roots (a hideous sight!) were clotted with fragments of the flesh of the **scalp**⑧ — sure **token**⑨ of the prodigious power which had been exerted in **uprooting**⑩ perhaps half a million of hairs at a time. The throat of the old lady was not merely cut, but the head absolutely **severed**⑪ from the body: the instrument was a mere razor.

送来金币这一事实就不仅仅是个巧合了。它将是谋财害命的确证。但就本案目前的情况，如果我们认为凶手的动机是金币，那么我们同时还要想象凶手是个拿不定主意的白痴，把到手的金币连同最初的动机一并抛弃了。

"我提醒你注意的那几点一定要牢记于心——那奇特的嗓音，那不寻常的矫捷，如此暴戾的罪行居然惊人地缺乏动机——让我们看看这惨不忍睹的凶案现场。一个女人被徒手掐死，头朝下被塞进烟道。普通的凶手不会采用这种手段。至少不会如此处理被害人。单凭将尸体楔进烟囱这个方法，你就得承认此中必有蹊跷——即便我们把行凶者想象成穷凶极恶的人，这一做法也与一般观念中的人类行为全然不相容。再试想，把尸体紧紧地塞入那么狭窄的烟道，几个人合力才能勉强把它拉出来，这得需要多大的力气啊！

"从其他一些迹象也能看出凶手使用的力量奇大无比。壁炉旁边有几缕长发——很粗的几缕长发——灰白色的头发，都是被连根拔掉的。要知道，即便是从头上同时拔下二三十根头发都需要很大的力气。和我一样，你也看到那几缕头发了。那发根（触目惊心！）还凝结着头皮上的血肉——一次拔下的头发也许有几十万根，的确是惊人力量的象征。老夫人不仅喉咙被割断，就连整个脖子也完全被割断，以至身首异处：所用工具只是一把剃刀。我也希望你注意到这残忍暴行的兽性。不用我说，你也知道勒斯潘纳耶夫人身上的瘀伤。仲马先生和他可信的助理艾蒂安先生均证实那是钝器伤；到现在为止，这两位先生的判断一直是正确的。所指钝器显然就是小

① outrage ['autreidʒ] *n.* 暴行

② vacillating ['væsileitiŋ] *a.* 犹豫的

③ atrocious [ə'trəuʃəs] *a.* 残暴的

④ strangle ['stræŋgl] *v.* 掐死，勒死

⑤ dispose [dis'pəuz] *v.* 处理，处置

⑥ irreconcilable [i'rekənsailəbl] *a.* 矛盾的

⑦ depraved [di'preivd] *a.* 道德败坏的，堕落的

⑧ scalp [skælp] *n.* 头皮

⑨ token ['təukən] *n.* 标志，象征

⑩ uproot [ʌp'ru:t] *v.* 连根拔起

⑪ sever ['sevə] *v.* 割断

I wish you also to look at the *brutal* **ferocity**① of these deeds. Of the bruises upon the body of Madame L'Espanaye I do not speak. Monsieur Dumas, and his worthy coadjutor Monsieur Etienne, have pronounced that they were inflicted by some obtuse instrument; and so far these gentlemen are very correct. The obtuse instrument was clearly the stone pavement in the yard, upon which the victim had fallen from the window which looked in upon the bed. This idea, however simple it may now seem, escaped the police for the same reason that the breadth of the shutters escaped them — because, by the affair of the nails, their perceptions had been **hermetically**② sealed against the possibility of the windows having ever been opened at all.

"If now, in addition to all these things, you have properly reflected upon the odd disorder of the chamber, we have gone so far as to combine the ideas of an agility astounding, a strength superhuman, a ferocity brutal, a butchery without motive, a *grotesquerie* in horror absolutely alien from humanity, and a voice foreign in tone to the ears of men of many nations, and **devoid**③ of all distinct or intelligible syllabification. What result, then, has ensued? What impression have I made upon your fancy?"

I felt a **creeping**④ of the flesh as Dupin asked me the question. "A madman," I said, "has done this deed — some **raving**⑤ **maniac**⑥, escaped from a neighboring *Maison de Santé*."

"In some respects," he replied, "your idea is not irrelevant. But the voices of madmen, even in their wildest **paroxysms**⑦, are never found to **tally with**⑧ that peculiar voice heard upon the stairs. Madmen are of some nation, and their language, however **incoherent**⑨ in its words, has always the coherence of syllabification. Besides, the hair of a madman is not such as I now hold in my hand. I disentangled this little **tuft**⑩ from the rigidly clutched fingers of Madame L'Espanaye. Tell me what you can make of it."

"Dupin!" I said, completely **unnerved**⑪; "this hair is most unusual — this is no *human* hair."

"I have not asserted that it is," said he; "but, before we decide this point,

① ferocity [fə'rɔsiti] *n.* 暴
行，残忍

② hermetically
[hə:'metikəli] *ad.* 密封
地，密闭地

③ devoid [di'vɔid] *a.* 缺乏
的

④ creeping ['kri:piŋ] *n.* 有
虫爬的感觉，毛骨悚然
的感觉

⑤ raving ['reiviŋ] *a.* 狂乱
的，精神错乱的

⑥ maniac ['meiniæk] *n.* 疯
子

⑦ paroxysm ['pærəksizəm]
n.（疾病等的）突然发作

⑧ tally with 与……符合

⑨ incoherent
[,inkou'hiərənt] *a.* 语无
伦次的，不连贯的

⑩ tuft [tʌft] *n.* 一撮

⑪ unnerved [,ʌn'nə:vd] *a.*
烦恼不安的

院里的铺路石，被害人是从床头的窗户被扔出去的。然而这些想法看似简单，但出于和警方忽略了百叶窗的宽度同样的原因，也逃过了警方的侦察。——因为在钉子这件事上，警方认为窗户不可能被打开过，因而思路被这两颗钉子给牢牢钉死了。

"除了这些事情之外，如果你适当回想一下那卧室里的异常凌乱，那么我们就可以将下面这些要点都综合起来：异常敏捷，超人的力量，残暴的兽行，毫无动机的残杀，异于人性的恐怖手段，各国人都听不懂的异国口音，毫无清晰可辨的音节。那么能推出什么结论呢？我的描述在你的想象中产生了什么影像？"

杜宾问我这个问题的时候，我感到一阵毛骨悚然。"一个疯子，"我说，"疯子才能干出这种事——从附近疗养院逃出来的狂怒的疯子。"

"单看有些方面，"他回答，"你的想法也不无依据。但是即便是在癫狂发作时，疯子的声音也不会和人们在楼梯上听到的奇怪声音相符。疯子也属于某个国家，他说话时无论多么语无伦次，也能听出连贯的音节。再说了，疯子的头发也不会像我现在手里拿的这样啊。这是我从勒斯潘纳耶夫人紧扣的手指间解下的一撮毛发。说说你的理解吧。"

"杜宾！"我失色惊呼道，"这种毛发太罕见了——这不是人类的头发。"

"我没说它是，"他说，"但在我们确认之前，你先看看我在纸上画的这幅素描。这是我按照部分证词的描述临摹的草图，其中一份证词说勒斯潘纳耶小姐的喉部有'深色瘀青和深陷的指甲印'，另一份证词（由仲马先生和艾蒂安先生提供）则

I wish you to glance at the little sketch I have here traced upon this paper. It is a *fac-simile* drawing of what has been described in one portion of the testimony as 'dark bruises, and deep indentations of finger nails,' upon the throat of Mademoiselle L'Espanaye, and in another, (by Messrs. Dumas and Etienne,) as a 'series of livid spots, evidently the impression of fingers.'

"You will perceive," continued my friend, spreading out the paper upon the table before us, "that this drawing gives the idea of a firm and fixed hold. There is no *slipping* apparent. Each finger has retained — possibly until the death of the victim — the fearful grasp by which it originally imbedded itself. Attempt, now, to place all your fingers, at the same time, in the respective impressions as you see them."

I made the attempt in vain.

"We are possibly not giving this matter a fair trial," he said. "The paper is spread out upon a plane surface; but the human throat is cylindrical. Here is a billet of wood, the **circumference**① of which is about that of the throat. Wrap the drawing around it, and try the experiment again."

I did so; but the difficulty was even more obvious than before. "This," I said, "is the mark of no human hand."

"Read now," replied Dupin, "this passage from Cuvier."

It was a minute **anatomical**② and generally descriptive account of the large **fulvous**③ Ourang-Outang of the East Indian Islands. The gigantic **stature**④, the prodigious strength and activity, the wild ferocity, and the imitative **propensities**⑤ of these **mammalia**⑥ are sufficiently well known to all. I understood the full horrors of the murder at once.

"The description of the digits," said I, as I made an end of reading, "is in exact accordance with this drawing. I see that no animal but an Ourang-Outang, of the species here mentioned, could have impressed the indentations as you have traced them. This tuft of tawny hair, too, is identical in character with that of the beast of Cuvier. But I cannot possibly comprehend the particulars of this frightful mystery. Besides, there were *two* voices heard in contention, and one of

提到'一串显然是指印的乌黑斑点'。

"你会发现，"我的朋友说着把那张纸平铺在我们面前的桌子上，"这幅草图说明那一掐有多牢固、多结实。手明显没有移动。每根手指都一直——可能直到被害人死亡——保持在最初掐住脖子时嵌入的位置。现在你试试把你的手指同时放在对应的指印位置。"

我试了一下，根本做不到。

"我们可能尝试的方式不当，"他说，"这张纸是一个展开的平面；但人的脖子是柱形的。这是一段木头，周长和脖子差不多。把草图围在上面，再试一次。"

我照做了，但比上次更费力气。"这，"我说，"不是人手的印记。"

"现在来看看，"杜宾答道，"自然学家居维叶教授的这段文章吧。"

那段文章从解剖学细节和一般概况这两方面对东印度群岛的黄褐大猩猩进行了描述。这类哺乳动物以其体型巨大、力量惊人、行动敏捷、异常凶残，以及爱好模仿等特点为世人所知。我立刻明白了这起凶案的恐怖之处。

看完文章后，我说："这段话对足趾的描述与你所画完全相符。我看除了书里提到的这种大猩猩，不会有别的动物能够抓出你所画的指印。这簇黄褐色的毛也正与居维叶教授描述的那野兽的特征一致。但这恐怖谜案中我仍有一些细节不太理解。人们听到两个声音在争吵，其中一个确定是法国人的声音。"

"对，你还记得证词显示几乎所有人都听到了一句话，那句话是'我的天！'，在当时的情况下，这句话已经被其中一名证人（蒙塔尼，糖果店老板）正

① circumference [sə'kʌmfərəns] *n.* 周长

② anatomical [,ænə'tɔmikəl] *a.* 解剖的

③ fulvous ['fulvəs] *a.* 黄褐色的

④ stature ['stætʃə] *n.* 身材

⑤ propensity [prəu'pensiti] *n.* 倾向

⑥ mammalia [mæ'meliə] *n.* 哺乳动物

them was unquestionably the voice of a Frenchman."

"True; and you will remember an expression attributed almost unanimously, by the evidence, to this voice, — the expression, '*mon Dieu!*' This, under the circumstances, has been justly characterized by one of the witnesses (Montani, the confectioner,) as an expression of **remonstrance**① or **expostulation**②. Upon these two words, therefore, I have mainly built my hopes of a full solution of the riddle. A Frenchman was cognizant of the murder. It is possible — indeed it is far more than probable — that he was innocent of all participation in the bloody transactions which took place. The Ourang-Outang may have escaped from him. He may have traced it to the chamber; but, under the agitating circumstances which ensued, he could never have re-captured it. It is still at large. I will not pursue these guesses — for I have no right to call them more — since the shades of reflection upon which they are based are scarcely of sufficient depth to be appreciable by my own intellect, and since I could not pretend to make them intelligible to the understanding of another. We will call them guesses then, and speak of them as such. If the Frenchman in question is indeed, as I suppose, innocent of this atrocity, this advertisement which I left last night, upon our return home, at the office of 'Le Monde,' (a paper devoted to the shipping interest, and much sought by sailors,) will bring him to our residence."

He handed me a paper, and I read thus:

CAUGHT — *In the Bois de Boulogne, early in the morning of the — inst.,* (the morning of the murder,) *a very large, tawny Ourang-Outang of the Bornese species. The owner, (who is ascertained to be a sailor, belonging to a Maltese vessel,) may have the animal again, upon identifying it satisfactorily, and paying a few charges arising from its capture and keeping. Call at No.—, Rue —, Faubourg St. Germain — au troisième.*

"How was it possible," I asked, "that you should know the man to be a sailor, and belonging to a Maltese vessel?"

"I do *not* know it," said Dupin. "I am not *sure* of it. Here, however, is a small piece of **ribbon**③, which from its form, and from its **greasy**④ appearance,

确地定性为是在劝告或者告诫。因此这几个字就是我解开全盘谜团的希望所在。有一个法国人知晓这桩谋杀案。很有可能——事实上远不只可能——他是无罪的，并未参与已经发生的血腥屠杀。那只大猩猩很可能是从他那里逃出去的。也许他追踪大猩猩到了那个大卧室；但随后发生了激怒大猩猩的情景，他没能再捕回那猩猩了。它仍逍遥在外。我不再继续猜测下去了——除了猜测，我现在还无权使用别的词语——因为凭我自己的智力尚无法鉴别这些推理的基础依据，因为我不能装作我的想法已经简单明了到其他人都能理解。我们就暂且把它叫猜测吧。倘若这个法国人真如我猜测得那样在这桩血案中是无辜的，那么我昨晚在回家的路上去《世界报》（致力报道航运事件的报纸，很受水手们欢迎）刊登的这则启事将把他带到我们的住所。"

他递给我一份报纸，这则启事内容如下：

招领——某日清晨（凶案当天早上）在布洛涅市灌木丛中捕获一体型庞大棕色婆罗洲大猩猩。失主（经查为马耳他籍商船水手）若验明猩猩确为本人所有，便可将其领回，但须支付少量捕获及留养费用。认领地址：圣杰曼郊区，××街，××号，请上三楼。

"你怎么可能，"我说，"你怎么可能知道那个人就是水手，还在马耳他籍商船上工作？"

"我并不知道，"杜宾说，"我并不确定。但是你看，这有一小根缎带，从款式和油腻的样子来看，显然是用来系水手们很喜欢梳的长辫子的。况且这种结除了水手，很少有人会系，而且是马耳他特有的绳结。我在避雷针下面捡到的这根缎带。它不可能是两位被

① remonstrance
[ri'mɔnstrəns] *n.* 抗议
② expostulation
[ik,spɔstju'leiʃən] *n.* 规劝

③ ribbon ['ribən] *n.* 缎带
④ greasy ['gri:zi] *a.* 油腻的

has evidently been used in tying the hair in one of those long *queues* of which sailors are so fond. Moreover, this knot is one which few besides sailors can tie, and is peculiar to the Maltese. I picked the ribbon up at the foot of the lightning-rod. It could not have belonged to either of the deceased. Now if, after all, I am wrong in my induction from this ribbon, that the Frenchman was a sailor belonging to a Maltese vessel, still I can have done no harm in saying what I did in the advertisement. If I am in error, he will merely suppose that I have been **misled**① by some circumstance into which he will not take the trouble to inquire. But if I am right, a great point is gained. Cognizant although innocent of the murder, the Frenchman will naturally hesitate about replying to the advertisement — about demanding the Ourang-Outang. He will reason thus: — 'I am innocent; I am poor; my Ourang-Outang is of great value — to one in my circumstances a fortune of itself — why should I lose it through idle apprehensions of danger? Here it is, within my grasp. It was found in the Bois de Boulogne — at a vast distance from the scene of that butchery. How can it ever be suspected that a brute beast should have done the deed? The police are at fault — they have failed to procure the slightest clew. Should they even trace the animal, it would be impossible to prove me cognizant of the murder, or to implicate me in guilt on account of that cognizance. Above all, *I am known*. The advertiser **designates**② me as the possessor of the beast. I am not sure to what limit his knowledge may extend. Should I avoid claiming a property of so great value, which it is known that I possess, I will render the animal at least, **liable**③ to suspicion. It is not my policy to attract attention either to myself or to the beast. I will answer the advertisement, get the Ourang-Outang, and keep it close until this matter has **blown over**④.'"

At this moment we heard a step upon the stairs.

"Be ready," said Dupin, "with your pistols, but neither use them nor show them until at a signal from myself."

The front door of the house had been left open, and the visitor had entered, without ringing, and advanced several steps upon the staircase. Now, however,

① misled [ˌmis'led] v.
（mislead 的过去式）误
导

② designate ['dezigneit] v.
指定，指派

③ liable ['laiəbl] a. 很有可
能的

④ blow over 平息

害人的。即便我通过缎带认定那个法国男人是马耳他籍商船上的水手这一推断是错的，这对于我在启事上所说的内容也并无妨。如果我真的说错了，那他也仅仅会认为我是被某种情况误导，也不会费神追究。但如果我对了，那我就实现了一个重要目的。那个法国人虽然无罪，但也目击了那桩凶案，自然会犹豫该不该回应这则启事——该不该认领那只大猩猩。他会这样想：'我是无罪的，我穷，我的大猩猩很值钱——对于像我这样处境的人来说它是一笔财富——我凭什么要失去它，就凭我胡思乱想出来的危险吗？它就在那儿，触手可及。它是在布洛涅市的灌木丛里被发现的——那里距离凶案现场远着呢。人们怎么会怀疑犯下这罪行的是一只野兽呢？警方也手足无措——尚未掌握丝毫线索。就算他们追查到了这个畜生，也不可能证明我对凶案知情，即便知道我对此知情，也不会因此给我定罪吧。最重要的是，已经有人知道我了。刊登启事的人已经指认我是那畜生的所有者。我还不确定他知道多少。别人已经知道它是我的，如果我不去认领这一大笔财富，那么至少会使那畜生遭到怀疑。我现在的原则是既不能让别人注意到我，更不能让别人注意到那畜生。我就去回应那则启事，领回大猩猩，把它关起来，直到这件事的风声过去。'"

就在此时，我们听到楼梯上响起脚步声。

"准备好手枪，"杜宾说，"但没看到我的信号千万别开枪，也别让他看到枪。"

房子的大门一直开着，来人没按铃就进来了，往楼梯上走了几步。然而他好像犹豫了。马上听到他往楼下走去。杜宾迅速走到我们正说话的卧室门口，这时我们又听到他走上来了。这次他并没有犹豫，步子很坚定，像是下定了决心，走到我们所在的卧

he seemed to hesitate. Presently we heard him descending. Dupin was moving quickly to the door, when we again heard him coming up. He did not turn back a second time, but stepped up with decision, and **rapped**① at the door of our chamber.

"Come in," said Dupin, in a cheerful and **hearty**② tone.

A man entered. He was a sailor, evidently, — a tall, stout, and muscular-looking person, with a certain **dare-devil**③ expression of countenance, not altogether **unprepossessing**④. His face, greatly **sunburnt**⑤, was more than half hidden by **whisker**⑥ and *mustachio*⑦. He had with him a huge **oaken**⑧ **cudgel**⑨, but appeared to be otherwise **unarmed**⑩. He bowed awkwardly, and bade us "good evening," in French accents, which, although somewhat Neufchatelish, were still sufficiently indicative of a Parisian origin.

"Sit down, my friend," said Dupin. "I suppose you have called about the Ourang-Outang. Upon my word, I almost **envy**⑪ you the possession of him; a remarkably fine, and no doubt a very valuable animal. How old do you suppose him to be?"

The sailor drew a long breath, with the air of a man relieved of some intolerable burden, and then replied, in an assured tone:

"I have no way of telling — but he can't be more than four or five years old. Have you got him here?"

"Oh no, we had no conveniences for keeping him here. He is at a **livery stable**⑫ in the Rue Dubourg, just by. You can get him in the morning. Of course you are prepared to identify the property?"

"To be sure I am, sir."

"I shall be sorry to part with him," said Dupin.

"I don't mean that you should be at all this trouble for nothing, sir," said the man. "Couldn't expect it. Am very willing to pay a reward for the finding of the animal — that is to say, any thing in reason."

"Well," replied my friend, "that is all very fair, to be sure. Let me think! — what should I have? Oh! I will tell you. My reward shall be this. You shall

室门口，他敲了敲门。

"请进，"杜宾说，带着一种欢快热情的声调。

进来一个男人，显然是个水手——高大、魁梧、肌肉发达，一副不怕天不怕地的表情，整体看着并不讨人厌。晒得黝黑的脸一大半都被浓密的胡子遮挡着。他拿着一大根橡木棍，但除此之外好像没有别的武器。他笨拙地鞠了一躬，用法语对我们说"晚上好"，虽然带些纽夏特口音，但仍足以听出他原籍巴黎。

"请坐，我的朋友，"杜宾说，"我想你是来认领那只大猩猩的吧。说实话，我真羡慕你有这样一只猩猩，非常漂亮，不用说，肯定很值钱。你说它几岁了？"

那水手长出了一口气，如释重负的样子，然后用一种放心大胆的语气回答说："我也说不清——但它肯定不超过四五岁。你们把它关在这儿了？"

"啊，没有，我们这儿不方便关它。它现在在杜堡街一家马车行的马厩里，就在附近。明早你就可以把它领走。当然，你准备好认领它了吗？"

"当然，先生。"

"放它走我还真有点舍不得。"杜宾说。

"我不会让你白忙活一场的，先生，"那水手说，"我不会有那样的奢求。我愿意付一笔报酬来感谢你们找到那畜生——只要合理，多少都行。"

"好吧，"我的朋友回答，"那的确很公平。我想想啊！——我该要点什么呢？哦！告诉你，我要的报酬是，你把你所了解的所有关于魔阁街凶杀案的信息都告诉我。"

杜宾说最后那句话时声调很低，语气很平静。亦如他平静地走到门口，锁上屋门，把钥匙放在衣袋里。然后他从怀里掏出手枪，不动声色地放

---

① rap [ræp] v. 敲击

② hearty ['hɑːti] a. 热情友好的

③ dare-devil 蛮勇的

④ unprepossessing [ˌʌnpriːpəˈzesiŋ] a. 不讨人喜欢的

⑤ sunburnt ['sʌnbəːnt] a. 晒黑的

⑥ whisker ['hwiskə] n. 腮须

⑦ mustachio [məˈstɑːʃiəu] n. 髭，蓬松胡子

⑧ oaken ['əukən] a. 橡木制的

⑨ cudgel ['kʌdʒəl] n. 棍棒

⑩ unarmed [ʌnˈɑːmd] a. 没带武器的

⑪ envy ['envi] v. 嫉妒

⑫ livery stable（出租马车、马匹的）代养马房

give me all the information in your power about these murders in the Rue Morgue."

Dupin said the last words in a very low tone, and very quietly. Just as quietly, too, he walked toward the door, locked it and put the key in his pocket. He then drew a pistol from his bosom and placed it, without the least **flurry**①, upon the table.

The sailor's face flushed up as if he were struggling with **suffocation**②. He started to his feet and grasped his cudgel, but the next moment he fell back into his seat, **trembling**③ violently, and with the countenance of death itself. He spoke not a word. I pitied him from the bottom of my heart.

"My friend," said Dupin, in a kind tone, "you are alarming yourself unnecessarily — you are indeed. We mean you no harm whatever. I **pledge**④ you the honor of a gentleman, and of a Frenchman, that we intend you no injury. I perfectly well know that you are innocent of the atrocities in the Rue Morgue. It will not do, however, to deny that you are in some measure implicated in them. From what I have already said, you must know that I have had means of information about this matter — means of which you could never have dreamed. Now the thing stands thus. You have done nothing which you could have avoided — nothing, certainly, which renders you **culpable**⑤. You were not even guilty of robbery, when you might have robbed with **impunity**⑥. You have nothing to conceal. You have no reason for concealment. On the other hand, you are bound by every principle of honor to confess all you know. An innocent man is now imprisoned, charged with that crime of which you can point out the perpetrator."

The sailor had recovered his presence of mind, in a great measure, while Dupin uttered these words; but his original boldness of bearing was all gone.

"So help me God," said he, after a brief pause, "I will tell you all I know about this affair; — but I do not expect you to believe one half I say — I would be a fool indeed if I did. Still, I am innocent, and I will make a clean breast if I die for it."

到桌上。

那水手突然涨红了脸，好像憋得喘不过气。他惊得抓起橡木棒一跃而起，但下一秒他又跌回到椅子上，浑身发抖，面如死灰。他一言不发。我发自内心地同情他。

"我的朋友，"杜宾用缓和的语气说，"你没必要惊慌——真的没必要。我们并没有伤害你的意思。我以法国绅士的名誉向你担保，我们不想伤害你。我完全了解你在魔阁街凶案中是无辜的。但这并不能否认你与此案还是有些牵连。从我的话中你也能了解我用我的方法能获得有关此事件的信息——你做梦都想不到的方法。现在事情是这样的。你没有犯任何你可以避免的错误——当然你是无可指责的。当你可以拿走金币还免于惩罚的时候，你并没有抢劫那些金币。你没什么值得隐瞒的。你也没有理由隐瞒。换个角度来说，从道义上讲，你有责任坦白交代你所知道的一切。现在有个无辜的人因此入狱，受到谋杀的指控，而你可以指出真凶。"

听了杜宾这番话，那水手的神智恢复了不少，但已不像初来时那样放心大胆。

"上帝为证，"他稍停了一下说，"我会把我知道的全部告诉你；但我不指望你能信一星半点——傻瓜才会这样指望。但我是清白的，哪怕死我也要坦白一切。"

他的陈述大概是这样的：不久前，他曾航行至印度群岛。包括他在内的一伙人在婆罗洲登陆，远足到岛屿深处游玩。他和同伴抓获了一只大猩猩。他的同伴死了，这只大猩猩就属他一个人所有了。归来途中这只被擒野兽凶猛异常，难以驯服，几经周

① flurry ['flʌri] *n.* 慌张

② suffocation [ˌsʌfə'keiʃən] *n.* 窒息

③ tremble ['trembl] *v.* 发抖，战栗

④ pledge [pledʒ] *v.* 保证

⑤ culpable ['kʌlpəbl] *a.* 有罪的

⑥ impunity [im'pju:nəti] *n.* 不受惩罚

What he stated was, **in substance**①, this. He had lately made a voyage to the Indian **Archipelago**②. A party, of which he formed one, landed at Borneo, and passed into the interior on an **excursion**③ of pleasure. Himself and a companion had captured the Ourang-Outang. This companion dying, the animal fell into his own **exclusive**④ possession. After great trouble, occasioned by the **intractable**⑤ ferocity of his **captive**⑥ during the home voyage, he at length succeeded in **lodging**⑦ it safely at his own residence in Paris, where, not to attract toward himself the unpleasant curiosity of his neighbors, he kept it carefully **secluded**⑧, until such time as it should recover from a wound in the foot, received from a **splinter**⑨ on board ship. His ultimate design was to sell it.

Returning home from some sailors' **frolic**⑩ the night, or rather in the morning of the murder, he found the beast occupying his own bed-room, into which it had broken from a closet adjoining, where it had been, as was thought, securely confined. Razor in hand, and fully **lathered**⑪, it was sitting before a looking-glass, attempting the operation of shaving, in which it had no doubt previously watched its master through the key-hole of the closet. Terrified at the sight of so dangerous a weapon in the possession of an animal so ferocious, and so well able to use it, the man, for some moments, was **at a loss**⑫ what to do. He had been accustomed, however, to quiet the creature, even in its fiercest moods, by the use of a whip, and to this he now resorted. Upon sight of it, the Ourang-Outang sprang at once through the door of the chamber, down the stairs, and thence, through a window, unfortunately open, into the street.

The Frenchman followed in despair; the ape, razor still in hand, occasionally stopping to look back and **gesticulate**⑬ at its pursuer, until the latter had nearly **come up with**⑭ it. It then again **made off**⑮. In this manner the chase continued for a long time. The streets were profoundly quiet, as it was nearly three o'clock in the morning. In passing down an alley in the rear of the Rue Morgue, the fugitive's attention was arrested by a light **gleaming**⑯ from the open window of Madame L'Espanaye's chamber, in the fourth story of her house. Rushing to the building, it perceived the lightning rod, clambered up with **inconceivable**⑰

① in substance 基本上，事实上

② archipelago [ˌɑːkiˈpeləgəu] n. 群岛

③ excursion [ikˈskəːʃən] n. 短途旅行

④ exclusive [ikˈskluːsiv] a. 独有的

⑤ intractable [inˈtræktəbl] a. 难驯服的

⑥ captive [ˈkæptiv] n. 俘虏，捕获物

⑦ lodge [lɔdʒ] v. 安置

⑧ secluded [siˈkluːdid] a. 隐蔽的

⑨ splinter [ˈsplintə] n. 碎片，尖片

⑩ frolic [ˈfrɔlik] n. 欢乐的聚会

⑪ lather [ˈlɑːðə] v. 涂以泡沫

⑫ at a loss 不知所措

⑬ gesticulate [dʒesˈtikjuleit] v. 用姿势示意

⑭ come up with 赶上

⑮ make off 逃走

⑯ gleam [gliːm] v. 发微光，闪烁

⑰ inconceivable [ˌinkənˈsiːvəbl] a. 不可思议的，难以置信的

折，终于还是成功地把它安放到他在巴黎的住所。为了不招来邻居们的好奇心而带来不愉快的麻烦，他小心翼翼地不让猩猩被人看见，想着等到大猩猩脚上被甲板碎片割破的伤口恢复了，最终还是要把它卖掉的。

凶杀案当晚，应该是凌晨，他从水手们的集会散场回家，本以为那野兽该安全地关在卧室旁边的小屋里，可谁知却发现它逃了出来，跑到了卧室，手里拿着剃须刀，脸上涂满肥皂沫，坐在梳妆镜前，正尝试着刮脸呢；它肯定是之前从锁孔看到主人这样做过，现在模仿呢。看到一只凶猛的动物拿着那么危险的武器，还那么熟练地使用，水手吓坏了，一时间慌乱无措。以前在猩猩最狂暴的时候，他习惯了使用鞭子令它驯服，于是现在他又拿起鞭子。岂料这次这大猩猩一看到鞭子，惊得一下蹿出门外，跑下楼，从一扇碰巧开着的窗户又蹿到了大街上。

那法国水手跟在后面绝望地追逐；那猩猩手里拿着剃刀，时不时地停下来回头看看，再朝这位追赶者手舞足蹈一番，就在水手快追上它时，又继续跑开。就这样亦步亦趋地追了很久。夜晚的街道静悄悄，当时已经快凌晨三点了。逃经魔阁街后面的小巷时，那大猩猩注意到了勒斯潘纳耶夫人大卧室开着的后窗口投射出的灯光，就在那幢房子的四楼。冲到那栋楼下，大猩猩看到了那根避雷针，异常敏捷地爬上去，抓住完全打开已经靠在墙上的那扇百叶窗，顺势把自己一下荡到窗边的床头。整个过程不过一分钟。它进屋时又把那扇百叶窗踢开了。

这时水手既欢喜又担心。欣喜的是现在他大

agility, grasped the shutter, which was thrown fully back against the wall, and, by its means, swung itself directly upon the headboard of the bed. The whole feat did not occupy a minute. The shutter was kicked open again by the Ourang-Outang as it entered the room.

The sailor, in the meantime, was both rejoiced and **perplexed**[1]. He had strong hopes of now recapturing the brute, as it could scarcely escape from the trap into which it had ventured, except by the rod, where it might be **intercepted**[2] as it came down. On the other hand, there was much cause for anxiety as to what it might do in the house. This latter reflection urged the man still to follow the fugitive. A lightning rod is ascended without difficulty, especially by a sailor; but, when he had arrived as high as the window, which lay far to his left, his career was stopped; the most that he could accomplish was to reach over so as to obtain a glimpse of the interior of the room. At this glimpse he nearly fell from his hold through excess of horror. Now it was that those hideous shrieks arose upon the night, which had startled from **slumber**[3] the **inmates**[4] of the Rue Morgue. Madame L'Espanaye and her daughter, **habited**[5] in their night clothes, had apparently been occupied in arranging some papers in the iron chest already mentioned, which had been wheeled into the middle of the room. It was open, and its contents lay beside it on the floor. The victims must have been sitting with their backs toward the window; and, from the time elapsing between the ingress of the beast and the screams, it seems probable that it was not immediately perceived. The flapping-to of the shutter would naturally have been **attributed to**[6] the wind.

As the sailor looked in, the gigantic animal had seized Madame L'Espanaye by the hair, (which was loose, as she had been combing it,) and was **flourishing**[7] the razor about her face, in imitation of the motions of a barber. The daughter lay **prostrate**[8] and motionless; she had **swooned**[9]. The screams and struggles of the old lady (during which the hair was torn from her head) had the effect of changing the probably **pacific**[10] purposes of the Ourang-Outang into those of wrath. With one determined sweep of its muscular arm it nearly severed her

有希望再次擒获那野兽，因为它很难从铤而走险进入的陷阱里逃脱，要想逃脱，只能借助避雷针，而只要从那里一下来，它就会遇到阻截；令他担心焦虑的是不知道那家伙会在屋里干出什么事。这担心使水手紧紧跟着大猩猩来到了楼下。对于一个水手，爬上避雷针不难；但爬到左边窗户那么高时，他发现根本够不着窗户；他所能做的就是尽可能探过头去瞥一眼屋内的情况。这一看不要紧，吓得他险些没抓住避雷针掉下去。紧接着就听见那深夜里将魔阁街的居民们从睡梦中惊醒的恐怖尖叫。勒斯潘纳耶母女穿着睡衣，显然正在以前提到的那个金属保险箱处整理一些票据，保险箱被推到了屋中央，打开着，里面的东西摆放在旁边的地板上。被害人当时肯定背对着窗坐着；从那野兽闯入到听到尖叫之间的这段时间来看，它似乎没有马上被发现。屋里的人自然地认为百叶窗的声音是风吹发出的。

当水手向屋里看时，那巨大的野兽已经抓住了勒斯潘纳耶夫人的头发（头发散着，因为她已经在睡觉前梳理过了），正模仿理发师刮脸的动作在她脸上挥舞着剃刀。勒斯潘纳耶小姐早已吓晕过去，倒在地上一动不动。那大猩猩可能原本并无恶意，但老夫人的尖叫挣扎刺激得它勃然大怒。它那强壮的胳膊使劲一挥，差点把老夫人的脖颈彻底割断。喷洒的鲜血使大猩猩由大怒变成了狂暴，咬牙切齿，眼中喷射出凶残之光，扑到那姑娘身上，用那有力的爪子掐住她的咽喉，紧紧掐着直到姑娘窒息而死。此刻，它错乱而蛮狂的目光扫向床头，它认出了主人那惊呆的脸。那野兽无疑还记得鞭子的威力，立

① perplexed [pə'plekst] *a.* 不知所措的

② intercept [ˌintə'sept] *v.* 拦截

③ slumber ['slʌmbə] *n.* 睡眠

④ inmate ['inmeit] *n.* 居民

⑤ habited ['hæbitid] *a.* 穿着衣服的

⑥ attribute to 把……归因于

⑦ flourish ['flʌuriʃ] *v.* 挥舞

⑧ prostrate ['prɔstreit] *a.* 俯卧的

⑨ swoon [swu:n] *v.* 晕厥

⑩ pacific [pə'sifik] *a.* 平静的

head from her body. The sight of blood **inflamed**① its anger into **phrenzy**②. Gnashing its teeth, and flashing fire from its eyes, it flew upon the body of the girl, and imbedded its fearful **talons**③ in her throat, retaining its grasp until she **expired**④. Its wandering and wild glances fell at this moment upon the head of the bed, over which the face of its master, rigid with horror, was just **discernible**⑤. The fury of the beast, who no doubt bore still in mind the dreaded whip, was instantly converted into fear. Conscious of having deserved punishment, it seemed desirous of concealing its bloody deeds, and skipped about the chamber in an agony of nervous agitation; throwing down and breaking the furniture as it moved, and dragging the bed from the bedstead. In conclusion, it seized first the corpse of the daughter, and thrust it up the chimney, as it was found; then that of the old lady, which it immediately **hurled**⑥ through the window **headlong**⑦.

As the ape approached the casement with its mutilated burden, the sailor shrank aghast to the rod, and, rather gliding than clambering down it, hurried at once home — dreading the consequences of the butchery, and gladly abandoning, in his terror, all **solicitude**⑧ about the fate of the Ourang-Outang. The words heard by the party upon the staircase were the Frenchman's **exclamations**⑨ of horror and **affright**⑩, **commingled**⑪ with the fiendish **jabberings**⑫ of the brute.

I have scarcely anything to add. The Ourang-Outang must have escaped from the chamber, by the rod, just before the break of the door. It must have closed the window as it passed through it. It was subsequently caught by the owner himself, who obtained for it a very large sum at the *Jardin des Plantes*. Le Don was instantly **released**⑬, upon our narration of the circumstances (with some comments from Dupin) at the bureau of the Prefect of Police. This **functionary**⑭, however well disposed to my friend, could not altogether conceal his chagrin at the turn which affairs had taken, and was **fain**⑮ to indulge in a sarcasm or two, about the propriety of every person minding his own business.

"Let him talk," said Dupin, who had not thought it necessary to reply. "Let him discourse; it will ease his conscience, I am satisfied with having

① inflame [in'fleim] v. 加剧
（愤怒、兴奋等情感）

② phrenzy ['frenzi] n. (作
者改写的 frenzy 的变
体）狂怒

③ talon ['tælən] n. 爪

④ expire [ik'spaiə] v. 断气

⑤ discernible [di'sə:nəbl] a.
看得见的，看得清的

⑥ hurl [hə:l] v. 用力投掷

⑦ headlong ['hedlɔŋ] ad.
头朝前地

⑧ solicitude [sə'lisitju:d] n.
焦虑，担心

⑨ exclamation
[,eksk
lə'meiʃən] n. 惊叫

⑩ affright [ə'frait] n. 惊吓

⑪ commingle [kə'miŋgl] v.
混合

⑫ jabber ['dʒæbə] v. (猿猴
等）叽里咕噜地叫

⑬ release [ri'li:s] v. 释放

⑭ functionary ['fʌŋkʃənəri]
n. 官员

⑮ fain [fein] a. 不得不的

刻由狂怒转为恐惧。意识到自己做的事情会受到惩罚，它似乎急切地要掩饰血腥的罪行，焦虑不安地在房间里跳来跳去；把家具扑腾得倒的倒，坏的坏，把床垫也从床架上掀翻下来。最后它抓着勒小姐的尸体，塞进了烟囱，就像被发现时那样；接着把老夫人的尸体一头扔出窗外。

当大猩猩抓着凌乱的尸体来到窗前，水手早吓得缩回头从避雷针连滑带爬地掉在了地上，跌跌撞撞地跑回了家——害怕受到血案牵连，吓得把那大猩猩的去向早就抛到九霄云外了。冲上楼梯的那群人听到的所谓争吵声其实是这个法国水手惊惧的喊声混杂着那野兽凶残的吼叫声。

我没什么可补充的了。那大猩猩肯定在众人破门之前顺着避雷针逃跑了。而在穿过窗户时把窗户碰得落下关紧了。后来大猩猩被主人再次擒获，卖给了植物园，挣了一大笔钱。我们去警察局长办公室讲述了事情经过（杜宾加了一些评论）后，勒邦立即被无罪释放。这位局长，纵然十分青睐我的朋友，但得知事情的经过后仍掩饰不住懊恼，少不得对我们冷嘲热讽几句，说什么各人管好各人的事，谁都搅和警务着实不妥等等。

"随他说吧，"杜宾说，似乎觉得无须理会。"让他发发牢骚也好；这样他心里好受点，在他自己的堡垒里把他打败，我已经满足了。尽管如此，他没能解开谜案，并非像他想的那样是什么难以置信的事；因为，事实上，我的这位局长朋友太过狡猾却造诣不足。他的智慧之花缺少雄蕊。就像拉薇尔娜女神的画像有头无身——或者，最多也就像鳕鱼一

defeated him in his own castle. Nevertheless, that he failed in the solution of this mystery, is by no means that matter for wonder which he supposes it; for, in truth, our friend the Prefect is somewhat too cunning to be profound. In his wisdom is no *stamen*. It is all head and no body, like the pictures of the Goddess Laverna, — or, at best, all head and shoulders, like a **codfish**[1]. But he is a good creature after all. I like him especially for one master stroke of cant, by which he has attained his reputation for ingenuity. I mean the way he has '*de nier ce qui est, et d'expliquer ce qui n'est pas.*'" *

* Rousseau — Nouvelle *Heloise.*

样只有头和肩膀。但它毕竟是个不错的家伙。我尤其喜欢他巧言善辩的本领，他也因此而获得了足智多谋的好名声。我的意思是他很善于'否认事实，强词夺理'。"[1]

① codfish ['kɔd,fiʃ] *n.* 鳕鱼

1　出自卢梭的小说《新爱洛伊斯》。